The Struggle for Cooperation

AUSA Books
Series Editor: Joseph Craig

The Struggle for Cooperation

LIBERATED FRANCE AND THE AMERICAN MILITARY, 1944–1946

ROBERT L. FULLER

UNIVERSITY PRESS OF KENTUCKY

Scholarly publisher for the Commonwealth,
serving Bellarmine University, Berea College, Centre
College of Kentucky, Eastern Kentucky University,
The Filson Historical Society, Georgetown College,
Kentucky Historical Society, Kentucky State University,
Morehead State University, Murray State University,
Northern Kentucky University, Transylvania University,
University of Kentucky, University of Louisville,
and Western Kentucky University.

Editorial and Sales Offices: The University Press of Kentucky
663 South Limestone Street, Lexington, Kentucky 40508-4008
www.kentuckypress.com

Cataloging-in-Publication Data is available from the Library of Congress.
ISBN 978-0-8131-7662-8 (hardcover : alk. paper)
ISBN 978-0-8131-7664-2 (pdf)
ISBN 978-0-8131-7663-5 (epub)

This book is printed on acid-free paper meeting
the requirements of the American National Standard
for Permanence in Paper for Printed Library Materials.

Manufactured in the United States of America

ASSOCIATION of UNIVERSITY PRESSES

Member of the Association of
American University Presses

Contents

Abbreviations

ABD	Airborne Division
AFA	Aide aux Forces alliées (Aid to Allied Forces; the French office supervising the material needs of Allied armies)
AMGOT	Allied Military Government of Occupied Territories
ARC	American Red Cross
AWOL	absent without leave
CFLN	Comité français de Libération nationale (French Committee of National Liberation)
CIC	Counter Intelligence Corps
CID	Criminal Investigation Department (division of the Office of the Provost Marshal)
COMZ	Communication Zone (zone through which military supplies must pass to reach the front)
CRS	Compagnies républicaines de sécurité (Interior Ministry troops)
DPs	displaced persons
DST	Direction de la Surveillance du territoire (French counterintelligence agency)
ETO	European theater of operations
FFI	Forces français de l'Intérieure (French Forces of the Interior; resistance fighters)
FTP	Francs-Tireurs et Partisans (Communist-dominated resistance fighters)
G-4	US Army designation for Logistics
G-5	US Army designation for Civil Affairs
GI	"government issue" (an American soldier of lower rank)
GPRF	Gouvernement provisoire de la République française (provisional government of Charles de Gaulle, 1944–1945)
IG	inspector general
IOU	I owe you (debt acknowledgment)
IRCC	International Red Cross Committee
JAG	Judge Advocate General (oversees justice within the US Army)

LVF	Legion des Volontaires Français contre le Bolchevisme (unit of the German army made up of French who volunteered to fight the Soviets)
MMLA	Mission militaire de Liaison administrative (French liaison to Allied armies)
MP	military police
NCO	noncommissioned officer
OPM	Office of the Provost Marshal
OSS	Office of Strategic Services (American intelligence agency)
PC	Bureau des Ponts et Chaussées (Department of Bridges and Roads)
PCF	Parti communiste français (French Communist Party)
PDR	[Ministry of] Prisoners, Deportees, and Refugees
PM	provost marshal
POW	prisoner of war
PPF	Parti populaire française (a French fascist party)
PTT	Postes, Télégraphes et Téléphones (French telephone company and post office)
PX	post exchange (army store)
QM	quartermaster
R&R	rest and recreation or rest and recuperation
RG	Renseignements Généraux (French domestic intelligence agency)
SFIO	Section française de l'Internationale ouvrière (the main French socialist party after 1905)
SHAEF	Supreme Headquarters Allied Expeditionary Force
SNCF	Société national des chemins de fer français (French national railroad company)
SS	Schutzstaffel (German military units that answered to Heinrich Himmler rather than the army high command)
STO	Service du travail obligatoire (labor conscription instituted by Vichy)
UK	United Kingdom
USAAF	United States Army Air Force
USO	United Service Organizations (volunteer organization created to assist and entertain troops)
USSR	Union of Soviet Socialist Republics
VD	venereal disease
WAC	Women's Army Corps

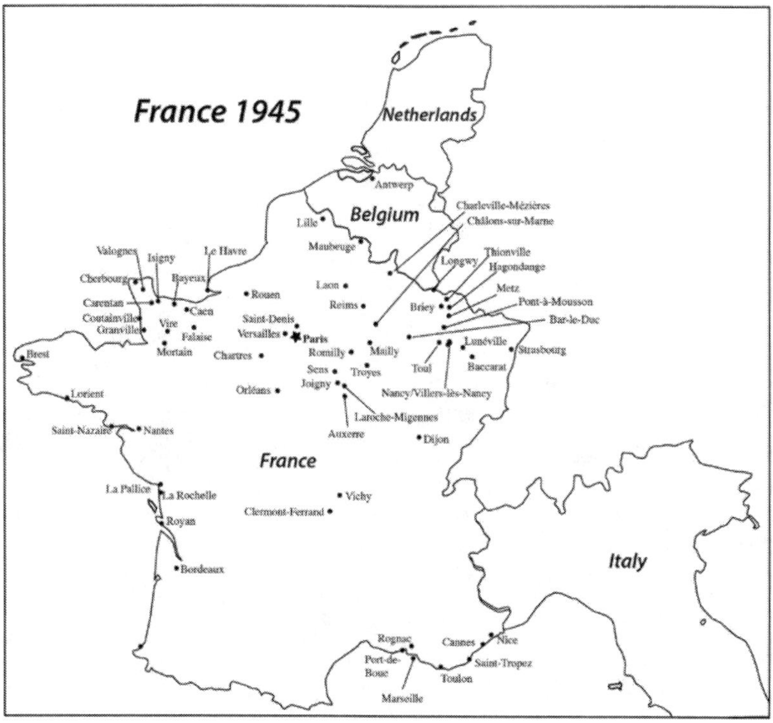

Created by Mia Paltrow.

Introduction

In February 1945 French dockworkers in Marseille went on strike. An argument between a French timekeeper on the docks and an American guard had turned into a fistfight, and American military police (MPs) arrested the timekeeper, taking away his logs, watch, papers, and money. This led the French dockworkers to stop all work and demand the release of their comrade. The MPs summoned French police, who, pistols drawn, threatened to arrest anyone who failed to get back to work. Even after the French police grabbed a foreman and two others, the men refused to return to work unloading Allied ships. Finally, US Army Major Marcus arrived on the scene. He talked to the workers and promised that all the Frenchmen who had been taken away would be released. Marcus was well known, well liked, and trusted by the French dockworkers, who accepted his word and resumed their work. Marcus had played this part before and would do so again, trying to keep the peace on the docks of Marseille so that supplies kept flowing to Allied soldiers fighting to expel the Germans from Alsace. He did his best to convince US guards on the docks that the Nazis were the real enemy, not the French dockworkers, who should be treated like friends. For his trouble, French officials in charge of the Marseille docks recommended Marcus for a French medal, L'Ordre du Mérite Maritime, awarded to those who rendered distinguished assistance to French maritime services. Many American officers served the same function as Major Marcus, working to keep the US Army supplied, housed, and entertained while the war slogged on. Like good labor relations on the Marseille docks, cooperation often proved elusive and demanded constant nourishing from both sides. Without the active effort of French officials and US officers determined to smooth over problems and make the system work, the alliance would not have succeeded, and the war could have ended much differently.[1]

When the US Army arrived in France along with the other Allied armies, they came not to liberate France but to defeat the Germans. The Allies, nonetheless, did indeed liberate France, and even if much of the rhetoric about the liberation was intended to gain the support of the French people, liberating

France was seen as a worthy goal by the American government, military leaders, and the soldiers who did the liberating. The French view was not much different. They had endured the hardships of war on their soil, which inflicted great suffering and enormous physical damage, to achieve not just liberation but the ultimate defeat of Nazi Germany. Both the French and the Americans shared the same goal and measured their lost blood as part of the price of achieving victory over Hitler's Germany. To reach their shared goal, the French people and the American military had to cooperate and get along as best they could.

President Franklin D. Roosevelt had planned to subject France to a military government (the Allied Military Government of Occupied Territories, or AMGOT) that answered to General Dwight D. Eisenhower, and he pushed that plan on both Prime Minister Winston S. Churchill and General Eisenhower even after the D-Day invasion in June 1944. Charles de Gaulle implanted his own administration on French soil in liberated Bayeux (in the British zone of Normandy) as early as 14 June, and the British forces under General Bernard Montgomery were happy to deal with it as the legitimate government of liberated France. Eisenhower shared Montgomery's view and treated de Gaulle's Republican Commissioner François Coulet as the legitimate civil authority in liberated France, despite Roosevelt's wishes. In 1942 Roosevelt had urged Eisenhower to act as the satrap of North Africa after the Allied invasion, a responsibility he dreaded and managed to avoid. When Eisenhower's chosen French leader for North Africa, General Henri Giraud, revealed himself to be maladroit and thoroughly ill-suited for the job, Eisenhower watched with relief in the spring of 1943 as the position slid into the hands of de Gaulle. Eisenhower got along with de Gaulle well enough, even if President Roosevelt did not. Having handed responsibility for governing French North Africa to de Gaulle, Eisenhower was pleased to do it again in France in the summer of 1944, despite Roosevelt's insistence that Eisenhower was in charge.[2]

Both the civilian populace and the French administrators put in place by General de Gaulle after June 1944 understood the reasons for their sacrifices. France was an Allied power too, and it had strived mightily to defeat the German foe. After the violence had passed, privations, requisitions, shortages, cold homes, high prices, and curbs on their sovereignty were the price the French had to pay. They accepted the sacrifices exacted by the Allied presence. While de Gaulle may have been in charge in liberated France, the Allies were still there, and they made many demands on the French in order to use France as a base to conquer Germany. Living with the liberators posed challenges for the French, and the Americans and the French did not always see eye to eye on many issues of common concern. The Americans and the French were (and remain) different people with their own ways of doing things, and those differences did not always mesh neatly. Thousands of reports, letters, memos, and telegrams from French to Americans, Americans to Americans, and especially French to French contained in the French and American archives reveal a clear pattern of concerns that preoccupied officers in the US Army and French officialdom. I have separated the principal subjects of these discussions between the two powers into chapters, even though the objects of mutual concern frequently overlapped. I say little about some topics that came up repeatedly, such as the lack of food and coal, because, for the most part, the two sides agreed that the situation was bad and there was little either of them could do about it in the short run. The French had to make do with limited supplies, and the US Army did what little it could to help. I examine other issues that might seem less crucial, such as a shortage of gas cans for the US Army, because they produced friction between the two sides. The shortage of these cans, for example, became a major irritant because of the ham-fisted way the US Army addressed it. The US Army not only confiscated gas cans possessed by French civilians but also subjected French automobiles—including those belonging to police and government administrators—to searches at armed roadblocks to find these cans. Needless to say, this inflamed the French and became the subject of scores of irate letters, memos, and reports, mostly generated by French police and other officials.

Both the French and the Americans expected there would inevitably be some conflicts bred by the friction between two mutually uncomprehending societies forced into close contact. Yet such low-level conflicts threw sand into the gears of two national machines trying to accomplish something big—victory over their common enemy. Both the French and the Americans claimed captured German supplies as rightfully theirs. The Americans insisted on setting aside roads and railroads for the exclusive use of Allied military convoys, which the French government agreed to, but as it turned out, neither authority had the ability or the will to enforce the monopoly. French civilians caught rides from GIs who were happy to help out, even though hundreds of MPs and French police were detailed to prevent them from doing so. At times, even the police took pity on stranded civilians and offered to help them find a way home. Differing attitudes toward the treatment of Axis prisoners of war (POWs) separated the two Allies until the end of the US presence in France. The Americans insisted on adhering to the Geneva Convention's rules on feeding, clothing, housing, and employing Axis POWs while French civilians lacked sufficient food, adequate clothing, and warm housing and were performing dangerous work, such as digging up land mines, which the French authorities believed should be left to German POWs. The Germans had violated so many of the Geneva agreements that the French saw little reason to abide by them when dealing with German POWs. After skeletal American POWs, some of whom had suffered forced marches in freezing weather, began to tell their stories to American interrogators, Generals Eisenhower and George Marshall also saw fewer reasons to abide by the Geneva Convention. Even though some German POWs were set to digging up land mines, luckier prisoners were still employed by the US Army as truck drivers on French highways—much to the disgust of the French.

Both the Americans and the French wanted to stamp out the black markets that thrived on stolen US Army property. But the mutual interest of the two authorities proved less powerful than the interest of GIs and civilians in profiting from the diversion of massive amounts of US Army property. Much of that diversion was fairly innocent—a few cigarettes for some apples or a bag of coffee as a simple thank you for help rendered—but it was all illegal and subject to punishment. In such cases, the punitive actions of law enforcement bound GIs and French civilians together rather than pushing them apart. Both the French and the Americans cooperated to see that the port of Marseille operated as smoothly as possible as the largest supply base for the Allies. However, mutual incomprehension—few French spoke English, and few Americans spoke French—led to numerous clashes between French workers and GIs, who sometimes made little effort to get along. These unfortunate incidents offered opportunities for exceptional American and French officials to put their extraordinary talents to the test at the right place and the right time. Having the right people on the job, like Major Marcus, accomplished wonders.

Many French, both officials and ordinary citizens, expressed the surprising sentiment that the German occupiers behaved more "correctly" than the Americans who replaced them. Although the German occupation was unpleasant, discipline in the German army was severe, and punishment was sure and swift—until June 1944, anyway. Until the summer of 1944, the German army (distinct from the SS and Gestapo) made a real effort to get along with the French people and cause them no more irritation than necessary, not out of benevolence but to make its occupation duties easier. The Americans also tried to avoid inconveniencing the French, but American GIs were subject to slacker disciplinary standards than the German soldiers were. Most GIs behaved themselves, but the small number who acted like brutes created a negative impression among the French, who saw no reason to tolerate berserk GIs. The French did not abide drunken GIs smashing up cafés, slugging French civilians on the sidewalks, and harassing French women and girls in public. To some extent, this misbehavior was encouraged by the American policy that placed all French bordellos off-limits to GIs, forcing them to seek sex elsewhere. Hordes of illicit streetwalkers who serviced GIs illegally (under both French law and American policy) horrified the French, who were exasperated by both the puritanical army and the boorish GIs. Pleas to change the policy went unheeded. In addition, large numbers of GIs had little experience with alcohol—especially strong drink such as cognac and calvados—and drank to excess to alleviate their loneliness and stress. GI drunkenness and its accompanying rowdiness annoyed the French and often led to vandalism, petty theft, and fighting, which attracted the attention of the French police. French police and US Army MPs often cooperated and got along quite well, but not always. On occasion, they engaged in fisticuffs and even brawls, leading to French police arresting MPs and vice versa.[3]

The American military remained in France and intruded on the French as long as the war raged. French officials understood that even when the war in Europe ended, American soldiers would be in France for many months to come. Despite much windy rhetoric about the Americans' deliverance of freedom to the French, most people understood that the Americans remained in France in 1945 to defeat Germany. With France ravaged by the war and Nazi occupation, the French needed American help to get back on their feet. American engineers and signal corpsmen lent many helping hands in 1944 that benefited the French administration and population. Much of that aid, such as repairing roads and railroad tracks, was rendered to advance the war effort, and any relief it provided to the civilian population was ancillary. However, other aid was selfless and not directed principally at the war effort, such as feeding and clothing French refugees and fixing broken waterworks and sewage systems. Although the Americans benefited from not being stationed among an epidemic-ravaged population, the benefit to the French was immeasurably greater than that to the American troops. Nonetheless, many French had an exaggerated belief about how much the Americans were going to improve their lives. The French government, however, understood the limitations on imports imposed by a finite number of ships and berths in ports to unload them. The war was a priority, and all available shipping and port facilities had to be used to achieve victory. Without victory, all other assistance would be futile in the long run. Regardless, the presence of American soldiers on French soil and demands made by Supreme Headquarters Allied Expeditionary Force (SHAEF) for the control of French roads, railways, and telephone lines unavoidably caused problems.

After the liberation and even after victory was achieved, the differing interests of the French civilian population and the US military inevitably produced friction. The US military took over many hotels, schools, and public buildings, and the French patiently endured this intrusion as long as they believed victory was not far off. The French were generally good-natured about the many irritations imposed by the Americans, until the misbehaving GIs wore out their welcome. GIs who got drunk, smashed up cafés, and abused French civilians and police had an unfortunate impact on the French perception of Americans but ultimately had no impact on the course of the war. Armed GIs who broke into people's houses in search of prostitutes made a very bad impression on the French but delayed victory by not a day. Despite such problems, the cooperation between French officials and American officers, all tasked with getting along and getting the job done, proved to be the more important Franco-American interaction. Their goal was to win the war, and they needed each other to do it. It is unfortunate that boorish GIs offended the French, but if the US Army officers tasked with cooperating with their French counterparts had failed as badly, the impact on the war would have been significant. In fact, cooperation and accord won the war. Friction and discord annoyed and angered people with only minor lingering effects, and the failure of Roosevelt and de Gaulle to see eye to eye had little influence on relations between the men and women who ultimately answered to them both.

The many points of contact between the French and the US military offered plenty of opportunities for both cooperation and discord. Some contested issues were not really subject to mediation—someone was going to get the upper hand or the better deal. Nevertheless, even such irreconcilable collisions of interests could be managed by professionals on both sides who were tasked with getting along. Yet even American officers assigned to work closely and cooperatively with French civilian officials were still concerned primarily with US interests and ensuring that the US Army got what it needed from the French. They were not in France to serve the French but to help the US Army. Reading letters, memos, and notes written by French officials similarly tasked with cooperating with the Allies makes it abundantly clear that their first loyalty was to France and not to the Allies (of which France was one). Despite the clear loyalties of all the professionals involved, without their sincere commitment to victory and their determination to make the alliance work, the outcome of the war could have been different. Victory on the western front could have been delayed, with unforeseeable consequences for Europe produced by an unambiguous Soviet triumph over Nazi Germany.

This work examines how the French and Americans in liberated France handled various issues that demanded cooperation: requisitions of French property to benefit the war, the treatment of Axis POWs, the care of displaced persons, the disposition of war booty, the flourishing black market, the utilization of French transportation networks, GI relaxation and recreation, GI crime, and the effective American takeover of the port of Marseille. All these issues offered possibilities to work together either amiably or at odds. Most produced both agreement and disagreement, but more often, accord and cooperation won out.

1

France and the United States, Allies in War

On 23 October 1944 the three principal Allied powers—the United States, the United Kingdom, and the Soviet Union—simultaneously announced their recognition of the provisional government of Charles de Gaulle as the legitimate government of France. Joseph Stalin and Winston Churchill had favored establishing formal ties to the de Gaulle government for many months, and in Churchill's case, for more than a year. Even US Secretary of State Cordell Hull had favored formal recognition since early in the year, leaving President Franklin D. Roosevelt as the sole leader opposed to it. Despite withholding de jure recognition from the French provisional government, the Americans had been treating de Gaulle's government as the de facto authority since the spring of 1943. The United States and the Gaullist regime had signed scores of agreements, and the Americans had loaned the French hundreds of millions of dollars—soon to become billions—through Lend-Lease operations. Indeed, the United States had been dealing with the French on practical matters without interruption since the beginning of the Second World War in September 1939. Even though the United States entered the war in December 1941 and had been fighting alongside French soldiers since January 1943, France and the United States became allies only in October 1944. Between the French military debacle of June 1940 and the reopening of the American embassy in Paris in 1944, much uncertainty and dissonance occupied Franco-American relations. Yet, after the Vichy regime was sidelined as inconsequential in November 1942, many (and soon most) French struggled for the same ends as the Americans: a defeated Germany and a restored France.

After the fall of France in June 1940, General Charles de Gaulle declared that "Free France" would continue the battle from London under his leadership. Both the Free French and the defeated regime of Marshal Philippe Pétain, based in Vichy, tried to win the sympathy of the American people and their government. De Gaulle sent representatives to New York and Washington to woo expatriate French and sway opinion within the Roosevelt administration. His agents had an uphill fight because of large reservoirs of sympathy in the United States for defeated France and unflattering news coverage of de Gaulle. At the same time, Pétain sent a new ambassador and launched a concerted propaganda campaign to court American opinion. Both de Gaulle and Pétain met with some success, but ultimately, events in Europe more profoundly shaped US opinion than newspaper columns or speeches at rallies by proponents of the two warring French camps. Churchill's embrace of de Gaulle and his tiny cadre of followers in the United Kingdom promoted de Gaulle's name recognition in the United States, but little more.

American sympathy for the Free French ebbed and flowed throughout 1940 and 1941 with each success and reversal. The disastrous attempt by British and Free French forces to seize Dakar in French West Africa convinced many Americans, especially President Roosevelt, that de Gaulle was a bungler and not to be trusted. But winning the allegiance of Chad, Cameroon, French Congo, and most of the French Pacific islands lent him greater credibility. Simultaneously, new policies adopted by the Vichy regime that more closely aligned Vichy France with Nazi Germany swayed many Americans to believe that the Pétain regime was turning fascist. In response, some Americans began to view de Gaulle more favorably, even if American journalists and unimpressed French living in the United States repeatedly denounced de Gaulle, too, as a fascist. In early 1941 Vichy agreed to sell military supplies to the Italians in North Africa, where Mussolini was engaged in a bitter fight with the British based in Egypt. Soon afterward, Vichy allowed Axis ships to unload war materials in Tunisian ports, thus using French North Africa as a base to support operations against the British. Members of the Roosevelt administration regarded Axis encroachments into French Africa with alarm because they believed that Dakar and French West Africa were ideally positioned to dominate Atlantic shipping lanes and offered the Axis powers a perfect springboard for invading South America.[1]

Thinking among some members of the Roosevelt administration drifted favorably toward the Free French as US relations with Japan deteriorated during 1941. This shift occurred because the Free French commanded the loyalty of Pacific islands that offered potentially valuable bases for military operations in the Far East. Talks were opened with de Gaulle's chief representative in the United States, René Pleven, in the fall of 1941 to extend Lend-Lease aid to the Free French, leading to an agreement in November. Still, Roosevelt was adamant that this aid and mutual agreements about military bases did not constitute formal recognition of de Gaulle's French National Committee as the legitimate sovereign of France. The United States still recognized Pétain as the French head of state and maintained an embassy in Vichy. By the time the United States entered the fight against the Axis powers in December 1941, the adroit and talented Pleven had been replaced by an irritable and truculent socialist labor union official, Adrien Tixier, who exasperated almost as many Americans and French in the United States as de Gaulle did. Ultimately, world events pushed the United States toward the Free French and achieved what neither Pleven nor Tixier could.

With the United States drawn into the war by Japan's reckless attack and Hitler's foolish and gratuitous declaration of war, the mutual interests of the American military and the Gaullists persuaded the US War Department to develop many contacts with Free French agents and armed forces. When General Dwight D. Eisenhower set up his headquarters in London, he and his staff came into contact with Free French personnel almost immediately. The British encouraged warm relations with the Free French, and mutual cooperation proved useful early on, especially in Africa and the Pacific and on intelligence matters in Europe. In late July 1942 de Gaulle met with Generals Eisenhower, George Marshall, and Mark Clark and Admiral Ernest King in London, establishing formal military-to-military ties between the United States and the Free French. State-to-state ties were unchanged, however; de Gaulle's representative in Washington, Tixier, was still received as a "delegate," which gave him no official standing. This status continued until October 1944, with relations largely limited to coordination between the US military and Free French military and civilian staff. The US military met with and signed cooperation agreements with French civilian administrators based on the "local authorities doctrine"; that is, Americans were free to work with whatever authority they happened to encounter in any locale. If Gaullists were in charge of an area, such as a Caribbean island, the War Department or State Department was free to treat them as the recognized sovereign and sign binding agreements with them. The United States was willing to recognize de Gaulle's representatives as the legitimate authorities in the Caribbean and Central Africa but not in France, which was still controlled by Vichy.

Roosevelt and American war planners were focused on Axis intentions in Africa, where they sought to neutralize threats to the North Atlantic posed by African territories that were still loyal to Vichy. Thus, in the summer of 1942 the British and Americans made plans to invade French North Africa; the Free French were kept in the dark. Assured by Roosevelt's chief representative in North Africa, Robert Murphy, that de Gaulle was loathed and considered a traitor by both the populace and the Vichy military in Africa, the Americans sought some other Frenchman who could command loyalty and was willing to cooperate with the Allies. They alighted on General Henri Giraud, who had recently escaped from a German POW camp and was attracting attention in Vichy as an enemy of Germany and a possible friend of the United States. Discreet talks between American diplomats and Giraud led to an agreement for Giraud to cooperate with the American invasion of Morocco and Algeria sometime in 1942 (British participation was not disclosed). Allied commanders revealed little to Giraud, including his exact role in the operation and its date, even though it was set to occur just a few weeks after discussions with him began. When Operation Torch unleashed the Anglo-American invasion of North Africa on 8 November 1942, General Giraud had just disembarked from a British submarine in Gibraltar and was being disabused of his notion that *he* was in charge of the whole operation. The Allies wanted Giraud to take command of the French military in North Africa and, if possible, the civil administration as well, but he was not to play a leading part in the North African campaign against the Axis military. The Allies doubted the ability of the French army in North Africa to contribute much to the fight that would soon begin. After hours of arguing with Generals Eisenhower and Clark, Giraud agreed to assume command of French forces, but he had no interest in being a satrap in French North Africa. As events unfolded, he need not have worried about that. By chance, the ex-premier of Vichy France, Admiral François Darlan, was stranded in Algiers by the invasion, and the French looked to him to take charge.[2]

Admiral Darlan assumed command of all French forces from French General Alphonse Juin, who would have cooperated with the Allies had they taken him into their confidence. Darlan assessed the situation and, with Juin's encouragement, quickly agreed to a cease-fire with the invaders. Unfortunately, the admiral was reluctant to act against the orders of Marshal Pétain, who had sent instructions to resist the Allies but not the Axis troops then flooding into Tunisia. After Pétain replaced Darlan as commander of French forces in North Africa with the governor-general of Morocco, Auguste Noguès, Darlan attempted to retract his cease-fire order, but it was too late to prevent German forces from crossing the "armistice line" in France. On 11 November German and Italian troops occupied all of southern France, which had previously been free of Axis troops. With all of France occupied, Darlan declared Pétain a "prisoner" who was unable to make decisions for the good of France. In the name of Pétain, but without his assent, Darlan took back command of North Africa and agreed to cooperate with the Allies. Noguès did not object. This was the "Darlan deal" that outraged so many in the United States and the United Kingdom: the Allies had come to an agreement with a "fascist" out of expediency and would recognize his civilian and military authority so long as it was convenient to do so. This was exactly how Roosevelt saw the Darlan deal, which he called "a temporary expedient."

De Gaulle was among the most outraged, so in an effort to mollify the Free French, Roosevelt agreed to meet Tixier at the White House on 20 November. Hoping to lessen the sting of the Darlan deal, Roosevelt assured Tixier that Admiral Darlan was not the ultimate authority in North Africa, General Eisenhower was! This was exactly what de Gaulle had come to expect and fear from Roosevelt.[3]

To govern North Africa, Darlan formed an Imperial Council that brought together numerous high Vichy officials serving in Africa, plus General Giraud. The Vichy regime remained alive and well in North Africa, with 8,000 political prisoners still languishing in Vichy prisons and concentration camps, including French officers who had conspired to help the Allies in Operation Torch. President Roosevelt remained under the mistaken impression that General Eisenhower was in charge of events in North Africa. Eisenhower was not in charge; nor did he want to be. He had hoped that Giraud would shoulder much of the Allies' burden in Algiers, only to be disappointed at almost every turn by the mulish and sullen general who wanted only to command soldiers. Giraud's skittishness about assuming greater responsibility came to an abrupt end after Christmas 1942, when Admiral Darlan was assassinated by a young royalist who believed he was part of a larger plot. Dilatory efforts to unmask any such plot were quashed by members of the Imperial Council for obscure and probably divers reasons, which remain in doubt to this day. After Darlan's murder, Eisenhower successfully promoted Giraud to head French affairs—civil and military—in North Africa. However, when Giraud proved to be maladroit as a leader, Eisenhower had to seriously consider recommendations by Churchill and his representative in Algiers, Harold Macmillan, to insert de Gaulle into North African affairs. Churchill also assiduously lobbied Roosevelt to admit de Gaulle into the French regime in Algiers and succeeded in adding him to the agenda of the January 1943 Casablanca Conference, held to make decisions about Allied plans for the war. When Roosevelt and Churchill met in Casablanca, the latter arranged for de Gaulle to be flown to Morocco, where he reluctantly met Giraud. Churchill was unable to cajole the two Frenchmen into negotiating about the leadership of liberated North Africa, but he persuaded them to shake hands for press photographers. Roosevelt, who met de Gaulle for the first time in Casablanca, was fooled by this stunt and believed de Gaulle and Giraud had come to an agreement on governing North Africa, when in fact they had agreed on nothing.[4]

It took another six months of wheedling and shuttle diplomacy to arrange an accord to merge Giraud's Imperial Council with de Gaulle's Free French Committee in London and move the headquarters of the "Fighting

French" to Algiers. An expanded committee, renamed the French Committee of National Liberation (Comité français de Libération nationale, or CFLN), consisted of members nominated by de Gaulle and Giraud but retained most of the Vichyist holdovers. De Gaulle quickly proved his skill at committee politics and outmaneuvered Giraud and the Vichyists to place Gaullists in key positions in Algiers. Having neither the taste nor the skill for politics, Giraud accepted de Gaulle's invitation to head the French military and quit the CFLN. This left de Gaulle with an absolute majority in the CFLN, which he immediately used to purge his Vichyist opponents. In December 1943 de Gaulle expanded the CFLN to include all colorations of political parties that had seats in the French National Assembly before the war, except the far right. The expanded committee, which included a large delegation of Communists, was heavily tilted to the left, which de Gaulle used to have the ex-Vichyist officials arrested for treason. This move outraged Roosevelt, who ordered Eisenhower to intervene and get the former leaders released. Eisenhower, fully absorbed in the Italian campaign, had no interest in stepping back into French politics, and in any event, he knew he could not force de Gaulle to release the prisoners. Despite diplomatic approaches by Robert Murphy, they remained in prison at the end of the war. Oblivious to events, Roosevelt assumed that Eisenhower was in charge in North Africa until the day Eisenhower transferred his headquarters to London in anticipation of the invasion of France.

Roosevelt's belief that he could impose an Allied Military Government of Occupied Territories (AMGOT) on France, replacing the German occupation with an Anglo-American one, led him to set in motion plans for the use of military governors. The British had gained experience administrating occupied enemy territory when they overran Italian East Africa in 1941 and found themselves responsible for large swaths of Italian colonial territory and thousands of Italian colonists. In 1941 the British had established the first of several schools for training military officers as civil affairs officers responsible for dealing with civilians in liberated or occupied areas. Just what "dealing with" meant in practice would depend on the circumstances encountered in these territories. Italian territories were hostile until the fall of 1943, when Italy became a cobelligerent with the Allies. By 1943, the British had opened several specialty schools focusing on various areas of civilian relations and had invited Americans and Canadians to attend them. The Americans opened their own civil affairs school for officers in Charlottesville, Virginia, where hundreds of officers took courses in politics, history, sociology, law, and other presumably helpful fields. The Allies realized early in the war that they would need to reach an accord with the French about handling civil affairs in France once it was brought back into the war by an Allied invasion. In September 1943 they presented a document to the CFLN outlining terms for the administration of France after an Allied invasion. The British and Americans had signed similar treaties with the governments-in-exile of Norway, Belgium, and the Netherlands. The Allies sought the CFLN's agreement that Allied civil affairs officers would be the ultimate civil authorities in liberated France, in consultation with whatever authority happened to be in place, until the French could freely choose a new government for themselves. The CFLN was invited to attach a *military* committee to Eisenhower's Supreme Headquarters Allied Expeditionary Force (SHAEF) to advise on civil affairs, but with the understanding that it would have no civil authority in liberated France. In return, the Allies promised they would not recognize the authority of the Vichy regime and would seek to liquidate its rule wherever encountered—something they had made no effort to do in North Africa. Not surprisingly, de Gaulle and the committee rejected the proposal out of hand. That the Allies' proposal offered less authority to the French in their own country than they already exercised in the liberated empire raised alarms among all Free French, not just de Gaulle. It compelled the CFLN to recognize that seizing control of the interior administration of France at the moment of liberation would be their primary concern. The Allies, especially the Americans, gave them as much cause to worry as the Germans did.[5]

Roosevelt remained adamant that the United States would treat de Gaulle as an ally on a military level but would not recognize him or his committee as a provisional government. Eisenhower, encouraged by his chief of staff Walter Bedell-Smith, saw the wisdom of recognizing *some* French entity to represent legitimate authority in France upon the German withdrawal, and the Gaullists offered the most obvious candidate. SHAEF also believed that de Gaulle was widely popular and commanded loyalty among the occupied French—an opinion promoted by the American Office of Strategic Services (OSS), which had agents in France—making him the preferred option. Neither Eisenhower nor Bedell-Smith had any interest in imposing any government—American military or French—on liberated France. Roosevelt insisted that SHAEF should come to an agreement with *any* French entity that offered to aid the Allies, which at least did not exclude the CFLN. However, Washington ordered SHAEF not to deal with any French authority unless it guaranteed the restoration of traditional French liberties, had no intention of retaining power indefinitely, and agreed to seek a constitutional mandate from the French people. The CFLN satisfied all these criteria, but arguably the French Communist Party (Parti communiste français, or PCF) did not, so this directive could have been seen as anti-Communist rather than pro-Gaullist. In March and again in April 1944, the Consultative Assembly in Algiers voted to hold an election for a constitutional convention, with universal adult suffrage (including women, who had never before voted in France), within one year of the Germans being evicted from the majority of French departments; once convened, the Consultative Assembly would dissolve and hand over all authority to the constitutional convention.[6]

De Gaulle recognized the necessity of giving Allied military authority wide latitude in France many months before the Allies landed, and in September 1943 he proposed to Roosevelt and Churchill a draft accord on cooperation in France once the Allies invaded. Eisenhower was eager for such an agreement but deferred to Roosevelt, who was uninterested and made no reply to de Gaulle's suggestion. Churchill also thought it was a good idea, but he too deferred to the president and allowed the proposal to languish on his desk. In December 1943 Eisenhower told de Gaulle that he wanted no part in any military government in France and hoped the French would assume full responsibility for their own affairs. Eisenhower had no interest in interfering in French political matters, and he ordered civil affairs officers under his command to stay out of political squabbles among the French. To ensure French influence with the Allied forces and to promote the effectiveness of the Allied cause, de Gaulle agreed to the creation of the Mission militaire de liaison administrative (MMLA) to serve as a liaison with Allied civil affairs officers in France. This corps of 170 English-speaking Frenchmen and 50 Frenchwomen was headed by Colonel Claude Hettier de Boislambert, a spirited and able officer who had rallied early to de Gaulle's cause.[7]

It was vital that the Allies reach an agreement with the CFLN about civil authority—to determine who would be in charge—*before* invading France. And because de Gaulle was more worried about sovereignty than the Allies were, it was important to him that any agreement respect the CFLN's authority within France. Eisenhower was equally interested in gaining the cooperation of French authorities in obtaining goods and services in France that would be necessary for the success of the Allies' military project. Therefore, Eisenhower directed Allied officers to meet with CFLN officials in Algiers in March 1944 to negotiate an agreement on acquiring and paying for services in France after D-Day. The committee offered and Eisenhower accepted an accord on mutual aid in time of war. The French proposed to establish an office, Aide aux Forces alliées (Aid to Allied Forces, or AFA), to ensure not only that the Allied armies would receive the local assistance they required to win the fight but also that such assistance would be provided only with the CFLN's permission. The committee resolved to appoint an official in every department and region (a group of three or four related departments) to receive requests for aid and see that it was provided. The committee recognized that Allied requisitions would be necessary in liberated France and wanted to ensure that, to the extent possible, those requisitions would be made through French authorities and under French law. This was similar to Vichy's frantic efforts to control the assistance rendered to the Nazis, such as making arrests or confiscating Jewish property, so that the French could control the process rather than ceding it to foreigners. According to the AFA agreement, Gaullist prefects would appoint people to receive military requests for billeting or goods, such as fresh meat or vegetables, and French officials would find the housing or the food and establish a price. Price schedules for almost every kind of exchange were to be worked out by French administrators and delivered to the appropriate Allied officers. Payment was to be rendered to the AFA and not directly to vendors, except under special circumstances agreed to by the French. In active war zones, Allied units could request supplies and billeting from mayors to meet only their immediate, temporary needs, not long term. Regional and departmental financial officers were to be appointed by the CFLN to deal with all financial transactions and questions. Some transactions were to be treated as "reciprocal aid," that is, rather than accepting payment from the Allies, the amount would be subtracted from French debts incurred under Lend-Lease. A metaphorical gigantic ledger would be kept by both sides, adding the costs of American aid to the French and subtracting French aid to the Americans.[8]

The CFLN also recognized that military necessity would demand de facto Allied authority over some parts of France while the fighting continued. The accords acknowledged that the Allied military might have to retain substantial control over some port facilities and communication lines in France. In all cases, French liaison officers would be attached to Allied military staff at various levels to act as intermediaries between French and Allied authorities. Once French civil and judicial administration had been reestablished, Allied civil affairs officers would operate through French officials rather than deal directly with French civilians or low-level French public servants. The accords signed by the Allies in April 1944 required them to cede authority to French civilians as soon as the military situation permitted. Delegates of the CFLN would assume governmental functions until such time as a popularly elected republican government could be restored. This came very close to recognizing de Gaulle's CFLN as the provisional government of France. The accords certainly acknowledged that de Gaulle's committee would most likely be the authority in liberated France and was seemingly the preferred sovereign to treat with the Allies. In any event, the US State Department was determined that any agreements between the CFLN and SHAEF about authority in liberated France would be a matter for the Department of War. Agreements signed by SHAEF were military matters, *not* matters of state. All these measures, of course, were just castles built on clouds until France was liberated from Nazi rule.[9]

Liberating France

On the morning of 6 June, Raymond Triboulet, the head of the local underground resistance in the region around Caen, rode his bicycle to the landing beaches to meet the British. He hoped to establish useful communications between his group and the invading British but could find no one to take him seriously. He tried again the next day after finding a senior intelligence officer on the scene, but he had no more success than on D-Day. On 9 June Triboulet finally met a British civil affairs officer who had no idea what to do with him. Learning that the local subadministration office had been liberated, Triboulet set off on his bicycle for Bayeux to set in motion a prearranged plan for a new Gaullist administration, only to find that the British had already made agreements with the Vichy-installed subprefect, M. Rochat, who was as ready to work with the Allies as they were to accept him. Triboulet managed only to meet with another local Gaullist agent, Maurice Schumann, and they discussed their common plight.[10]

In anticipation of the Allied invasion of France, the CFLN in Algiers had voted on 26 May to become the provisional Government of the French Republic (Gouvernement provisoire de la République française, or GPRF). De Gaulle still feared that the Allied governments would treat liberated France as they had French North Africa and Italy after the surrender in September 1943. In both cases, the Allies had made agreements with leaders who were badly tainted by prior associations with fascist regimes—Admiral Darlan in North Africa and Marshal Pietro Badoglio in Italy—preserving their authority within Allied occupied territory. De Gaulle was determined to avoid such a fate for France and planned to plant the flag of the GPRF on liberated French soil as soon as possible after the Allied landings. He and many in his administration believed they were in a race against the Allies and the French Communists to install a new government, even though all the alternatives to de Gaulle were alarming to the Allied leaders and most of the French populace, leaving de Gaulle as the only realistic option. In the mind of President Roosevelt, there remained an even better choice: an AMGOT. However, Roosevelt was almost entirely alone in hoping for an AMGOT. His top military staff opposed it, especially General Eisenhower, who would have been responsible for implementing it; he had no more interest in being proconsul in France than he had in running North Africa, condemning the idea to irrelevance. Eisenhower's experience with French politics in Algiers convinced him to avoid any repetition in France, and because Roosevelt had given him wide latitude in dealing with French civil affairs, the general had the freedom to bow out. He was happy to recognize any cooperative French official as the authority for civil affairs, and as long as the Americans acknowledged French sovereignty over France, the officials appointed and put into place by de Gaulle were equally happy to cooperate with the Allied militaries.[11]

Despite the weak prospects of the alternatives to de Gaulle's provisional government, the GPRF became established in France only because actions taken by de Gaulle and his associates ensured it. Gaullist agents-turned-functionaries assiduously grabbed the reins of authority in every town and region as it was liberated by Allied armies. General Leclerc's 2nd Armored Division was brought into Normandy with the specific objective of liberating Paris. With the landing of French divisions under General Jean de Lattre de Tassigny on the southern coast of France in August 1944, the liberating Allies included more French units. As more of France was overrun by Allied soldiers and the liberated zone expanded, the GPRF gained not only more territory and citizens to govern but also more confidence in its ability to exercise control. Nevertheless, so long as the war raged, the GPRF was willing to cede all reasonable authority to the Allied military.

When the much-anticipated D-Day arrived, de Gaulle directed that none of Boislambert's corps of liaison officers participate in the invasion. He had been kept in the dark about the date and details of the landings until 4 June and, in a fury, ordered the MMLA not to cooperate, but it was too late to recall the thirty MMLA officers who accompanied Allied soldiers onto the beaches. He initially refused to make a radio speech on the BBC on 6 June, asking the French populace to cooperate with the invaders. Still furious, de Gaulle was determined to establish GPRF authority on French soil at the earliest opportunity. At dawn on 14 June he boarded the French destroyer *La Combattante* at Portsmouth along with Commissioner of the Republic (Commissaire de la République) François Coulet, Colonel Pierre de Chevigné, and other aides to steam to Normandy. After landing on a beach crowded with Canadian soldiers, de Gaulle set out in a small procession to tour the narrow strip that had been liberated by the British and Canadians. De Gaulle's first stop was to pay a call on General Bernard Montgomery, who received him with great courtesy and briefed the French general on the progress of the invasion thus far. De Gaulle, however, failed to bring along Commissioner Coulet and introduce the British commander to the face of the new government in France. As de Gaulle toured the liberated zone, few of the French men and women he met recognized him, although his name was familiar and they all announced their delight at meeting him once they knew who he was. The frustrated de Gaulle then asked two gendarmes on bicycles that he encountered on the road to go to Bayeux and announce that General de Gaulle was coming so that he would be greeted with a proper reception. He also dispatched Coulet to establish himself—and the French Republic—in Bayeux in advance of his arrival. After he arrived, de Gaulle promised victory and liberation for France to an enthusiastic crowd that had gathered in front of the Hôtel de Ville. De Gaulle's next stop was Isigny in the American zone. Unlike Bayeux, which had been captured by the British relatively unscathed, Isigny had been nearly razed by American bombers on 6 and 7 June, and the dead were still being dug out of heaps of rubble when de Gaulle came upon the sobering scene. Before dark, de Gaulle returned to *La Combattante* and sailed back to Portsmouth, leaving Commissioner Coulet and Colonel Chevigné behind in Bayeux to represent the GPRF in liberated France.[12]

Once situated in Bayeux, Coulet's authority was more theoretical than real. He struggled to assert French sovereignty when it clashed with Allied military policy. When he heard that both the British and the Americans were delivering food and supplies directly to French grocers and charging the deliveries to the French government, he insisted that they stop and that all deliveries go to Ravitaillement Général (General Supply), a government body charged with buying and distributing civilian goods. The Allies agreed to work through General Supply and keep accounts with the AFA when its offices were fully functioning; in the meantime, they delivered supplies to whomever was best situated to receive them. By July, the French had revived inspections of food sold to the Allied armies, and in the opinion of the US Quartermaster Corps officers in charge of buying the goods, they were disqualifying dairy products acceptable to the US Army. Civil affairs officers asked Coulet to allow his inspectors to set lower standards for sales to the Allied armies. This demonstrated that at least the Allies recognized that the French government set standards and that any deviation had to be authorized by the French.[13]

General Pierre Koenig, in charge of the French military, was eager to reestablish French justice in the liberated zone and dispatched five military judges to Normandy to direct the trials of accused collaborators detained by French Forces of the Interior (FFI) and French police (France had been under martial law since September 1939). When Koenig arrived in Normandy for an inspection tour on 7 July, the law courts in Bayeux were operating. Two spies were being tried before judges, and within days they were found guilty and sentenced to life in prison. To help him shoulder the burden of administration, Coulet relied on some very talented Frenchmen. Colonel Pierre Laroque, who had been in charge of training French liaison officers for the MMLA, was dispatched from London to help Coulet establish the new French state in the liberated zone. He had been an administrative mandarin in Paris before the war and went on to greater achievements in shaping the postwar French welfare state. Coulet asked Laroque to assume responsibility for liberated Cherbourg in late June.[14]

When General Omar Bradley's armies finally broke the German lines on the west of the Cotentin Peninsula at the end of July, American troops quickly overran large swaths of France, adding them to the liberated zone. With a doomed counterattack at Mortain, the Germans played their last card in Normandy but failed to cut the American forces in two. Those Germans who escaped the great massacre at Falaise made a mad rush for the German border and the safety of the Siegfried Line. Although Allied armies remained in close pursuit of the fleeing Germans, they had too few soldiers to occupy the territory being evacuated, leaving a vast void of dubious authority in much of France. In some areas, Vichy officials continued to exercise their functions if left unmolested by local and regional liberation committees and the FFI. In other towns and villages, the FFI sprang into action, often assuming power in competition with local police and gendarmes. Few members of the Vichy paramilitary police, the Milice, stuck around to contest the FFI, who quickly found themselves in charge of large territories. Often, local and regional liberation committees filled the vacuum of authority that opened as the Germans disappeared. In many areas, Vichy-appointed administrators were ousted or arrested by the FFI, whose ranks swelled with eager new recruits. De Gaulle's provisional government was determined to take control of newly liberated areas and demanded the loyalty of the FFI units that were seemingly in control. Fortunately, almost all FFI immediately pledged their allegiance to the GPRF, so de Gaulle's agents met little resistance. Colonel Boislambert followed behind the American armies and made contact with the resistance and liberation committees emerging from the underground to ensure their loyalty to General de Gaulle. Advised by the liberation committees, he made case-by-case judgments about who would serve the new order well and who should be replaced. Coulet visited the newly liberated zones as soon as possible to confirm officials in their posts. In Coutances he met an assistant prefect, M. Endelin, a recent Vichy appointee who had remained at his post during the worst of the fighting to help the anti-Nazi resistance. He favorably impressed Lieutenant Colonel Gunn, a civil affairs officer, as cooperative and helpful when he greeted the Americans as liberators. Endelin also impressed Coulet, who pronounced him "a courageous true patriot" and confirmed him in his post. Other officials appointed by Vichy were deposed and had to await the results of an inquest to determine whether they were fit to serve the new regime; some others remained in office until Coulet could find qualified replacements.[15]

The US Army recognized the authority of the GPRF over civil matters and generally cooperated with the new French government. Civil affairs officers had a clear incentive to defer to the Gaullists: it meant fewer responsibilities and headaches for the US Army. The army's eagerness to hand over civilian matters to the GPRF helped Coulet and other newly arrived commissioners and prefects to establish their rule in recently liberated areas. The Allies usually stayed out of internal French affairs, turning a blind eye to summary executions of collaborators and mostly ignoring kangaroo courts run by liberation committees and the FFI. The menace of ill-disciplined and sometimes vengeful FFI members and liberation committees also convinced many liberated French to embrace Gaullist officials as they arrived in the wake of the Allied armies. Following the orders of French lawyers who had spent the last three years in London was almost always preferable to following orders from armed young FFI fighters who had spent the previous six months stealing chickens from farmers.[16]

Sometimes the new authorities proved too eager to cooperate with the Americans. The newly appointed Gaullist commissioner at Rennes, Victor Le Gorgeu, agreed to allow French technical experts to work directly with their American counterparts to make quick decisions about what needed to be done with roads, electricity, water, and other infrastructure. Laroque, on an inspection tour, feared this would allow the Americans to do whatever they wanted, bypassing the new commissioner and thus the GPRF. He was further distressed to learn that the French military commander for the newly liberated area, Colonel Chevigné, had issued public orders (*arrêtés*) that deviated from government policy on the military powers of arrest. Laroque was stupefied because Chevigné was a trusted subordinate and had more experience than most in dealing with the Allied military. To ensure that French sovereignty was unquestioned, Laroque called a meeting in Rennes of American civil affairs officers, heads of the French technical services, and Commissioner Gorgeu to explain that the civil affairs officers and the French section heads were just liaisons between SHAEF and the provisional government, and everyone had to respect the lines of authority and the agreements in force between SHAEF and the GPRF. Assuring compliance by French officials who were eager to help the Allies defeat the Germans proved to be a challenge for de Gaulle's new administrators as they tried to assert control.[17]

The FFI supposedly composed the French army in France, awaiting the day of liberation to take up arms in the name of General de Gaulle. The CFLN in Algiers created a formal armed organization headed by General Koenig in March 1944 not only to establish the CFLN as a formal partner in the liberation of France but also to assert control over the armed groups of the interior. De Gaulle worried that French Communists would build up an active army that was loyal to them alone to challenge de Gaulle's claim to leadership of newly liberated France. Guerrilla bands organized by French Communists, the Francs-Tireurs et Partisans (FTP), posed a potential challenge to de Gaulle's authority among the Free French resistance. Although de Gaulle included members of the PCF in the CFLN and then the GPRF, this did not guarantee that Communist partisans would not form an independent army within France, possibly to attempt a coup when the moment was right. However, the FTP agreed to accept the authority of General Koenig, avoiding a rift within the armed resistance and assuring the FTP a recognized role in the Allied invasion. French Communists wanted to avoid infighting among guerrilla groups and were glad to be recognized as one of the players in the Allied forces of liberation. Until the invasion occurred, the FFI had many important tasks to perform: gathering intelligence, sabotaging infrastructure crucial to the Germans, circulating pro-Allied propaganda, and helping downed fliers to escape, among other responsibilities. General Eisenhower was happy to accept General Koenig as a formal part of his command. This gave the Allies a valuable tool to use against the Nazis, and it made it more likely that the FFI could be subjected to discipline and would not act as freebooters. The FFI also formed the most important French arm of the invasion until French army troops landed in southern France in mid-August 1944.[18]

Regardless of the organizational charts that graced General Koenig's walls in London, the FFI were mostly ad hoc and ragtag bands of youths trying to stay out of the clutches of the Vichy Milice and the Germans. Most resisters in France were more or less freelance men and women who took up arms during the Allied invasion and did not take orders from superiors in London. They were volunteer guerillas, known as *maquis,* who operated in small groups under their own commanders. The term *maquis* was applied to those who had fled their homes and made precarious lives for themselves in the bush (*maquis* is a brushy vegetation common in the south of France) and outside the law. *Maquis* bands grew in number and size after labor conscription (Service du Travail Obligatoire, or STO) was introduced by Premier Pierre Laval in late 1942 to send French workers to German war plants. As Allied bombers rained greater destruction on German factories, this service became increasingly dangerous in late 1943 and early 1944. The best way for young men to avoid being sent off to Germany was to take to the hills, which thousands did. Living by their wits in forests, hills, and swamps, many sustained themselves through poaching, petty thievery, and helping themselves to produce on farms. Because of this filching, many were not on good terms with local farmers or the police. This varied greatly from band to band, however, as some received assistance from both farmers—who were sometimes relatives—and the local police. Most *maquis* were unarmed, although a lucky few wielded hunting rifles, shotguns, or weapons left over from past French wars. Only as the invasion approached did the British, Americans, and Canadians make serious efforts to drop arms, supplies, and commando leaders (known as Jedburghs, after their principal British training site) to give the FFI a fighting chance. Even then, they were ordered not to engage in suicidal battles with German regular soldiers.[19]

General George Patton's tanks ran out of gasoline just as they reached Nancy, the ancient capital of Lorraine, on the Moselle River. With Patton's offensive suspended in early September, the Germans took the opportunity to reinforce their armies in eastern France. The war continued in Alsace and Lorraine, which were not fully cleared of German troops until March 1945. Other German soldiers holed up in ports on the Atlantic coast—Saint-Nazaire, Lorient, La Rochelle, Royan, and the Channel Islands—until May 1945 because neither Eisenhower nor de Gaulle was willing to spare the soldiers or supplies to liberate those places. American and French armies endured some severe fighting in the hills and mountains of eastern France in the winter of 1944–1945 to push the Germans out of Alsace and Lorraine. However, most of France was liberated and more or less under the control of de Gaulle's GPRF by December 1944.

Liberated France

De Gaulle's provisional government slowly asserted control. The FFI, mostly working in close coordination with clandestine liberation committees that emerged from the forests and hills, assumed control of areas and awaited further instructions from de Gaulle's GPRF. Ugly incidents involving head-shavings of women and summary executions of *collabos* (collaborators) or supposed *collabos* occurred in many departments, but for the most part, discipline and order reigned. Some FFI, who had lived by snatching food from farmers who had supposedly been hoarding crops, "requisitioned" food from the same farmers at gunpoint after liberation. It took weeks for de Gaulle's commissioners to find quarters and appoint officials to install the GPRF in the liberated zones of France. The authority of de Gaulle's GPRF was accepted everywhere, even if its ability to control events was weak in some regions, such as the far southwest of France. Nevertheless, de Gaulle was eager to assert his rule in place of the FFI, so he ordered all FFI to be incorporated into the regular French army. This was easier said than done. Many FFI were married fathers or teenaged boys and girls with no interest in joining disciplined units and sitting in foxholes in eastern France. They melted away just as quickly and easily as they had joined the *maquis,* in some cases only weeks before. The remaining FFI were herded into the army slowly and with difficulty, partly because the French lacked everything needed to equip their rapidly expanding army: uniforms, boots, arms, ammunition, food, transport, and the like.[20]

The newly liberated French had expected the Americans to linger and help reestablish civil society, but they rarely stayed for more than a few hours as Patton's Third Army swept to the south of Paris toward Germany. Some towns, such as Chartres in the Eure-et-Loir, became supply or communications bases for US military units; their presence lent an air of stability, even if the US Army offered only limited assistance to civil authorities. The Quartermaster Corps officers who remained in Chartres and elsewhere were mostly interested in acquiring the resources they needed to do their job and happily cooperated with local officials to acquire such things as fresh water or wood for bridges. Such towns were likely to host civil affairs officers to assist the Quartermaster Corps, and these officers also helped French administrators whenever possible. Thus, towns with a US presence were more likely to receive help from the Army Corps of Engineers, Signal Corps, Transportation Corps, and similar units with skills and supplies that were useful to the French. However, such towns were the exception.

The first town in France to be placed under US Army supervision was Carentan, in the department of the Manche, in Normandy. The Germans were evicted in mid-June by American paratroopers of the 101st Airborne Division and tanks of the 2nd Armored Division, leaving behind a devastated and charred town that had no working water system, no electricity, and no telephone service. Most of the town's inhabitants had fled, and its mayor and nineteen others had been killed in an American air raid in early June. The vice mayor emerged after six days in a cellar to greet Carentan's new manager, Major John J. Maginnis, a civil affairs officer who had served in France with the US Army during the First World War and spoke French. Acting Mayor Joret promised his complete cooperation to Maginnis, and they immediately got to work, putting out fires and clearing debris from the main roads so US troops, equipment, and supplies could get through. The Herculean tasks facing Maginnis, his small staff, army engineers, and French civilians rounded up by Joret were made more difficult because Carentan remained on the front line for weeks and was subjected to German shelling, causing new fires to break out and more debris to block the roads. Teams set to work locating and burying the dead bodies of soldiers, civilians, and farm animals. US Army sappers were kept busy for weeks locating and disposing of land mines and unexploded ordnance scattered everywhere. Joret and Maginnis had no trouble finding farmers who volunteered to round up stray cows and look after them; the real problem was keeping the farmers out of their still very dangerous fields. Local FFI members were recruited to act as security—a move that was not greeted with unanimous joy, as some of the locals viewed the FFI as thugs and bullies.[21]

There was little food in the town, and many of its inhabitants had lost everything they owned in the battle, leaving few resources. The French looked to the US Army for help, but Maginnis explained that supplies for civilians were very limited. Even so, he managed to scrounge up 3,000 bags of regular and buckwheat flour, boots, and blankets from the Quartermaster Corps. Army engineers supplied several water trucks to haul potable water from a nearby reservoir. Unfortunately, the water had been fouled by seawater washing in from broken locks on a canal linking Carentan to the English Channel, so the engineers fixed the locks. Usable bricks, tiles, stones, and wood were salvaged from smashed houses and buildings to effect repairs, but French civilians had to compete with the US Army as they both scavenged for useful materials. Major Maginnis did what he could to reserve materials for civilian use, but under battlefield conditions, he had only limited success. He promised to compensate the civilians for these "irregular requisitions," as battlefield scavenging was called. By mid-July, German forces had been pushed far enough from the town that it was safe from all but the largest German cannons, which were occupied with worthier targets. Finally, "permanent" repairs could be made to roads, wires, and waterlines. Unhappily, the large American supply trucks that constantly roared through the town quickly chewed up the repaired roads and crushed the new water pipes, which had been buried too close to the surface. The hastily fixed sewer lines mixed effluent with fresh water, rendering the town's water undrinkable.[22]

The first six weeks of liberation for Carentan showed that the front lines of battle were no place for civilians to live. Daily existence for the French who remained in Carentan was difficult. However, the civil affairs operation led by Major Maginnis also showed that goodwill on the part of admittedly amateur military administrators, who were still learning on the job, could produce swift improvements in living conditions. The civil affairs officers easily gained the cooperation of local officials, who were grateful for any help they could get in these dire circumstances. Many small business owners enthusiastically volunteered to help and accepted aid once it became clear that the Americans intended to treat them fairly. Over time, they proved to be valuable allies and resources for Maginnis in his struggle to revive Carentan. Friction caused by young GIs stealing chickens, tools, and building materials was smoothed over by Maginnis, who compensated the victims of these "irregular requisitions." MPs did what they could to dampen the ill effects of good Norman calvados (apple brandy) on GIs seeking relief from the tensions of war. Major Maginnis, working closely with Mayor Joret, assumed the position of local administrator, making quick decisions about what should be done and by whom. This was well within his mandate as prescribed by the US Army. Maginnis continued in this role until the town was returned to French sovereignty on 29 August and the major took up his next posting in the Marne.

As Carentan was the first town liberated and placed under American control, Cherbourg was the first French city taken over by the American armies and used as their main supply base until larger English Channel ports were liberated in September. Cherbourg lay far behind the front lines, and although it was damaged by Allied bombing and heavy fighting, it was not as badly mauled as Carentan, and restoring it to usefulness proved less onerous. Repairing Cherbourg was important to the Allies because it served as the principal supply base for the war effort for many months. Both Cherbourg and Carentan were patched up to make them minimally livable rather than permanently repaired. Because Cherbourg was larger, the problems faced by the Allies there were correspondingly larger as well. Both the Americans and the French faced myriad difficulties that had to be addressed to allow the port and the city to play a crucial part in the war. The Americans almost completely dominated the city; many of its buildings were requisitioned to house GIs, forcing the inhabitants to live in quickly erected temporary housing outside the city. When the scattered population tried to return to the city and resume their lives, MPs and French gendarmes had the distasteful duty of evicting them again. Yet the Americans accommodated the French to the extent possible, and the French cooperated in many ways to make the city an important element in the liberation of France.

A battered and exhausted France provided the setting for French and Americans to work together to win the war. American soldiers stationed in northern France used it as a base of operations from which to launch the final assault against Germany. Marseille was an important port in terms of supplying the war effort to the north and also housed large numbers of Allied soldiers. Resort towns on the southern coast were enlisted to provide rest and recovery areas for war-weary GIs in the spring of 1945. Biarritz, in the far corner of southwestern France, was even asked to provide a location for an

American university where GIs could take courses while waiting for ships to transport them back to the United States or on to the Pacific theater of war. The Americans and the French had to get along while GIs drove the roads of France, drank in French cafés, and negotiated for and bought supplies for the army from French farmers and businesses. Relations had to be managed in liberated France so that the war could be won and ended; only then could the Americans leave.

2

Requisitions

Requisitions were an unpleasant yet necessary fact of life during wartime, but any friction they caused between French and American authorities was insufficient to ignite any fires. Although the requisition process presented challenges to French authorities and their US counterparts, it posed no real obstacles to good relations, and on the whole, each country dealt with the other in good faith and with goodwill. Most of the acrimony that flared up involved French civilians and their own government, which set compensation rates and handled all payments to citizens whose property was requisitioned.

French citizens' private property became subject to requisition beginning in September 1939, when the French military started requisitioning properties deemed essential to the conduct of the war. To save on expenses, the government set compensation rates very low. The Germans took over many previously requisitioned properties and took some more when they occupied northern and western France in 1940 and then all of France in November 1942. The German military hewed to a fairly legal path when assuming French properties. They conducted thorough inventories in the presence of owners and French officials. Goods removed from premises were carefully stored, and thievery and vandalism seem to have been kept to a minimum, at least until June 1944. As the 1940 armistice stipulated that the French would be held financially liable for all occupation costs, any costs associated with the German requisitions were borne by Vichy. French officials continued to set compensation rates, just as they had since 1939, and they continued to keep rates low. Marie-Louise Osmont and Xavier de Guerpel in Normandy were inconvenienced by the German soldiers who were forcibly billeted in their homes, but they were allowed to remain in rooms set aside for them. Such was also the case of Gustave Sabatier. When his house near Toulon was requisitioned in 1943 by the Germans, they provided him with a list of the contents of his home and their value. Sabatier estimated the rental value at 3,000 francs per month; Vichy paid him 1,500 francs per month.[1]

After the Allies arrived in France, the requisition policies put in place by the new Gaullist regime changed little. By agreement with the Allies, the French presented monthly tallies of monies owed by SHAEF, and these were forwarded to the Lend-Lease office. The US Treasury then subtracted those amounts from the total Lend-Lease bill in the form of "reverse lend-lease" or "reciprocal aid." Both the Americans and the French kept ledgers of American aid to the French and French aid to the Americans, and little actual money ever changed hands between Paris and Washington. The hope that the ledgers would have a zero balance at the end of the war proved unrealistic, but the true source of many problems was the vast amount of money Paris owed to its own citizenry. According to the Aid to Allied Forces (AFA) agreement signed in Algiers in March 1944, Gaullist-appointed prefects assigned people to receive military requests for billeting or goods, locate the necessary items, and negotiate a price. Price schedules for almost every kind of exchange were worked out centrally by French officials and delivered to the appropriate Allied officers, with payment rendered to the AFA and not to the vendors. In special circumstances, Allied units could ask mayors for supplies and billeting to meet only their immediate and temporary needs. The agreement provided for regional and departmental financial officers appointed by the CFLN to handle all financial transactions and questions. The agreement also provided for mixed juries of French and Allies to hear appeals. The April 1944 agreement between the CFLN and the Americans stated that all vehicles in France had to be registered with the Bureau des Ponts et Chaussées (Department of Bridges and Roads) and were subject to requisition *by the French* to be placed at the disposition of the US Army; the rental rate would be determined by the bureau, depending on the age and condition of the vehicle. In July 1944 both the French and the Americans decided that the French authorities needed the vehicles more than the Allies did, so they agreed that all requisitioned and captured civilian vehicles would be turned over to the French.[2]

Until the breakout in August, all of liberated France remained in a war zone and, as such, was subject to emergency requisition rules that allowed the Allied armies wide discretion. Requisitions that occurred outside the agreement between French and American authorities fell under the catch-all rubric of "irregular requisitions." Pilfering by front-line soldiers was one form of irregular requisitions, and an agreement was eventually worked out with de Gaulle's authorities on how to handle it. Both sides recognized that procurement by soldiers on the move would not always conform to regulations, and little could be done to stop it. They realized that irregular requisitions were necessary to keep men in the field provisioned and fighting, so they agreed that soldiers could requisition pretty much whatever they wanted, with payment to be determined later. In mid-August "later" arrived, and the Americans had to adjust to working under French rules. Many properties that had been requisitioned in war zones under emergency conditions had to be returned, or the requisitions had to be regularized with the appropriate French authorities. A new agreement was signed that approved cash payments by US Army "town majors"—the army liaison with civil authorities—to French mayors, who would then pay French civilians for services rendered according to a schedule set by the French government. Whenever possible, a French army liaison officer would act as the go-between for French civil authorities and American military officers. This agreement replicated what had been previous practice in Normandy, while reflecting that combat conditions frequently did not allow application of the letter of the law. It recognized that town majors would not always have cash on hand to pay French mayors, so IOUs (requisition orders) would have to be accepted and countersigned by French liaison officers when possible. However, the agreement insisted that French officials act as mediators in all transactions and that the US military give IOUs directly to French civilians for purchased goods—milk or vegetables, for example—only in "dire circumstances" or if the mayor were unavailable. This put American officers in the awkward position of not being allowed to pay cash to farmers or shopkeepers for goods, requiring them to pay with IOUs *only.* One might think this would make American requisition officers unwelcome customers for French civilians with something to sell, but I found few civilian complaints against American requisition officers (complaints by French officials are another matter); however, there were many civilian complaints against French officials responsible for payments.[3]

The French government initially struggled to ensure that US Army purchases and rentals followed the agreed-upon rules. Throughout the American presence in France, irregular requisitions were a constant irritant. The American liaison in Paris delegated to handle this problem, Colonel Wadsworth Cresse, practically threw in the towel at a meeting with French officials, conceding there was little he could do to make US officers conform to the regulations. He admitted it had been a big problem in the United Kingdom before D-Day, when officers in new units were unfamiliar with the rules. He could only suggest that French vendors submit statements to "claims offices" and hope for eventual compensation. Once AFA offices were opened, all purchase orders were supposed to be funneled through them. When the US Army section headquarters in Lyon discovered it was being charged retail prices for fruits and vegetables by a wholesaler in Nice, as well as a delivery fee, even though the army supplied the trucks and drivers, it complained to the AFA. The AFA responded that the army should stop doing business with that company and, in the future, should seek the AFA's advice

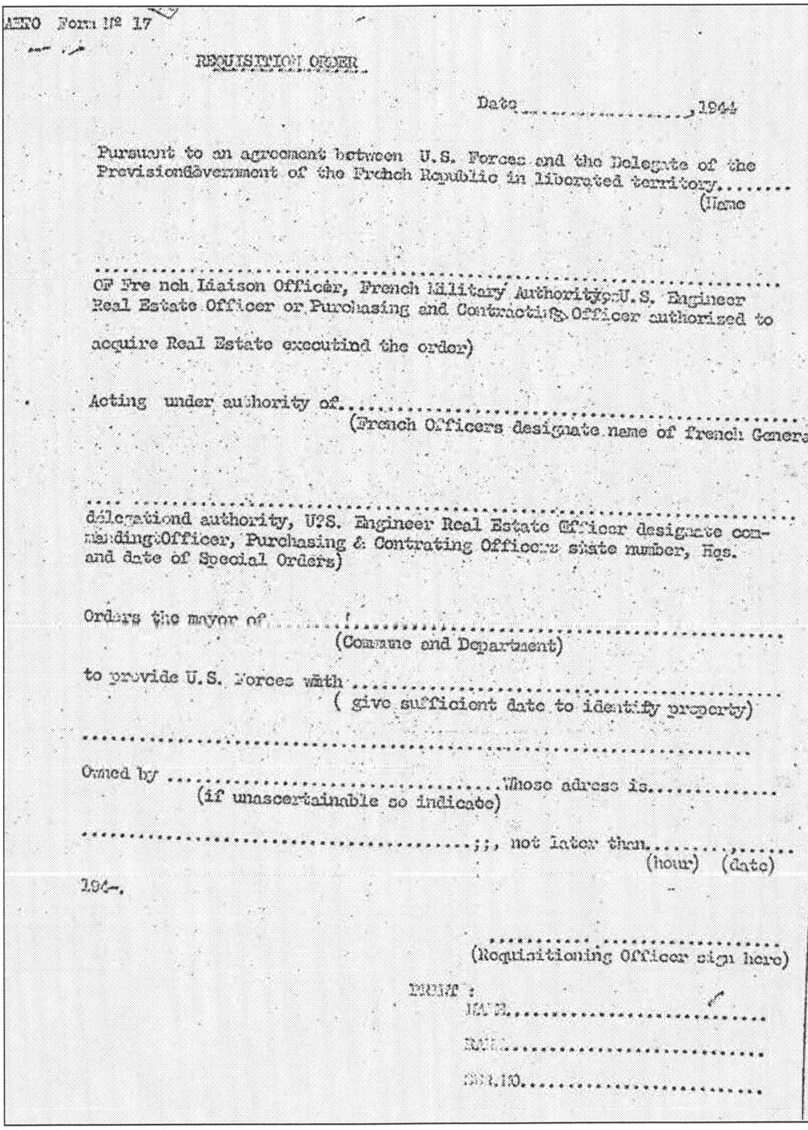

AEEO Form N° 17

REQUISITION ORDER

Date ....,1944

Pursuant to an agreement between U.S. Forces and the Delegate of the ProvisionGövernment of the Frehch Republic in liberated territory........ (Name

....

OF Fre nch Liaison Officer, French Military Authority or U.S. Engineer Real Estate Officer or Purchasing and Contracting Officer authorized to acquire Real Estate executind the order)

Acting under authority of.. (French Officers designate name of french Genera

....

délegationd authority, U?S. Engineer Real Estate Officer designate commanding Officer, Purchasing & Contrating Officers state number, Hqs. and date of Special Orders)

Orders the mayor of .... (Commune and Department)

to provide U.S. Forces with .... (give sufficient date to identify property)

....

Owned by ....Whose adress is............. (if unascertainable so indicate)

...................................;;, not later than..................... (hour) (date)

194-.

.... (Requisitioning Officer sign here)

PRINT :
NAME..........................
RANK..........................
SER.NO........................

Blank US requisition order attached to Col. Wayne Allen, general purchasing agent, US Army, to Col. Laroque, office of Commissaire de la République, Bayeux, 16 August 1944. (Courtesy of the Archives nationales de France)

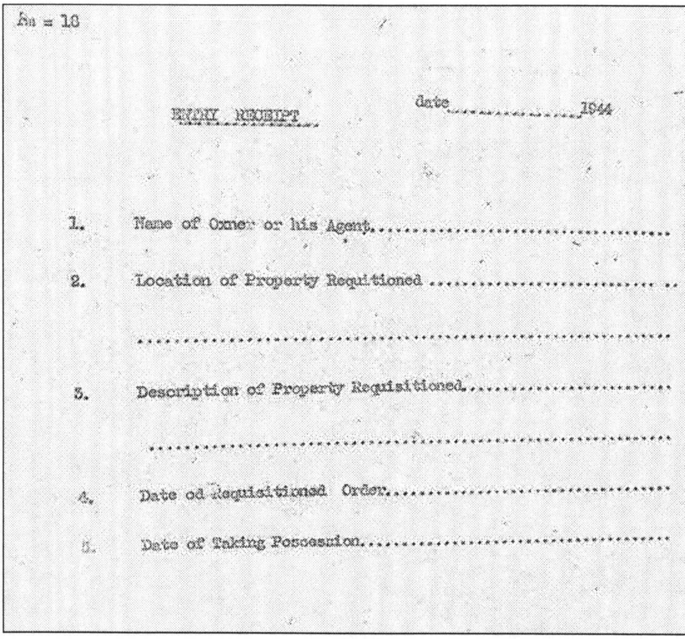

Blank US requisition receipt attached to Col. Wayne Allen, general purchasing agent, US Army, to Col. Laroque, office of Commissaire de la République, Bayeux, 16 August 1944. (Courtesy of the Archives nationales de France)

on reliable vendors. Even though the Americans were allowed to buy fresh meat, it was so scarce after the great slaughter of farm animals in northern France from June to September 1944 that the army agreed to reserve French meat for the French people. Minister of Supply Paul Giacobbi reminded government officials that it was illegal for French to sell or rent facilities outside of AFA supervision (except under certain agreed-upon circumstances), and merchants were warned not to sell food to American soldiers. The French army was just as guilty (or perhaps more so) of irregular requisitions, buying coffee, dried beans, vegetables, and cheese directly from shopkeepers in Auxerre rather than going through army procurement. A national supply plan that went into effect on 1 January 1945 reserved most foodstuffs for civilian consumption; the French army was supposed to receive its rations from the Americans under Lend-Lease. Rumors circulated in Nancy in December 1944 that butter was unavailable to civilians because the Americans had bought it all; in fact, they bought little butter and few eggs from the French. Although individual GIs bartered cigarettes and coffee for eggs and butter

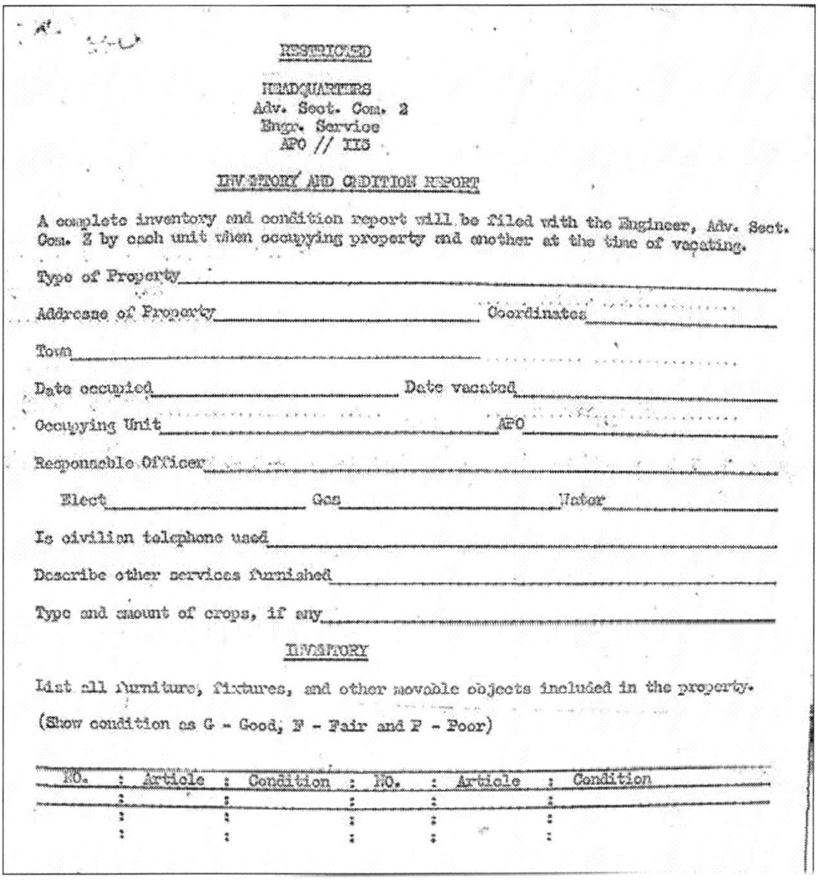

RESTRICTED

HEADQUARTERS
Adv. Sect. Com. Z
Engr. Service
APO // 113

INVENTORY AND CONDITION REPORT

A complete inventory and condition report will be filed with the Engineer, Adv. Sect. Com. Z by each unit when occupying property and another at the time of vacating.

Type of Property__________

Address of Property__________ Coordinates__________

Town__________

Date occupied__________ Date vacated__________

Occupying Unit__________ APO__________

Responsible Officer__________

Elect__________ Gas__________ Water__________

Is civilian telephone used__________

Describe other services furnished__________

Type and amount of crops, if any__________

INVENTORY

List all furniture, fixtures, and other movable objects included in the property.

(Show condition as G - Good, F - Fair and P - Poor)

NO.	Article	Condition	NO.	Article	Condition

Blank inventory sheet attached to Col. Wayne Allen, general purchasing agent, US Army, to Col. Laroque, office of Commissaire de la République, Bayeux, 16 August 1944. (Courtesy of the Archives nationales de France)

unofficially, the Quartermaster Corps did not buy these items wholesale in France. Allied commanders in Lorraine went so far as to forbid their troops from buying any food from civilians. SHAEF denied that Allied troops had any responsibility for the shortages that plagued the population of the Nord in November; it blamed the lack of transport and the French government's devotion to stamping out the black market, which was where most people acquired scarce goods such as butter and milk.[4]

With so many shortages in France, requisitions of scarce goods caused real hardships for civilians. This was particularly true when it came to transport. In the winter especially, the Americans requested large numbers of horses and mules, which had proved their value in Italy. But the Germans had already taken so many French horses that few were left. If the Americans requisitioned those that remained, what were French farmers to do? The government in Paris felt obliged to intervene. The same was true of cars and trucks: the Germans had already taken so many that if the Americans (not to mention the French army and FFI) took all they needed, there would be none left for civilian use. In Châlons-sur-Marne the US Army requested twenty touring cars from the French, provoking the exasperated prefect to point out that the Marne probably did not contain twenty such automobiles. Once requisitioned vehicles crossed the Rhine into Germany, owners' prospects of seeing their property again were not good. Wrangling over the use of French vehicles, especially trucks, by the US Army in Germany occupied an excessive amount of time and energy for both American and French officers. Still, it is hard not to feel sympathy for the two French owners of a truck "bought" by the Germans and then seized by the Americans and taken into Germany, where it disappeared from records.[5]

The most irregular of requisitions were those by the FFI in the early, chaotic days of liberation. De Gaulle had endowed local liberation committees with consultative powers, meaning that officials appointed by de Gaulle had to listen to the committees' advice, even if they did not follow it. This led local committees to believe they also had the power to requisition properties, which they did with abandon in the early days of liberation. As the prefect in Colmar stated to the minister of the interior during this chaotic period, "One can excuse some level of irregularity [in requisitions]." Their favorite targets were buildings previously requisitioned by the Germans or properties belonging to people accused of collaboration. Frequently, there was little difference between a local liberation committee and the FFI, so FFI "sequestrations" were done in the name of the local committee, or vice versa. These sequestrations were irregular requisitions that were most easily reversed by replacing them with regular requisitions made by the American or French army, if available. Most often, there were no French military units available to displace the FFI or the local committees, so mayors or prefects relied on Americans to issue requisition orders. That proved easier with buildings and almost impossible with automobiles, which were frequently just driven off, never to be seen again. FFI units also had to be fed, so they took to requisitioning supplies directly from local farmers, giving them unofficial "requisition orders" for potatoes, vegetables, and the like. When farmers presented these orders to mayors and prefects, they were sometimes honored. Often, however, the hapless farmers were given the runaround and were told to present the order to General Supply, which was responsible for providing the FFI with whatever they needed, aside from military equipment. Though sympathetic to their plight, the director of supply in the Yonne could do nothing to help the luckless farmers. He told the FFI to come to him for supplies, which he would buy from the farmers, but this did little good. When packs of armed FFI showed up at their doors demanding eggs, cheese, and beets, the farmers were in no position to refuse. Nevertheless, a farmer in Arces-Dilo convinced the prosecutor's office in Joigny to press charges against five FFI who forcibly took food and cash from his house in September 1944. When police were alerted to FFI members walking six cows down a lane in Champignelles (west of Auxerre), the police assumed the cows were stolen; however, investigation revealed that the FFI were acting under orders of General Supply to escort the cows to town. Jacques Soustelle, the commissioner in Bordeaux—a region hardly touched by Allied requisitions but subjected to many irregular seizures by the FFI—wanted all requisitions stopped as soon as the war was over. He proposed that civil authorities be given the same power of requisition as the military and that prefects be granted the authority to requisition supplies and equipment, such as trucks, from the army to serve civilian needs. With the war in Europe won, he believed that economic reconstruction should be approached with the same urgency as the war against Germany. Such a plan would have pleased the liberation committees but had no chance of adoption by the provisional government.[6]

One hundred and fifty farmers unfortunate enough to have flat land near les Grandes-Chapelles, north of Troyes, had their fields requisitioned by the French air force in 1939, then by the Germans in 1940, and finally by the Americans in September 1944. The US Army Air Force (USAAF) immediately contracted with local builders to make repairs and build new facilities to accommodate the American fighter planes and medium bombers that would use the bases. As the provisional government became firmly established in Paris, it moved quickly to assume control over such matters. The Bureau des Ponts et Chaussées (PC) in Troyes was tasked with supervising all such work and was instructed to forward all bills for work and materials to the Air Ministry in Paris. The bases were unambiguously French and on loan to the Americans for the duration of the war. The PC was also responsible for determining fair compensation for damages or alterations to farmers' properties and ensuring that modifications were reversed once the US military left. And, like any other requisition, changes to property had to be approved beforehand—in writing—by local authorities. The United States hung on to the fields until April 1945, when they were released to the French air force, which declined to use them. Rental rates were set by the PC, which also handled payments. One farmer, M. Dieudonné, was paid 246 francs (about $5) per month for the period of American occupancy for his 4 hectares (10 acres), or around $35. He appealed for compensation for his lost harvest but received nothing. M. Clement was paid $21 for his 6.5 acres; M. Choiselat received $37 for his 11 acres. One farmer asked for 12,000 francs ($240) for his lost crops; he got zero. Another farmer who asked for only 1,200 francs ($24) also received nothing. In reading through these appeals and petitions, I detected no bitterness toward the USAAF but plenty aimed at the PC. Shortly after the Allied invasion of France, Commissioner Coulet investigated whether it might be better to call farm fields taken for airfields "war damage" rather than requisitions, only to discover that war damages were not compensated by Lend-Lease. Later the Air Ministry wondered whether it might be better to expropriate the land rather than rent it. It received the same answer: Lend-Lease allowed the US Army only to rent real estate in France, not buy it. Ultimately, these paltry sums paid to farmers by the PC would be subtracted from the Americans' bill to France.[7]

Because Marseille provided one of the largest ports available to the Allies in continental Europe—only Antwerp was more important to Allied supply—the Allies built up an enormous establishment there, necessitating a large number of requisitions of all sorts. Starting in September 1944, the Allied militaries requisitioned thousands of apartments, garages, warehouses, hotels, restaurants, movie theaters, workshops, offices, and all manner of establishments deemed necessary to run the port and support facilities. One register of requisitions (there were many such registers) listed 1,087 rentals in September; by the end of 1944, 5,071 places had been requisitioned, including 88 hotels, 14 restaurants, and 8 bars. As per the agreement between the Allies and France, all requisitions were ordered and paid for by the French provisional government, but they benefited the French, British, Canadian, and American militaries. Commissioner of the Republic Raymond Aubrac was responsible for all requisitions in Provence, but he had only ad hoc administrative machinery to handle them until the creation of the AFA's regional office, which took over requisitions and payments in late October 1944 and maintained permanent contact with Allied officers appointed to supervise such matters. When French chief engineer for the port of Marseille, G. Le Bel, needed an office to handle all the Lend-Lease paperwork landing on his desk, he, too, requisitioned an office building previously requisitioned by the Germans.[8]

Owners of requisitioned properties had plenty of complaints. The owners of the hydraulic boat elevator in Marseille protested that the rates set by the French government and paid by the United States to use the dry dock did not even cover the cost of operations. Hotel owners on the Côte d'Azur were also unhappy about compensation rates, protesting they were only a fraction of prewar rates and did not cover their expenses. Besides, the Americans used the hotels extensively, pushing up costs beyond prewar levels. The French government was slow to compensate the hotels for their American guests, which proved catastrophic to the owners of smaller hotels, who could not pay their workers. When the US Army requisitioned four large hotels in Nice for R&R for soldiers, the hotels wanted the prices for drinks raised. This was not simply price-gouging: the hotels had been ordered to lower prices because their bars had previously served mostly French workers—whose wages were also set by the government—and the government wanted them to be able to drink cheaply. With French workers now barred from drinking in the watering holes reserved exclusively for GIs, the owners wanted to restore the old prices. One solution was to add live music: bars that offered entertainment could charge higher prices. Yet when GIs wandered into nonreserved bars and cafés, the commander of Delta Base, General John Paul Ratay, complained that the GIs were overcharged for drinks by crooked French proprietors. The American liaison officer, Colonel Lévy, replied that the army could not police French establishments and GIs should stick to bars run by the USO. Many French found themselves in the same unhappy plight as the farmers in the Yonne, who provided goods and services for which they could not receive payment. When US Army personnel seized three harbor boats from a harbor supply and service company for the port of Marseille without presenting any requisition order, the company was denied payment by the responsible French office. The company was simply out of luck.[9]

The US military looked around Marseille for buildings suitable for a hospital and found a municipal retirement home, La Tour Blanche (The White Tower), which it attempted to seize on 2 September by presenting an evacuation order to the resident manager, Mme. Mayrargue. An American officer told her she had six days to find other accommodations for the residents—220 bedridden invalids—and move them out. Part of La Tour Blanche had already been requisitioned by the French army in 1939; most of the rest had been taken by the Germans in March 1944, when they forced 300 ambulatory residents to be removed to a mountain resort in the Haute-Loire. When Mme. Mayrargue protested that the mountain resort was not only far away but also unheated, and that fall was almost upon them and winter not far behind, the prefect relented and asked whether the residents could be dispersed to various quarters within Marseille. Eventually, room was found for them at a Catholic hospital there. The prefect had tried to talk General Ratay and the district's French military commander out of the requisition, without success. In this case, the US Army was clearly in charge, although the French army sided with the Americans, undercutting the prefect's authority. When the municipal council voted in December 1945 to return La Tour Blanche to its old function as a public retirement home, the US Army was still in possession of the buildings. After the Americans finally quit La Tour Blanche in March 1946, the cost to restore just the grounds was estimated at 1.65 million francs (about $33,000), as the Americans had torn out all the shrubs, cut down many trees, demolished a greenhouse, and damaged the walls on the property. It would cost another 2.5 million francs ($50,000) to repair the buildings; most of the interior doors and windows needed to be replaced, as well as many bathroom and kitchen fixtures. The US Army had paid a total of 150,833 francs ($3,000) in rent during its occupancy, or about 3.5 percent of the estimated cost of repairs. The Americans had promised to restore the grounds and repair the interior, but in the end, the work was left to the French, and when it was finally completed in 1952, the French military received the bill.[10]

Starting with the first battlefield requisitions in Normandy, the American policy was to requisition buildings and lands previously requisitioned by the Germans. This made it easy to find suitable properties and avoided evictions. During the period of chaos and cloudy authority in June and July 1944, this system worked fairly well but was not without problems, especially in Cherbourg. Local authorities—usually mayors—were theoretically in charge of assigning or at least approving requisitions by the US military, but in practice, the military took what it needed and the mayors generally went along. However, as de Gaulle's provisional government established its authority, the practice was challenged by commissioners, prefects, officials in Paris, and even mayors. The French successfully evicted Americans from some historic buildings previously occupied by the Germans; however, historic buildings were just as vulnerable to military use as any others in a war zone. It is worth noting that officers reporting to General Patton apparently showed as much disdain for regulations as Patton did, so the Americans in Third Army's war zone were more likely to ignore rules and national agreements than Americans elsewhere.

With liberation, the French wanted to resume normal life as soon as possible. Mayors everywhere were particularly upset that schools appropriated by the Germans were not restored by the Americans. The Germans had favored using schools as barracks and had requisitioned nearly 40 percent of them in the Occupied Zone in 1941; they occupied two-thirds of the schools in Reims. Because the Americans followed the policy of simply taking over German requisitions to avoid acquiring new buildings, a lot of GIs were billeted in schools. The French were especially anxious to get students back into classrooms in the fall of 1944 and were disappointed when that did not happen. They were doubly shocked when the new French army continued the practice of using schools as barracks, filling classrooms with French soldiers. The Ministry of Education advised all prefects to urge the Americans—and the French military, too—to quit their schools in favor of anyplace else. This call was taken up by the office of AFA, which tried—more or less in vain—to convince the Americans not to use schools if other facilities were available. Unfortunately, schools also provided ideal spaces for hospitals, and during the Germans' Ardennes offensive, the US Army required a lot more hospital space quickly. In December and January the Americans proved to be somewhat flexible and accommodating in northern France, but despite the pleas of Commissioner Pierre Pène in Laon, the Oise section of the US Army requisitioned all secondary schools in the Aisne for hospitals. Still, the army tried to accommodate the French need for schools, and General John T. Lewis chose schools that were already being used for other purposes: a girls' lycée in Valenciennes being used to house political prisoners, two schools in Châlons-sur-Marne that had already been half requisitioned by the United States, and a school in Montesson (a suburb of Paris) housing juvenile delinquents. Numerous schools requested by the United States were religious establishments serving students. Perhaps the US Army believed—probably correctly—that French authorities would have fewer objections to disturbing education in religious schools. General Lewis suggested a meeting with the education minister to discuss how to transfer the schools with the least inconvenience to students and teachers. He showed tact and consideration, but as in all matters concerning the US Army in France, the war effort and victory came first, something the US government and the provisional government usually agreed on. The commissioner in Dijon was less pleased with American practices when General Larkin requisitioned the Lycée Carnot in November 1944 without notifying him first. The Americans had discussed the requisition with the school rector and the local French military commander and mistakenly believed that was sufficient. After some tough negotiations, the Americans agreed to return the dormitories to the students and leave half the school for education. But the affair left a bad taste in the commissioner's mouth, and he warned Interior Minister Adrien Tixier that the Americans had better change their ways, which were too reminiscent of Nazi methods. De Gaulle's commissioners almost always showed the same prickliness on questions of sovereignty and central authority as the provisional president did.[11]

With AFA offices up and running in all relevant departments and major towns, the amount of paperwork necessary to keep up with requisitions quickly became overwhelming. All requisitions prior to 31 August had to be reregistered and payments calculated. The central office in Paris had a backlog of 25,000 requisitions still outstanding in January 1945. Payments for requisitions not handled by reverse Lend-Lease were still unsettled and proved burdensome to local authorities. The French complained that the British had been quick to pay when presented with consolidated bills and requested in vain that the Americans adopt the same practice. Despite the lack of an American centralized system for handling bills, the French made few complaints about the Americans, reserving their ire for AFA officers who were slow to reimburse burdened French citizens. The prefect in Châlons-sur-Marne noted that the Americans in his district were quick to submit receipts to the AFA, but the ministries in Paris were slow to process them and approve payments. Hotel owners in the Marne were unable to pay their workers because they had received no compensation from Paris for requisitioned hotels. Many issues that had been postponed during combat had to be settled after January 1945. Who was to pay for goods transferred from the United States to France and subsequently destroyed by fire? The Americans agreed that they would not charge the French if the fire had been caused by enemy action, but if it were an accident, the French would still be liable for the goods. And what about goods purchased by the US Army in France that were not directly related to the war effort, such as musical instruments or rolls of paper for *Stars and Stripes*? Should they be subject to reciprocal aid? And should the French reimburse the US Army for taxes paid on 72,000 bottles of cognac purchased in Marseille? The French argued that alcohol should never be the subject of reciprocal aid, so why should taxes on it be rebated? Any tax-related matters would have to be settled between the French Ministry of Finance and the US Treasury. What about anchorage fees paid by US ships unloading war matériel in French harbors? That, too, would have to be taken up by higher authorities.[12]

American demands for wood became an irritant early on. French minister Raymond Haas-Picard, in charge of relations with the Allies, judged that the Allied armies should not requisition any wood because it belonged in a category with pharmaceuticals, livestock, fodder, lubricants, and some foods not subject to requisition. That came as news to most American supply officers, who requisitioned wood in large quantities all across northern France and, indeed, had no other source of fuel and construction materials. The US Army had been sensitive about using construction materials because of the great need for repairs in French towns and villages. Nevertheless, the war demanded wood: temporary structures of all sorts had to be constructed to meet the armies' needs, and little of it could be imported. In the fall of

1944 the US Army began replacing pontoon bridges with wooden bridges and requisitioned 284 million board feet of lumber for that purpose. Ninth Army alone operated thirty-five sawmills (in Belgium) in January 1945 for the purpose of producing lumber to build wooden bridges, giving some idea of the amount of wood necessary to keep an army moving. The commissioner in Orléans complained that wood needed to reconstruct the towns of Blois and Vendôme was being taken out of French forests and burned for fuel by the Americans. He feared civilians in the region would have inadequate fuelwood during the winter and asked the Americans to limit their consumption until March 1945, when the warmer weather would allow more wood to be diverted to other uses. In fact, the Americans were allowed to acquire wood for many purposes, but the amount remained in dispute. Third Army reached an agreement with the French Forest Service about how much it could use, but enforcing that agreement proved difficult. Stacks of logs in public forests near Toul kept disappearing, and people blamed the Americans, no doubt justly. In November an air force squadron near Ochey took wood set aside for the local population to use for fuel, leaving them without enough wood to heat their homes during the coming winter. For some reason, USAAF personnel were apparently the worst offenders. The region around Troyes hosted numerous air bases and was plagued by repeated thefts of logs from French forests, which civil affairs officers seemed powerless to prevent. They promised French authorities that the stealing would stop, but when it did not, the officers suggested that the French submit claims for these irregular requisitions. In one base just southwest of Nancy and within an active war zone, such requisitions would have been hard to prevent, as officers authorized whatever was necessary to keep the fight going. A pile of wrecked railroad cars in Châlons-sur-Marne looked like a good source of fuel to the US Army, but to French railroad officials, it looked like useful scrap material for repairing other cars. Disputes over how much wood the US Army was entitled to rose to the cabinet level and became the subject of debate in Paris. The prefect in Châlons-sur-Marne reported in January 1945 that the problem of stealing wood from forests had diminished not because the Americans had responded to his pleas but because the German offensive in the Ardennes had vastly reduced the number of US troops in his department and thus their demand for wood for heating. Only the end of the war dampened disputes over the US Army's enormous appetite for wood. The question of who had the right to use materials deemed essential for the war effort remained open and unresolved.[13]

In some cases, the French protested not the requisitions themselves but the way they were implemented. Factory owners and managers in the east clashed with US Army officers almost as soon as the Americans arrived and started occupying their buildings. When US troops occupied a factory in Hagondange, north of Metz, they amused themselves by breaking machinery, and someone took a blowtorch to the strongbox. GIs moved into factories in Lunéville that had been operating just a few days earlier and began "pillaging" whatever looked useful to them. When the owners alerted the subprefect, he met with US commanders, who promised the irregular requisitions would stop. Even after these requisitions became regularized by the reestablished French authorities, factory owners protested that they could not operate their facilities if they were occupied by Americans. In some cases, factories landed contracts to produce materials for the US Army but could not do so because the soldiers were using the buildings and grounds as warehouses or truck depots. Moreover, some factory owners discovered that when the Americans vacated the buildings, they left behind ruined machinery or stole stocks of materials necessary to fabricate goods. One American captain tried to get a French factory owner ejected from his own factory because running it would interfere with whatever the Americans were trying to do there. In this case, French authorities succeeded in overruling the Americans; the owner was allowed to remain and run his business. The French agreed that the Americans could use the Bugatti factory in Molsheim and even agreed that the machinery should be moved. However, when the delicate machinery was taken away, it was loaded onto trucks and left exposed to the elements, causing it to rust. Although the Americans admitted the soldiers should have taken greater care to protect the property, even French AFA officials noted that the French on the scene at the Bugatti factory should have objected to the way the machines were being moved at the time, rather than waiting until it was too late.[14]

Some regions were subjected to greater requisitioning than others. Port cities housed enormous numbers of GIs, and by the end of the war, the US Army had requisitioned buildings or other properties in ports to house 110,000 American servicemen and -women. The southwest of France mostly escaped the need to quarter US troops, except for an R&R center that hosted the American University in Biarritz, staffed by US professors who taught college courses to GIs. This prompted the requisitioning of every hotel in Biarritz (except for one reserved for French guests) and some neighboring towns to house the 5,000 GI students. The Americans proposed to requisition all the villas belonging to South Americans and Spaniards in the region, but this was successfully resisted by French authorities on the grounds that doing so would end the long tradition of Spanish-speaking tourists visiting the area. The Côte d'Azur provided a major R&R center for GIs, and the United States ended up requisitioning most of the hotels from Nice to Saint-Tropez. The

12,000 enlisted men and 3,000 officers on R&R in September 1945 occupied 172 hotels; some private villas, apartments, and garages; a bakery; numerous bars; a dry cleaner; and sporting grounds. The huge numbers of US soldiers being transferred from Europe to the Pacific theater caused an enormous surge in requisitions in northern France. For the most part, US troops were lodged in seventeen gigantic tent cities (known as the "cigarette" camps, such as "Old Gold," "Lucky Strike," and "Twenty Grand") erected in upper Normandy in November 1944 as staging camps to receive new replacements arriving in Europe. Even though these giant tent cities could house 138,000 troops, the GIs' presence placed enormous pressure on local French facilities. Normandy was not alone in feeling overwhelmed by GIs. The 45th Infantry Division set up new quarters in Burgundy, causing a housing crisis. In August 1945 Dijon was out of rooms to requisition and had no place to house displaced persons or workers and POWs returning from Germany.[15]

The Oise base section, headquartered in Châlons-sur-Marne and covering much of northeastern France, demanded huge numbers of buildings and French workers. To support the giant supply depots, airfields, truck parks, repair facilities, and the like, the Americans requisitioned 1,350 buildings and paid a monthly rent of 4.2 million francs ($84,000). They also rented 325 workshops, garages, warehouses, oil tanks, and similar facilities for an additional 3 million francs ($60,000). In addition, the Americans required automobiles, electricity, water, linens, laundry services, food, dishes, and furniture, all of which cost money. In May 1945 the AFA presented the Oise base section with a bill for 70 million francs ($1.4 million) to cover one month's worth of rents, utilities, provisions, and wages for 13,000 workers—1,550 itemized demands for payment. As early as March 1945 Commissioner Pène in Laon protested the heavy burden imposed on the French by Allied requisitions and convinced SHAEF that some important buildings in Givet and Charleville should be returned. At the same time, Commissioner Marcel Grégoire in Châlons-sur-Marne reported, "Our region . . . is supersaturated with the American Army, [and] the actions in the interior and those of the U.S. government on the exterior are received unfavorably. Housing is very short and requisitions here are much too burdensome. The conduct of the Americans in the requisitioned houses is [so] scandalous, that people fear to have their properties occupied by Americans. They frequently occupy a property without even notifying the owner. They hire way too many workers to the detriment of our economy." In June the commissioner characterized his region as "over saturated with Americans" and said he was looking forward to their departure, even though he found them cooperative and "sensitive to our plight." The June AFA bill for Lorraine was more than twice as large as May's—168.5 million francs ($3.37 million)—even though the commissioner noted that the American presence was diminishing. When all the numbers were finally tallied, the rental bill just for SHAEF headquarters in France came to $5 million, all of which was charged to reverse Lend-Lease (the Americans suggested the British pick up half the tab!). For all of France, the American rental bill totaled $100 million. The United States provided France with $2.3 billion in military aid and an additional $550 million in aid to civilians or for infrastructure repair before the end of Lend-Lease. The French furnished US forces with $868 million in reciprocal aid. Thus, the ledger did not balance at zero, and the $100 million rental bill was applied against US expenditures that benefited France.[16]

It should come as no surprise that the prolonged US Army presence in eastern France imposed a greater burden there than elsewhere, but these circumstances explain only a portion of the exasperation expressed by many French in the region. General Patton's way of doing things proved to be a problem for the French, and his requisition practices conformed to this pattern. Commissioner Paul Chailley-Bert in Nancy and the prefect in Metz both complained bitterly that Patton and the officers under him made unreasonable and excessive demands for space and supplies. Chailley-Bert concluded early on that the only way to get any satisfaction from Third Army was to deal with Patton personally, but this intimate contact failed to ease the burden on the population and administration of Meurthe-et-Moselle, even after the front line moved on in November 1944. He protested to Paris that the US Army monopolized all telephone lines between major towns and would not make them available even for official French communications. Despite repeated pleas to regularize requisitions, Third Army continued to occupy any and all buildings previously occupied by Germans. In reaction to the Germans' Ardennes offensive, Third Army requisitioned so many hospital rooms—20,000 by March 1945—that few were left to meet civilian needs. The prefect in Metz complained that while he found the commander of the 5th Infantry Division, General Stafford L. Irwin, likable and easy to get along with, the general's demands for requisitions were "onerous and unreasonable," and he concluded that "the Americans intend to be just as intrusive as the Germans were." The Americans demanded all barracks space in Metz, which, as a fortress city, had a lot to offer, as well as 150 rooms for a headquarters there. Irregular requisitions remained a problem. Americans seized thirty tons of coal from a working factory that needed it to carry on operations, and despite shortages in the region, the Americans demand as much coal as they could get their hands on. The prefect was especially perturbed when the Americans demanded that civilians evacuate two villages south of

Metz so soldiers could practice maneuvers with live ammunition. The people of these villages, which had just recently been liberated from the Germans, were allowed to return to their homes and retrieve their belongings, but they were upset that they were not allowed to stay. In contrast, Chailley-Bert had nothing but compliments for General Alexander Patch, the commander of Seventh Army, situated on the front to the south of Patton's Third Army. The commissioner found Patch and his chief of staff General Wilson very accommodating and easy to work with. Wilson did his part to improve the lot of French civilians in his zone.[17]

Relations between Third Army and industrial plants went more smoothly because Patton needed their products and services: numerous establishments serviced tanks and vehicles, and sawmills were fully employed by the US Army in coordination with the French Forest Service. However, the US Army demand for skilled workers quickly escalated beyond the French ability to supply them, especially because so many skilled technicians had been conscripted to labor in Germany. Commissioner Chailley-Bert feared he would be unable to find enough workers to carry out critical rebuilding and repairs around Metz. Repair shops and metalworking plants employed 9,000 men in January 1945, which was not enough to meet American needs, so Patton wanted the workweek extended to fifty-four hours to provide steel girders for bridges. To counter the German offensive in the Ardennes, Patton ordered more than 500,000 yards of white canvas for winter camouflage, which was more than mills in Lorraine could provide; the order was forwarded to Paris for handling. The US Army employed huge numbers of workers by March 1945: 6,000 in the Meurthe-et-Moselle and 12,600 in all of Lorraine. American demands for skilled workers strained the region's capacity because of the shortage: the Americans employed 5,000 skilled workers, half of whom were hard-to-find metalworkers; they employed another 500 workers in hospitals and 250 in offices, many of whom possessed valuable skills such as the ability to translate or to use American typewriters. In the spring of 1945 the Americans announced their intention to tender large new contracts for supplies and services, which the commissioner feared would monopolize Lorraine's industry and interfere with rebuilding. In February 1945 the payroll reached 20 million francs ($400,000), which surely would have been a welcome infusion into the region's economy, the prefect noted, if Paris could have speeded up the payment of wages.[18]

With Patton's successful push to the east of Nancy in mid-November, the Lorraine front moved east to Metz and beyond to the Saar. By mid-December, Patton moved his headquarters to follow the battle, which freed up space in Nancy. When Third Army headquarters decamped, this opened up 650 buildings and apartments for civilian use and 65 workshops, warehouses, garages, and the like. Third Army civil affairs officers turned out to be sensitive to the needs of the civilian population and released these buildings by early January 1945. The AFA opened a claims office in Nancy to settle claims for damages caused by the US Army during its residency in Nancy and began dispensing money right away.[19]

By early 1945, the provisional government in Paris was both firmly established and confident enough to take control of requisitions throughout France. De Gaulle instructed Interior Minister Tixier to oversee a complete inventory of requisitions by the Allies. He wanted to regularize all requisitions implemented under emergency circumstances and make sure that any goods or properties seized by the Allies under combat conditions were returned if no longer needed. In particular, de Gaulle challenged the seizure of ports, airfields, roads, and rail facilities, all of which he wanted returned to French control as soon as possible. He also objected to the direct recruitment of French workers by the Allied armies and instructed Tixier to see that all employment contracts were handled by the French government. Beginning on 5 February, all requests for requisitions had to be approved by the Ministry of National Economy to ensure that they conformed to the recently approved plan to restore the economy. Even enlisting all the commissioners of the Republic, prefects, and their staffs, this would be a mammoth undertaking that would take months to complete.[20]

When the war in Europe ended, the French expected to reclaim their properties occupied by American troops. Both the French government and SHAEF anticipated restitution as well, but both knew it would take many months for the US military to leave Europe and move to Asia. They tried to manage a smooth and speedy transfer of properties. The French government was especially anxious to get its schools back and asked that they be handed over first. Civil affairs officers considered this a reasonable request, but they wanted the French to find alternative quarters for troops that had to vacate schools. Not surprisingly, French authorities were not always able to locate suitable substitutes, and come September 1945, many schools in the Paris area were still occupied by American soldiers. The school inspector in Nancy was bewildered and frustrated that only twenty GIs continued to be billeted in the girls' school in Jarville in August 1945, depriving the pupils of their classrooms for no good reason at the start of the school year. The prefect convinced the Americans to vacate the building by mid-September. He was unable to perform the same magic for l'Ecole Jeanne d'Arc in Homécourt, which was not vacated by the US Army until the end of October. Prefects had similar experiences elsewhere: in Châlons-sur-Marne, the French army cleared out of a girls' school and moved into other quarters evacuated by the Americans, but the United States would not release the local teachers' college, provoking the prefect to ask Paris to urge the Americans to quit the school. On other matters, the prefect found the Americans reasonable and easy to deal with, even when it came to requisitioned hotels and industrial buildings. The University of Nancy faced the same problem as the primary schools: university buildings had been requisitioned for various purposes—not always by the US Army. With classes set to begin in September, university officials and professors wanted their buildings back. Because the dormitories had been requisitioned by the French government to house homeless refugees from Lorraine, local churches appealed to their parishioners to take in students as boarders. The director of one school suggested to the prefect that the government requisition hotels for the students to live in, but all the hotels had already been requisitioned. If the Americans had to keep the university buildings, maybe they could release some of the hotels. In the end, the Americans agreed to release some underutilized university buildings in Nancy, allowing them to revert to educational purposes.[21]

As the US military wound down its presence in France and closed its offices, the French government was supposed to step in and pick up the various functions. Claims for property damage caused by the US Army had previously been submitted directly by the aggrieved party to civil affairs officers in district claims commissions. But as these commissions closed up shop, many thousands of French with outstanding claims besieged French officials, asking where their compensation was. Local French authorities protested that they knew nothing about the claims; it was a matter for the French War Ministry. French hotel keepers on the Côte d'Azur complained that they had submitted 1,300 claims for theft, fire, vandalism, accidents, and "pillage" by the US Army, and only 30 had been settled by the time the claims commission in Nice disappeared in October 1945. The prefect in Nice protested that in addition to being besieged by the hotel keepers about their old claims, they were submitting 100 new claims per month, and his office had no means to settle them. In January 1946, with the Allies gone, hotel keepers on the Côte d'Azur were still clamoring to be paid rents owed to them by the French government for routine services rendered to Allied troops, as well as their claims for damages.[22]

Many people were still waiting to be paid for rentals to Americans after the expiration of Lend-Lease. The Bureau des Ponts et Chaussées, which was responsible for tabulating the bills, had not finished doing so by July 1946, at which time a new agreement was signed between France and the United States. Although people or entities that were still owed monies for wartime requisitions deserved sympathy, the PC staff must have been completely overwhelmed by the mountains of paperwork left over from the war, not to mention all the repair work required on roads and bridges damaged by the war and chewed up by giant American trucks. As the Americans wound down their presence in Normandy in late 1945, they released a steady stream of requisitioned properties, to the satisfaction of the commissioner in Rouen. Although the AFA handled routine requisition payments in a timely manner, dossiers of claims for damages mounted many times faster than they were paid. Farmers in particular, who had to deal with fields ruined by trucks, torn-down temporary buildings, or seas of pallets for holding supplies, had received little compensation. Only farmers whose fields had been used as landing strips by the USAAF in the Eure received anything at all by the end of 1945: 430,000 francs ($9,759), a mere pittance because of the low rents set for the use of their fields. In November 1945 the prefect in the Aube reported that his office still had 200 claims for irregular requisitions, and he would hold those dated after 2 September to await further instructions. The PC in the Aube was still settling accounts in September 1949: widow Fevre received 3,904 francs ($78) for renting a house, Louis Payen received 1,805 francs ($36) for damages to his house, M. Vignes eventually received 6,000 francs ($120) for damage to his furniture, and a river and canal transport agency finally got paid the 140,070 francs ($2,801) it was owed. The unfortunate Mme. Beuchat, who rented a property in Plan-de-Cuques, on the outskirts of Marseille, had to sue the French army and appeal her loss before she pried loose 7,829 francs ($157) for damages plus 859 francs ($17) in interest in 1955. The PC had a delicate task separating damages attributable to the Americans from those actually caused by the Germans. French citizens knew they had almost no likelihood of collecting compensation for damages caused by the Germans, except at the low rates for "war damages" established by the French government. People stood to reap much higher rates if they could blame the (real) damages on the Americans.[23]

The French chafed as requisitions continued through 1945. In July 1945 the US Army still held 70,000 hospital beds in France and planned to relinquish them steadily until the end of the year. But even come 1946, it still expected to have 3,000 hospital beds in France and 145,000 soldiers in the vicinity of Reims. French officials negotiated assiduously with their American counterparts to have requisitioned properties released. In June and July 1945 the Americans released a steady stream of properties in and around Nancy: 11 public buildings, 144 other buildings, 58 rooms in houses, and 23 fields. There is no way to know whether the Americans relented on some properties out of deference to French sensibilities—such as the release of two hospitals in Nancy in early September 1945 after lengthy discussions or the release of the Hôtel Thiers in Nancy soon after—or whether they the Americans simply no longer needed them. Probably both factors pushed and pulled the army to give up facilities that were no longer serving vital purposes. French officials in Lorraine were frustrated that the Americans were too slow to evacuate hospitals and other properties long after the war was over. The only mental hospital in Meurthe-et-Moselle was held by the Americans until September 1945, when it and another hospital were released. But in October the Americans still held a hospital in Nancy. An administrator for Alsace-Lorraine wanted to know why the French, who were in charge of requisitions, after all, could not simply re-requisition unutilized or underutilized properties from the Americans. As the president of the Constituent Assembly that met in Paris in December 1945, Félix Gouin, who was also the mayor of Istre, just west of Marseille, was well informed about problems posed by the enduring American presence. The US Army continued to occupy the dance hall and the casino in Istre, leaving local youths nowhere to go. Even requests by the president of the assembly could not move the Americans out of their officers' social club. General Ratay promised to release the club as soon as the Americans no longer needed it, which was the reply he gave to all French officials who wrote inquiring when a garage, office, or villa would be available. As late as October 1945, the Americans had released only 80 percent of their requisitioned real estate.[24]

According to French civil authorities and civilian property owners, the French army assumed too many requisitions that were relinquished by the Americans. Property owners and officials alike protested that the French army abused its requisition rights even more than the Americans had. When the Americans left Marseille in 1945, more than 100 establishments, including hotels, bars, and restaurants, were released to the French, but rather than reverting to civilian use, many were snapped up by the French military. A business association in the city protested to the commissioner that so long as businesses were occupied by one military after another, normal commerce could not resume, and the French recovery would be arrested. The Americans relinquished sixty-seven hotels; the French army took sixty-three of them. The Americans released eight bars; the French military took six. Only fourteen hotels remained available for occupancy by visitors to Marseille, although it is worth noting that many other hotels were housing people whose homes had been destroyed in the war. This same problem afflicted many towns in France. For example, the Americans were using the largest hotel in Auxerre as a barracks, leaving few rooms available for civilians, including traveling government officials. A French couple had to sleep in a shed in Auxerre for want of a hotel room, and they were robbed by two men claiming to be MPs.[25]

Local authorities were greatly relieved in August 1945 when the Americans finally relinquished the vast depot warehouses by the train station in Metz, only to have them snapped up by the French army to supply its troops in Germany. Although officials in Metz had dealt patiently with the US Army, their reaction to the French army's requisition was strident protest and demands that the warehouses be released for civilian use. There were so few vehicles, especially trucks, left in the Haut-Rhin that when the French military requisitioned all those it could find, the prefect in Colmar balked. The prefect in Bas-Rhin (Strasbourg) echoed this complaint about the military monopolizing all wheeled transport, leaving none to serve the public. The commissioner in Strasbourg claimed he could find neither office space for government functions nor places for officials to live because the army was occupying all the available space. The prefect in Metz made similar complaints about a civilian agency that served refugees; when barracks became available (in May 1945), the agency took all the available space to house homeless returnees. The Americans were chagrined to see that, in the Rhône, the buildings they had surrendered were quickly occupied by the French army. The prefect was equally chagrined and appealed to Paris to have the buildings returned to civilian use. It is possible the French army made more abusive requisitions than the Americans did, but it is just as likely that by the time the French army arrived on the scene, the Americans had already requisitioned every property previously taken by the Germans, leaving the French to take only untouched properties. Or perhaps the local population had suffered so much from military impositions that the French military requisitions were the last straw. Whatever the case, French requisitions seemed to engender more resentment among the locals than those by Americans. The owner of a banquet hall had the misfortune of having it requisitioned in October 1940, and with "one requisition after another," as the hapless owner complained in October 1945, it was still out of his grasp.[26]

Almost every type of complaint lodged against the US military was also lodged against the French army. The prefect in Metz complained to Interior Minister Tixier that the Americans had requisitioned the largest café in Metz as a social club for American servicemen, even though there were never more than fifteen people in it. In the same letter he protested that the only large hotel not requisitioned by the Americans had been occupied by the French army to house French women auxiliaries, but only five or six women lived at the forty-room hotel, costing the state 26,000 francs ($540) per month. Tixier took these complaints seriously and protested to President de Gaulle that now that the war was over, the "unlimited right of requisition" claimed by the army should be curbed. To restore the French economy, the army should give way to civilian needs; he cited telephone lines as an urgent example. Despite Tixier's protests, complaints of abusive requisitions by the French army continued to arrive from Strasbourg, including a demand that the army evacuate a tannery needed by local industry and of no use to the army. In June 1945 the prefect compiled a list of 245 buildings, 118 apartments, and 2,000 rooms in private houses occupied by the French army (and 30 buildings still occupied by the US Army), while 15,000 Alsatians remained homeless. That the French army still requisitioned schools, the Hôtel de Ville, the Chamber of Commerce, the largest brewery, and the largest department store in Alsace was "absolutely scandalous," the prefect claimed. An obviously frustrated Minister Tixier asked President de Gaulle again in July to intervene "energetically" with War Minister Diethelm to clear the French military out of facilities that were crucial to restarting the regional economy.[27]

The French civil administration also provoked resentment among the population; years after the war had ended, French citizens still clamored to be paid what they were owed. The French government was responsible for processing and settling all claims, many of which lingered for years. A female religious establishment in Marseille that had housed some of the unfortunate residents of La Tour Blanche finally pried 163,000 francs ($3,260) from the prefect's office in August 1947 to pay for repairs. Sister Marie was unhappy that it took fifteen months to get the money they were due, and she would have appreciated receiving interest on the amount to make up for the delay.[28]

US Army requisitions did not directly conflict with the interests of the French state. The US government and the provisional government of Charles de Gaulle both wanted to defeat Germany, and both agreed that requisitions in France were necessary to achieve victory. Requisitions pitted the personal interests of French civilians against both the French government and the US Army. The French government set compensation rates low in 1939 in order to save money, and those rates remained low until 1946. As a result, French civilians subjected to forced rentals focused most of their frustrations on their government rather than the US Army. Although the carelessness with which some American units treated the properties they occupied shifted blame directly to the US Army, most complaints were not about rough treatment of property but about low rates and sluggish payment. There was nothing the Americans could do about that, and most French civilians recognized that. The Americans also occupied many public buildings, which local and regional administrators needed to provide crucial public services. Requisitioned schools and hospitals occasioned the most complaints, and American officers tried to address these grievances to the extent they could, even though they could not always satisfy French wishes. Nevertheless, American efforts to meet French demands for the return of schools and other public buildings illustrated that their conflicting interests were negotiated in good faith, even if the conflicts could not be fully resolved until the Americans departed France.

3

Transportation

The Allies requisitioned more than hotels and schools; they requisitioned much of France's transportation network that connected the ports to the front. To guarantee free access from the Normandy invasion beaches and Cherbourg to the front in the east, the Allies took close to complete control of the roads and railroads connecting these sites. In late summer, when the Germans had been expelled from most of France, military control of the region between the English Channel and the war zone in the east was ceded to the French provisional government, and SHAEF designated that area the Communication Zone, or COMZ. As in most matters, SHAEF was glad to turn over responsibility for anything that did not directly impact the war effort. But because transporting supplies to the front was absolutely essential to the war effort, SHAEF retained control over transport to the extent necessary to win the war. That required cooperation and coordination on the use of roads and rails in France, with a mixed record of success. French officials generally agreed that it was necessary to keep war supplies moving to the front, but they became irate when the US Army interfered with their attempts to carry out their normal functions. Stubborn American insistence on implementing poorly thought out policies that infringed on French sovereignty damaged relations, but not enough to influence the course of the war.

Immediately upon landing in Normandy, the Allies took over all French roads in the small liberated zone and reserved their use for military purposes. They also took over responsibility for maintaining the roads, which would have quickly degenerated without constant attention from the Army Corps of Engineers. SHAEF had a plan to restore all requisitioned roads, railroads, ports, and inland waterways to French control in three stages. In stage one, which was in effect everywhere in the liberated zone in July, the Allied armies operated all transport systems with the assistance and cooperation of French technicians who answered to the French army, whether they were in uniform or not (the state of siege declared in 1939 was still in effect, granting the French military vast power and authority within France). In stage two,

French civilian personnel of the Bureau des Ponts et Chaussées (PC) would be in charge of the transportation networks, operating under Allied control and supervision. In stage three, the French government would be in charge of the networks and operate alongside Allied military liaisons attached to the PC. Each stage was to be implemented when and where possible, upon mutual agreement.[1]

Roads were requisitioned first and proved challenging to manage. Even though the US military's monopoly on the use of certain key roads proved inconvenient to the French during much of 1944, French authorities agreed to help enforce US control to the extent possible. The Americans and French decided that MPs should police the American military traffic on the roads, and the French police were assigned the unpleasant task of keeping civilians off those roads deemed essential to the war effort. Only civilians with permits issued by the French police were allowed to drive on any roads at all, and their vehicles were subject to inspection by both MPs and French police. As General Patton's tanks and trucks raced eastward in August and September 1944, they ran into roads clogged with French civilians traveling mainly by nonmotorized transport. Although a rare few drove cars, most were on foot, bicycles, horses, or wagons. OSS Colonel David Bruce recorded in his diary on 28 September that the roads leading to Paris from Vesoul (in Haute Saône) were packed with French: "many camions [trucks], most of them wood-burning, laden with victuals, especially wheat flour, making their way toward Paris. There were also the usual thousands of bicycles. Every automobile, cart, or carriage was thronged with people making their way back to the capital and bringing with them an assortment of household belongings ranging from canary birds to kitchen utensils. Children along the route have as yet abated little in their enthusiasm, and wave vigorously at every passing soldier." The Americans complained to the newly appointed prefect René Petitbon in Troyes that civilians were not only using roads that were important to the American advance but also traveling down the middle of the roads and not keeping to the margins. The Americans pleaded with French officials to keep civilians off the main roads and requested that if the French had to use the roads for government matters, they pull over and make way for convoys of US soldiers. The Americans sought to requisition National Route 60 (from Orléans to Troyes) and National Route 77 (from Auxerre to Châlons, via Troyes) for a week to ten days, after which the roads would be returned to civilian use. Prefect Petitbon complied and had posters mounted around the department of Aube asking the populace to stay off the main roads so they would be available to "our American friends" and the FFI.[2]

It was often difficult to determine who was in charge and what the rules were. In some zones, the Gendarmerie Nationale (an arm of the War Ministry) claimed that it was responsible for issuing all road permits, while the PC had responsibility everywhere else. The PC protested that the gendarmes had no such authority and that they often refused to recognize permits issued by the PC, sometimes ordering vehicles with PC permits off the roads. And some roads ceded to French control were snatched back by the US Army, such as when Patton's Third Army retook control of roads in Alsace-Lorraine in January 1945. In another case, when a former Third Army zone was handed over to General Patch's Seventh Army, restrictions on civilian traffic lifted by Patton were reimposed by Patch. As late as March 1945, Commissioner Paul Chailley-Bert in Nancy complained to Paris that his staff had to carry four permits issued by four different authorities to drive on roads in the Meurthe-et-Moselle. General Patch had instructed Seventh Army's Office of Civil Affairs to issue permits in his zone—without the legal authority to do so—and the two different American zones of operation implemented different rules for using roads in their sectors. Despite such irregularities and inconveniences, Commissioner Chailley-Bert reported that General Patch and his staff did everything in their power to accommodate the French and to ease the burdens imposed by US military control. Control over roads in the south of France was further complicated by bands of FFI who insisted that they controlled the public highways. When US Army vehicles in southern France proved reluctant to halt for FFI roadblocks, the FFI opened fire on several occasions. In an effort to avoid problems occasioned by French patrols (especially FFI) stopping US Army vehicles, the Americans of Delta Base in Marseille proposed that MPs accompany any French units controlling traffic on roads used by Americans. Representatives of the French ministries meeting in Paris at the end of October lamented the decision to hand over control of French roads and railroads to the Americans. The ministries may have been unaware of the extent to which lower-level French officials influenced these operations, but their real concern was the appearance of surrendering French sovereignty to the Americans.[3]

On the eve of General Patton's renewed offensive in Lorraine, public notices went up suddenly and without warning at 4:00 a.m. that all roads were reserved for military traffic and civilians were to stay off them. On 8 November a car with five French officials, all on government missions, was stopped by MPs on National Route 3 as they tried to leave the Marne and enter the Meuse. The MPs pointed to Patton's freshly posted announcements forbidding all nonmilitary traffic on the roads of Lorraine. The car, assigned to Chargé de Mission H. Heuzé of Strasbourg, flew a French flag and was clearly marked as a French government vehicle. Moreover, Heuzé carried a laissez-passer issued by the commander of US 20th Corps, allowing passage through US checkpoints in the combat zone. The two passengers in the car named on the laissez-passer were permitted to continue as far as Verdun, the next major town, where they were stopped at another checkpoint manned by less accommodating MPs and forced out of the vehicle; they had to walk the remaining two miles into Sainte-Menehould, leaving the car on the side of the road. Heuzé and the other officials were rescued by French army officers who had been sent to find them with a forged (*fantaisiste*) pass, and they were all able to reach Verdun but no further. Despite entreaties from the French liaison officer assigned to Third Army and pleas from US civil affairs officers, without an exemption signed by General Patton himself, the French officials could either stay in Verdun or return to Paris. They all returned to Paris except for M. Chenrion, in charge of economic affairs for the Moselle, who chanced riding in a French military vehicle with some French officers to Hayange (near Metz). This episode illustrates not only the extent to which the US Army dominated the roads of France but also the extent to which General Patton insisted on absolute control over all affairs touching his Third Army. Needless to say, at the outset of the offensive to evict the Germans from the rest of Lorraine, he was unavailable to sign passes for French administrators seeking to use French roads. Patton's insistence on doing things his own way and without consulting other interested parties (even General Eisenhower) frequently turned minor irritants into bigger problems and tried the patience of the French.[4]

After Germany surrendered and the movement of army traffic became less urgent, US officers in charge of routing trucks were more willing to accommodate French requests. When heavy truck traffic through the center of Troyes proved especially annoying to patients in the city hospital—shaking their beds as the trucks rumbled by—its administrator asked the prefect if the traffic could be rerouted. The prefect pointed out to the relevant army engineer that the roads in the center of town were entirely unsuitable for such heavy vehicles, without mentioning the hospital. It took several weeks to reroute the traffic (the availability of bridges may have dictated the route), but not long afterward, army trucks disappeared from the center of the city, to the great satisfaction of the hospital director.[5]

The cooperation of French engineers from the PC proved not only helpful to the Americans but also critical to their mission. When the Army Corps of Engineers used the rubble of old bridges to form the foundations for temporary bridges across the Seine River in the Aube, they blocked three-quarters of the riverbed, forcing the water to flow in narrow channels under the bridges. PC engineers pointed out that this worked fine in the dry summer season, but when the rains came in the fall, the volume of the Seine would increase massively and carry away the American-built bridges. They advised the French liaison to Third Army that the engineers should fix this problem while they still had bridges. Similarly, the PC advised the US Army that a tunnel in Pennes-Mirabeau, outside Marseille, had become dangerously weak. Because the tunnel was important to the Americans and French alike, the US Army agreed to supply engineers, equipment, and supplies to shore up the tunnel, but even with help, it was going to take PC four months to complete the work. The sheer amount of maintenance required for France's overburdened and neglected road system was beyond the abilities of either the French or the Allies, even working together. The United States agreed to maintain all through roads within the COMZ stretching from the English Channel ports to Germany. Although the Corps of Engineers was responsible for maintaining the roads and the army supplied much of the necessary equipment and fuel, French contractors performed most of the actual work. Whenever possible, captured German equipment and supplies were used. Roads and bridges that were not important to the US military were left to the PC, although the engineers helped the PC whenever possible and with the approval of SHAEF. SHAEF estimated that by February 1945, 3,800 miles of roads had been refurbished by the US Army, and it was maintaining 2,700 miles of French roads. The United States agreed to assume the cost of that work but proposed that the French pay for the rebuilding of bridges. Trying to divide up the real financial responsibility for all that work, the Corps of Engineers admitted, was impossible. Not all this work was welcomed by the French. When the big American trucks coming from the Normandy beaches to the slowly receding front in Calvados found the country lanes too narrow, the Corps of Engineers brought in bulldozers to widen the roads. The first time Xavier de Guerpel saw these monstrous machines, they were plowing down his apple trees and hedges and piling dirt in his hay fields that were ready for harvest. This work was performed with amazing speed, little planning, and no delicacy, much to the dismay of de Guerpel.[6]

In late August, when the US Army Transportation Corps started to rush huge amounts of materials from the Normandy beaches to the region around Chartres to support the upcoming push to the east, it quickly realized that the roads were not wide enough to accommodate two-way traffic consisting of big army trucks. Commanders suggested converting the principal roads into one-way routes and limiting traffic to supply trucks only. MPs and French police were assigned the task of controlling access to the routes and allowing only those trucks with a red ball painted on the door to use the roads. This operation to move huge quantities of supplies forward as quickly as possible became known as the Red Ball Express. By the time this suggestion was put into practice, the front had already surged forward beyond Chartres, and the trucks followed the routes of Patton's Third Army and Courtney Hodge's First Army beyond Paris. The extended routes went around Paris to the north and south but also passed through some very congested suburbs, such as Saint-Denis. Ultimately, roads northeast of Paris to Soissons and into the Aube were requisitioned for the Red Ball Express to support First and Third Armies. During its two and a half months of operation, the Red Ball Express monopolized 700 miles of French through roads to deliver 7,000 tons of supplies per day to troops in eastern France, and it consumed 300,000 gallons of gasoline and 800 tires a day. Trucks wore out quickly for lack of proper maintenance, so some units were called "truck destroyer battalions." The requisitioning of the roads was intended to be a temporary expedient, as the trucks were needed only until French rail lines could be repaired and rolling stock refurbished or replaced. It turned out that the damage inflicted by the air campaigns on rail lines east of Paris was minimal. Rail traffic from Normandy was sufficiently restored by mid-November that the battered and poorly maintained trucks of the Red Ball Express and their exhausted drivers could be retired from service. With railroads carrying the burden of delivering supplies to the front, the roads were released to two-way traffic, even though they remained under US military control. Additionally, by mid-November, Antwerp (much closer to the front) was available as a supply port, and gasoline pipelines had been laid from Normandy to eastern France to supply fuel.[7]

During the brief life of the Red Ball Express, French police cooperated with MPs to keep the trucks moving. However, they never succeeded in keeping all civilian traffic off the roads. A survey by French gendarmes revealed that bicycles, horse-drawn vehicles, and *gazogene* (charcoal-burning) vehicles still traveled on the requisitioned roads, slowing down Red Ball trucks. French authorities enlisted French newspapers to appeal to the populace to stay off the roads. They also used the press in an effort to reduce accidents caused by drunk American drivers, entreating readers: please do not give wine to the Americans driving trucks with a red ball painted on the door! Both the French police and MPs suspected that much of the wine and spirits that slaked the drivers' thirst was not presented out of gratitude for liberation but was sold or traded for the goods being hauled—especially precious gasoline. US authorities were just as upset about the unknown quantity of gasoline that disappeared en route and ended up on the black market as they were about drunk-driving accidents. They also uncovered a surreptitious system for transporting "refugees" under cover of the Ravitaillement Général

(General Supply). Either drivers in French government service were carrying illegal passengers for a fee, or trucks masquerading as General Supply vehicles were serving as buses for unauthorized movement, or perhaps both. It was not surprising that a black market in transportation arose at a time when civilian transport was largely unavailable. Bus service between towns was scarce in France in 1944, and French officials had to appeal to civil affairs officers for the right to reestablish civilian bus routes connecting towns within the COMZ. French civilians in the south of France were entirely dependent on the generosity of GIs and the rare French person with a motor vehicle to get from place to place. They routinely hitched free rides from GIs in trucks and jeeps and shared information on the best places to find rides—sometimes with the help of friendly MPs. When Janet Teissier du Cros (a Scotswoman married to a Frenchman) hitched her way from Nîmes to Paris, generous Americans loaded her with packs of cigarettes, coffee, and K rations and plied her with friendly banter. An MP posted at an intersection outside Dijon with orders to make sure French civilians stayed off US Army vehicles helped her find a ride on an army vehicle.[8]

While restricting their use of the roads inconvenienced the French, road accidents triggered many more complaints. French officials cooperated with the Americans to control traffic, but they got little cooperation in return when it came to solving problems caused by accidents. When French were injured or suffered losses, they expected the Americans to make restitution, which was sometimes hard to obtain. When a jeep knocked M. Guyot off his bicycle on a country lane in the Yonne, he was left lying injured in the grass until a French passerby discovered him and took him to a US medical facility, where he was treated. Guyot was told that an officer would contact him to see that his bike and ruined clothing were replaced, and he was promised compensation for ten workdays lost due to his injuries. He never heard anything from anyone. When the mayor of his village attempted to intervene, he was treated rudely and dismissed by the local American commander, and no follow-up was forthcoming. The prefect of Yonne had to intervene with the commander of US forces in the region, General Eldridge Chapman, to get an investigation opened, but there was little likelihood of locating the driver of the jeep, which would have been necessary for Guyot to be compensated. At least he was not as unlucky as Mme. Sibault, who was presumably knocked down and killed by persons unknown while walking on the side of the road. The French believed Americans were the most likely culprits, and the Americans promised to investigate, but such investigations rarely produced useful results; this only aggravated the French, who were already upset about the frequency of accidents. In late September 1944 a speeding US Army truck in the Aube struck a French bicyclist; he was taken to a French hospital in Troyes, where he died two days later. When his widow tried to find out what had happened to her husband, French doctors could only tell her that he had died of a broken skull. Efforts to pry information out of the US Army proved fruitless. At the time, the Americans were engaged in a rapid advance across Burgundy, and finding the unit responsible would have been a low priority for Third Army. Though a tragedy for the man's family, his death would not have garnered much attention from anybody other than the locals who might have known him. A railway employee hit by another US Army truck in the Aube in October was luckier: he landed in a hospital for three months. A stream of similar incidents steadily eroded any warm feelings the residents of Troyes had toward the Americans. A little girl run down and killed by a jeep in Troyes in the summer of 1945 occasioned much bitterness among the populace, and the gendarmerie warned the prefect that unless such accidents stopped occurring, the citizenry would be permanently disaffected toward Americans. When another young girl was killed by a speeding truck in Lille in November 1945, the truck stopped only because a crowd of witnesses forced it to. The occupants of the truck got out with weapons drawn, and the witnesses were convinced they would have used them if MPs had not intervened.[9]

Satisfaction could sometimes be pried from the US Army, but it required perseverance and luck. A young Algerian girl who was badly burned in an accident caused by an American truck mechanic obtained relief from the army only after her mother repeatedly appealed for help. The unfortunate girl, Renée Touboul, was playing near an army truck under repair in Algiers in February 1944. When a container of gasoline caught fire while a soldier was using it to clean a truck engine, he tossed the flaming can away from the truck and onto nine-year-old Renée, badly burning both her legs. The soldier smothered the fire by wrapping Renée in a blanket, and the captain in charge of the maintenance facility drove her to an army medical clinic. The staff there said she had to go to a civilian hospital, so an army ambulance drove her to Mustapha Hospital, where Renée stayed for the next three and a half months. The quartermaster (QM) troops at the army garage took up a collection for Renée and gave her mother—a widow with three other children—10,800 francs (about $216), but she had to sign a release absolving the US Army of any further responsibility to get the money. Renée's mother, Etoile Touboul, had to bring her daughter food every day, and her doctors recommended a diet that Etoile, a cloth cutter at a department store, could ill afford. She could barely afford to buy Renée milk, which cost 20 cents per can. Captain Lawrence of the QM Corps brought four cans of milk when he visited Renée in the hospital four days after she was burned, but he never returned. When Etoile pleaded at the garage that her daughter was not recovering in the hospital and needed more help, a lieutenant went to see her once but never went back; nor did anyone else from the army. Renée was eventually released and sent home, where a French navy doctor who lived in the building looked in on her regularly, but there was little he could do for her. She was confined to bed, her legs would not straighten out, and Etoile had to change her bandages three times a day. She had no access to antiseptic or sterilized bandages and used scraps of cloth she got from work. By July 1944, Renée still had unhealed sores and extensive scarring, was malnourished, and, according to a US Army doctor who visited her, was in a bad mental state. Etoile took her plight to the French authorities, who said the release she had signed was invalid under French law and the amount of compensation paid by the QM Corps was clearly inadequate. Finally, Etoile appealed directly to General Jacob Devers, in charge of Allied troops in North Africa. General Devers ordered an investigation, which found the army responsible for Renée's injuries. She was taken to a US Army hospital with experience treating burn victims. Army doctors estimated that Renée would need extensive skin grafting and a year of physical therapy in order to walk again. On 17 July 1944 General Devers wrote to Etoile promising that the US Army would work toward "restoring your daughter to full health and strength."[10]

Because of a general manpower shortage in the spring of 1945, the US Army used German POWs to drive trucks. This made many French irate. They became especially angry when German POW drivers caused accidents that killed or injured French citizens and damaged French property. The population of Carentan was reportedly outraged over three deaths in March 1945 caused by US Army vehicles driven by German POWs. Many people suspected the deaths were deliberate, and the prefect predicted that antipathy toward the Americans would increase because of them. In the south of France, officials repeated a complaint heard in the north: German drivers drove too fast, and they often failed to stop after an accident. American transport officers receiving these complaints responded that German drivers had better records than American drivers and caused fewer accidents. This may have been a backhanded compliment, as French officials complained bitterly about how carelessly Americans drove both jeeps and trucks.[11]

The French in upper Normandy, already agitated by the presence of hundreds of thousands of GIs in vast tent cities waiting to be shipped home or to the Pacific theater, became incensed when speeding American trucks smashed into French vehicles, bicycles, carts, pedestrians, and farm animals. The prefect in Rouen energetically protested to US commanders that the Americans drove too fast and too carelessly. The commissioner added that drunk Americans were killing French citizens and just driving off, and MPs did nothing about it. In September, when some drunk GIs got into an accident in Roubaix, they got out of their vehicle and attacked first the French civilians in the other car and then witnesses to the accident. The next day in nearby Tourcoing, GIs damaged some cars while trying to park, and when the French car owners protested, the soldiers beat them. A spate of accidents involving American vehicles resulted in the permanent posting of both French police and MPs at an intersection in Alizay, outside Rouen. The Americans claimed that some accidents resulted from the drivers' inability to read French warning signs, and they recommended that signs such as "Men Working" be posted in both English and French. In November 1945 the prefect in Beauvais, Oise, had a dossier detailing 622 traffic accidents involving US Army vehicles in his department alone (23 of the accidents involved British vehicles, and American authorities had made 22 counterclaims against French drivers). The prefect of the Marne also complained to Interior Minister Tixier that every day he received reports of French fatalities caused by American trucks. At the same time, the commissioner in Châlons-sur-Marne protested to Tixier that the amount of compensation the US Army offered for accidents was insufficient and had become a political issue. The newly elected General Council for the Marne raised the issue of restitution and expressed its dissatisfaction at the sheer number of accidents involving US Army vehicles. American trucks had knocked down utility poles twice in two weeks in the Aube. The first time, the Americans had collided with their own pole, and the Signal Corps had promptly replaced the damaged pole and lines. The second time, French electric lines had been downed, and the French wanted to know who was going to replace them. The French did, but they wanted compensation from the Americans. Usually, the amounts sought by French complainants were not very large. A house belonging to a man in Sens, Yonne, had been damaged by a truck inelegantly turning around—a witness testified the driver had been drinking in a café moments before—and he asked for 1,315 francs ($26) to replace a smashed window and repair the façade. A stream of reports of reckless GIs behind the wheels of cars and trucks flowed into Paris in 1945 and reached meetings between the US Military Mission (which had replaced SHAEF) and French ministers, who protested that GIs had caused more than 1,000 accidents between 15 June and September 1945. The Americans promised to establish a program of "highway safety" for drivers, and perhaps they did. However, in November 1945 the prefect in Troyes informed Paris that he still had a dossier containing demands for compensation for 500 accidents caused by American GIs.[12]

The Jerry-Can Controversy

In some matters, French and American interests clashed, and neither side proved willing to back down. The French often accepted Allied military interference in principle but expressed annoyance at how it was implemented. A controversy over the use and regulation of gas cans irritated Franco-American relations in the fall of 1944, revealing that sometimes neither side demonstrated understanding and goodwill. During the contest for North Africa, the British captured some well-designed gas cans from German forces—hence the name jerry cans—and asked British manufacturers to supply the British army with cans like them. The Americans also admired the cans and ordered millions from US manufacturers for the US Army. In the fall of 1944 careless handling by American drivers resulted in the loss of more than 1 million empty cans, abandoned by GIs along the roads of France. So many cans were tossed aside that an acute shortage developed and hindered the QM Corps' ability to furnish gasoline to army vehicles. The QM Corps, which was responsible for the cans, had no program to retrieve abandoned cans during the summer breakout, so they littered French roadways in the wake of the American surge across France. French famers discovered the cans—*bidons*—scattered along the roadsides, admired them, and found many uses for them on their farms. That is what happened to most of the cans abandoned by GIs. The QM Corps assembled teams in late August 1944 to pick up cans from the sides of roads and later to visit French farms, hoping to convince the farmers to return the cans. French officials were enlisted in the effort and appealed to citizens to turn in any cans they had found. FFI units were set to searching for the missing cans as a way to keep them busy and out of mischief. Schoolchildren were encouraged to forage for the cans and turn them over as their contribution to the war effort. The search teams and the appeal were successful, but it took many months to gather the wayward cans. By mid-January, 202,464 cans had been collected by the French in nineteen departments, 97,000 in the Seine-et-Oise alone. However, the process was too slow to meet the urgent need; the shortage became critical, and in October SHAEF authorized the requisitioning of cans from civilians. MPs erected checkpoints to search French cars for jerry cans and seize them, thereby affronting French sovereignty yet again. It is understandable that in October 1944, with the Red Ball Express speeding gasoline and supplies to the front as quickly as possible and with Patton's offensive stalled for want of gasoline, SHAEF would see recouping its gas cans as an urgent objective to be carried out aggressively.[13]

The QM Corps' urgent mission to gather the cans collided with the newly installed French provisional government's mission to assert its legitimacy and sovereignty within France, especially in the eyes of its allies. De Gaulle's government was, like him, supremely touchy about its right to control its own affairs and believed it was too little involved in the process of recouping the *bidons*. When the US Army instituted its policy of searching vehicles for jerry cans in late October, it clashed with the French government's obligation to protect its citizens from abuse by foreign troops—something Vichy had clearly failed to do. Army MPs began confiscating all German-style cans, on the theory that even if they were not of American provenance, they were war booty and thus US government property. The French quickly informed SHAEF that MPs had no right to stop or search any French government vehicle, and in fact, most French police vehicles carried the German-style cans. The Germans had confiscated all French *bidons* during the occupation, so when the Germans pulled out, French police routinely seized German cans as compensation for the *bidons* lost to the enemy. The MPs confiscated not only the jerry cans from French police but also the gasoline in them, and French officials wanted both returned. An education official in Paris questioned the MPs' right to search his car and seize his gas can, but like most French officials, he thought it better to relinquish the can and protest later. However, protesting to American officials or even French liaison officers produced no results. The American compromise, accepted by the Foreign Ministry, was to agree that French official cars with permits could keep German-style gas cans. This was rejected out of hand by Assistant Minister of the Interior Raymond Haas-Picard as an unwarranted infringement of French sovereignty. Under no circumstances were MPs to search vehicles with French government plates, and no gas cans of any kind should be surrendered by such vehicles to the Americans. SHAEF eventually capitulated and accepted this policy, but not before much hue and cry over the wayward jerry cans.[14]

One French official who took seriously his right not to be searched was Roger Wybot, head of the French counterintelligence agency (Direction de la Surveillance du territoire, or DST) and highly placed in the anti-Nazi resistance. In October he refused to stop at a checkpoint when ordered to do so by MPs, who then fired at his car and put three bullet holes in it. With that, Wybot stopped his car, got out, and confronted the MP in charge, Sergeant Chester Krol. According to a US Criminal Investigation Department (CID) report, Krol said he fired in the air before firing once at the vehicle, which he claimed was speeding and endangering the lives of the MPs at the checkpoint. A heated argument between Wybot and Krol ensued, and Krol suggested the two "settle this like men." When Krol waved a pistol in Wybot's face, the unarmed Wybot suggested that Krol give him a pistol too and they could settle it right there. Krol admitted that he grabbed Wybot by the lapel and "led him a few paces to the curb." Krol's commanders backed him up and claimed the respected sergeant had done nothing wrong and was entirely within his rights. Neither Wybot nor the CID agreed, the latter recommending that Krol be charged with assault with a deadly weapon. He was not charged. Brigadier General Thomas F. Bresnahan of the Oise base section wrote Wybot a letter of apology, but he also restated the facts as offered by Sergeant Krol and denied the MPs had done anything wrong. Wybot replied, reiterating his position that MPs had no right to stop French government vehicles, that Krol was in the wrong, and that the sergeant did not possess the necessary qualities to be an MP. Wybot pressed the issue with his superior, Interior Minister Tixier, calling the letter from General Bresnahan "not even a letter of excuses, no less a letter of apology."[15]

This sort of problem worked both ways. In April 1945 French police in Paris set up a checkpoint on the Boulevard Courcelle at 11:00 p.m. to enforce the curfew. By 2:00 a.m., the police had stopped and checked 212 cars, including 50 US military vehicles. At 2:05 a vehicle raced toward the barrier at high speed and did not slow down when French police blew their whistles and waved their flashlights. The car ran through two barriers before French police fired at the car, trying to hit the tires. It came to a stop after the second barrier, and two men exited the car. When they got back in and tried to drive away, an officer fired three more shots at the car, which stopped again. The vehicle carried three American officers and two WACs, one of whom was Lieutenant Grace Dito, a thirty-year-old nurse from Pennsylvania. Lieutenant Dito, struck in the back of the head by one of the bullets, was rushed to an American hospital by the police but was pronounced dead on arrival. All the other occupants were taken into custody by MPs, and the French heard no more about it.[16]

The Wybot incident faded away, but the jerry-can issue dragged on. SHAEF insisted that French vehicles with jerry cans had to carry permits issued by the French government, but it agreed that such vehicles were subject to search by French police alone and not by MPs. For its part, the French government informed SHAEF that it had no intention of issuing gas-can permits to its people, and even if French gendarmes accompanied MPs at checkpoints, the gendarmes had been instructed not to search for any kind of *bidons.* And that is where the issue ended in January 1945, with both sides insisting on their authority to set the rules. By then, the acute jerry-can shortage was over, and the US Army had placed orders with French manufacturers to produce 7.4 million gas cans for the US Army. By the end of the war, only 287,000 had been delivered, and the contract for the rest was canceled. The

French refused to compromise on the question of sovereignty in the fall of 1944 because the GPRF was still gaining control over France, and the Gaullist regime felt it had to show that the French were in charge of their own affairs and would brook no interference by the Americans.[17]

Civilian Transportation

When the German army quit France, it took an enormous number of French vehicles with it—buses, trucks, cars, railroad cars, wagons, carts, and bicycles—leaving the French with a dearth of transport. Anticipating this, the Allies had set aside trucks in the United Kingdom for civilian use in France. As of 1 August 1944, 2,000 trucks earmarked for French civilian use sat unused in England because the ships needed to move them to France were more urgently required to support the military. In any event, even the French agreed that the system of the US Army providing trucks, drivers, and gasoline to move civilian goods was working out well for the time being. If nothing else, getting those trucks to the French would have freed up army trucks and 3,500 drivers—but not gasoline—for military use. Civil affairs officers often interceded in attempts to wrangle more trucks for civilian use, and US forces found themselves besieged by requests for transport. By early September, about 1,000 trucks, along with tires and gasoline, had begun to arrive in France for civilian use, with about half allocated to supply Paris with food. To meet the dire shortage of trucking available for French civilian use, Sixth Army Group, operating in the south of France, agreed to provide 557 trucks to a French government–run transport company. French officials would decide how to use the trucks and which regions they would serve; they would also supply the drivers and fuel, and the United States agreed to supply 125 mechanics and officers to maintain the trucks. Without trucks, French manufacturers found it difficult to get back into production. When hosiery manufacturers in the Aube found themselves without cloth in October 1944, they turned to the US Army, seeking trucks to bring materials from Lille or Rouen so they could return to work. Even though French authorities were willing to pay the QM Corps for the deliveries, they were out of luck; the army had no spare trucks for them. By the fall of 1944, the US Army relied less on road transport in France and more on railroads, allowing the army to release control of most roads outside the war zones to French civil authorities. However, control of the roads did not mean control of the trucks on them. To move as much matériel as possible, the US Army had established rules for what moved by truck and what moved by rail. So, when the United States loaned trucks to General Supply, the French were stuck with US Army regulations about what they could transport and how far. This did not please officials of the PC, who chafed at having to follow US rules for using their own roads.[18]

The French railroad network (Société national des chemins de fer français, or SNCF) had been heavily targeted by Allied bombs in the months before liberation, but it was up and running with remarkable speed in 1944. Only a few short lines—all in northern France—were operational by September 1944; by November, a network of rails linking Brest to Biarritz and Marseille to Lille was functioning. Unfortunately, all roads led to Paris, which would have caused enormous congestion had there been enough locomotives, cars, coal, and electricity to allow a Parisian pileup. Before such a tangle could occur, a sufficient number of railroad bridges around France had been repaired to resurrect a network that was not dependent on Paris. After the system in western France was restored in mid-September, the US Army was eager to turn over railway operations to the SNCF so that US personnel could get to work repairing and maintaining rail service east of Paris. The rail network throughout France was mostly in French hands (stage two) by 1 October; only the lines within Normandy and a single line from Normandy to Paris were still under Allied military control. Even lines running to Belgium were entirely in French hands, and the army found it could rely on French civilians to run the trains. By 1945, SHAEF had restored all railroads to the French (stage three).[19]

Although train operations were back in French hands, the US Army still controlled security on the lines throughout northern France that supplied the Allies. During Patton's stranglehold on all movement in his zone, only French passengers with passes issued by the Counter Intelligence Corps (CIC) and French security services could travel past Bar-le-Duc and into the war zone of Meurthe-et-Moselle. French travelers from Paris without the required documents were forced off the trains at Bar-le-Duc. Because American MPs in Bar-le-Duc would not allow anyone to board a train to any destination without the necessary passes, passengers taken off trains from Paris could not return to Paris. The American and French armies had requisitioned all the hotel rooms in Bar-le-Duc, so these hapless French civilians could neither return to Paris nor find a place to stay while awaiting approval of their passes. Meanwhile, more French passengers without the proper documents continued to pile up in the Bar-le-Duc station, caught in a dilemma worthy of Franz Kafka. Such was the result of hurried wartime improvisation and numerous authorities in control of people's lives. Presumably, all the ill-fated travelers eventually returned to Paris.[20]

As long as both the US military and the French government had a voice in deciding what traveled where by rail, there would be confusion and discord over apportioning the limited space available on trains. French rail officials in Marseille were driven to distraction by competing rules for the shipment of goods to serve the civilian economy established by the French ministry in Paris. In February 1945 M. Dine, the chief rail official in Marseille, fulminated in frustration at the irrational orders from Paris that prevented him from authorizing shipments approved by the US military. He ranted that shipments had been easier when he dealt personally with the civil affairs rail transportation officer, whose office had been in the main train station in Marseille. Together, the two men could determine how many cars were available for civilian use in the coming days. When the US Army had absolute control of the rails in the south of France, it set aside for civilian use twenty to thirty boxcars per day to move food around the south. In October that number increased substantially and then doubled again in January 1945. However, rules established by Paris did not permit the movement of all the goods approved by the US military, so that capacity was wasted. Dine worried that when the US Army stepped aside entirely and returned complete control to the French—set to occur in March 1945—the supply system in the south would collapse. Among other things, the US Army took care of all emergency repairs, which were many, and the SNCF had no means to do this. The "strict coordination" between civil affairs officers and representatives of the Transportation Ministry that had been promised never occurred. In this case, French rail officials found American officers easier to deal with and more "supple" than French officials in Paris. The US military focused on immediate needs and problems and was not concerned about the future beyond a few narrow considerations, whereas French officials in Paris worried about many matters and were planning for the long-term recovery of the French economy. Rules governing how much oil or sugar could be transported over how many miles mattered to planners in Paris but made life miserable for managers like Dine in Marseille.[21]

In general, French and Americans share a relaxed attitude about rules and are willing to overlook them when they prove inconvenient. As a result, French officials and American officers sometimes made up their own rules as they went along to get an otherwise balky system to work. However, such nonchalance could also result in capricious and arbitrary decisions that worked against French interests and the smooth running of the railroads. In March 1945 an American rail liaison in Nancy tried to commandeer four coaches assigned to French deportees, returning POWs, and Russian POWs. When a French official refused to comply, the American threatened to have the Frenchman arrested, which MPs declined to do. When the American officer ordered Russians off the train, they pretended not to understand what was going on and refused to leave the coach. Commissioner Chailley-Bert interceded and convinced the American he could not commandeer the cars, but the fracas delayed the train's departure for three hours, upsetting the timetables for the whole line and irritating Franco-American relations in Nancy for a time.[22]

The rail system was resurrected throughout the country with remarkable speed, but the dearth of locomotives, rolling stock, and coal to fuel the trains meant that train transport remained a scarce resource subject to rationing well into 1946. From D-Day to January 1945, the US Army supervised the rebuilding of 14,282 miles of track in France and rebuilt 276 railroad bridges. The USAAF had destroyed or damaged many of those bridges; others had been blown by the FFI or by the departing Germans. But for reasons of tact, no one chose to make an accounting of who was responsible for the damage. The United States imported 22,080 tons of steel to rebuild them and paid for 2.18 million man-hours to do all the work, with most of the labor performed by French civilians or Axis POWs (who were still paid). By April 1945, the United States had also provided 148 diesel locomotives, 1,831 steam locomotives, 16,000 freight cars, 135 passenger coaches, 2,870 gondola cars, 1,150 mineral wagons, 670 cabooses, and 1,047 miscellaneous specialty wagons. When the war in Europe ended, rather than cart all that equipment back to the United States, the US Army proposed turning it over to the SNCF, charging the French Lend-Lease account, and then leasing it back from the French to provide transport for US forces that were still in France. SHAEF presumed that the equipment rental would more than cover what it cost the French to acquire it, giving the French a surplus. The US Army assumed that everyone would come out ahead in the deal. The French looked forward to acquiring all that rail stock and using it to benefit France rather than the Allies. The proposal was accepted by both sides, and the United States paid the French $1 per day per boxcar.[23]

When the Allies returned complete control of all the railroads in France to the SNCF on 1 August 1945, the Allied military accounted for only 18 percent of all traffic on the lines, with about three-quarters of that used by the Americans. The US Army used 51 trains per day to move men, equipment, and supplies from Germany to French ports, and most of the cars were taken from German stocks; the locomotives were French but of American origin, and the United States required only 450 French boxcars per day. American use of French rails and ports dropped dramatically in the fall of 1945. When the French resumed control of all port facilities in Cherbourg and Marseille in early 1946, American shipping requirements had dropped to a small fraction of what they had been a year earlier, when usage peaked. The same proved true for French railroads: by the time control of the rails was fully returned to the French, American needs had fallen to meager levels. However, the transport officer for Delta Base in Marseille was not happy with the service provided by the French. He complained that passenger railcars were lice-ridden and had to be fumigated, and when the French added new lousy cars to trains, the fumigated cars had to be fumigated all over again. The coaches were unheated, and even in the south of France, the winter was cold. When he protested to the SNCF that the cars had no water, it responded that there was no way to prevent the pipes from freezing and bursting, and there were no facilities in Nice to fix them. The trains also lacked lighting, so GIs resorted to candles, which were dangerous on a rocking train. Thus, at the end of their working relationship, which had been agreeable overall, small problems still cropped up. By January 1946, such problems would not last much longer.[24]

The Allied military usurpation of the transportation network was accepted by both the French people and de Gaulle's provisional government as a necessary sacrifice for the war effort. However, as was often the case, they bridled at the way the Americans implemented that control and chafed at its duration. The Red Ball Express lasted for only two months and taxed the French during its brief existence; that it was short-lived saved everyone involved from a descent into bitterness. The plan to return control of French transport in stages reveals the wisdom of Allied planners. Though successful, it did not prevent the inconveniences of war from turning into frustration as the war dragged on. Events revealed that routine difficulties could be resolved by officers and officials tasked with doing so, yet the process often left a bitter taste in the mouths of some of the Frenchmen involved. The interactions between responsible staffs on the two sides were not always happy, but the French transportation system was successfully harnessed to serve the war effort, which is what mattered in both the short and the long run.

4

The Port of Marseille

Franco-American cooperation in the war was imperative and effective, despite tension between the heads of the two governments. The American exploitation of the port of Marseille provides a superb example of the close cooperation between US and French officials working faithfully together, all pulling in the same direction to achieve a common goal. The French directors of the port worked diligently and cooperatively with their American counterparts to smooth over the inevitable problems that arose. Their collaboration was supremely important because Marseille quickly became the primary supply port for the US military in western Europe. Even after September 1944, when the Schelde estuary was cleared of German forces and the huge, modern, almost entirely intact port of Antwerp was opened, largely superseding the Normandy ports as supply depots, Marseille remained the most important port of entry for Allied military supplies into 1945. Even after it was surpassed by Antwerp in importance, the Allies still relied heavily on Marseille.

A shortage of labor on the southern coast of France posed the greatest problem for the US military, which had to scramble to find enough men to perform all the necessary tasks. With the assistance of French authorities, the manpower problem was solved, but getting French workers to cooperate with Americans and Axis POWs remained a challenge. The language barrier between the often overworked French and GIs who were anxious to get on with the job led to friction and sometimes bad relations on the docks. Only deft handling of these problems by American civil affairs officers and French administrators—all eager for success—made the port of Marseille perform better than expected. Just a few months after evicting the Germans from Marseille, the Allies were unloading more cargo than the port had handled before the war, even though the extensive sabotage carried out by the departing Germans had not been completely repaired. Some of the damage still had not been fixed and some of the sunken ships remained in the harbor by the time the Allies returned control of operations to the French in 1946.[1]

Table 4.1 Supplies Off-Loaded by Port (1,000 Long Tons), August 1944–April 1945

Month	Cherbourg	Rouen	LeHavre	Marseille*	Antwerp
Aug. 1944	267			174	
Sept. 1944	314			327	
Oct. 1944	366	27	62	525	
Nov. 1944	433	128	149	548	6
Dec, 1944	250	132	166	502	428
Jan. 1945	262	158	199	386	433
Feb. 1945	287	173	195	496	473
Mar, 1945	261	268	193	548	558
Apr. 1945	181	241	165	485	628

Source: Jeffrey J. Clark and Robert Ross Smith, Riviera to the Rhine (Washington, DC: US Army Center of Military History, 1993), 576.

*Figures for Marseille include Port-de-Bouc and Saint-Tropez.

Marseille had escaped direct involvement in the war until its occupation by the German army in November 1942. A few months later, when a plan concocted by SS chief Heinrich Himmler to round up 100,000 bad elements in Marseille for slave labor yielded only 2,000, the Nazis ordered that the old city around the Old Port (Vieux-Port) be razed. Vichy officials cooperated in this "urban renewal" that leveled hundreds of buildings and created thousands of homeless. An American bombing raid in May 1944 aimed at the rail yards and rail lines in the center of Marseille wrought more devastation, killing 2,000 Marseillais, injuring another 1,200, and damaging or destroying the homes of 18,000 people. The raid also killed or injured 400 German soldiers caught in the wrong place. When the Allies landed on the southern coast of France on 15 August 1944, they accorded the honor of liberating Toulon and Marseille to French soldiers—most of whom were Arabs and Berbers from North Africa—serving under General Jean-Marie de Lattre de Tassigny. The landings were more successful and overran more territory than cautious Allied planners had counted on, and de Lattre's troops seized Toulon and reached Marseille weeks earlier than anticipated. The Germans defended Marseille with a mixed force of around 13,000 soldiers of uneven quality; a large proportion of the Axis soldiers in southern France were unenthusiastic Balts and former Soviet POWs. The Germans did not evacuate the half a million inhabitants of Marseille, who grew increasingly restless and hostile as liberation drew nearer. Nervous Germans evacuated French from the port areas as German engineers placed explosives to wreck the harbor facilities. The head of the port was arrested and later released without explanation. As French forces surrounded Marseille, de Lattre ordered General Joseph de Goislard de Montsabert to hold off attacking until his whole force was in place and ready. However, FFI within the city did not wait and started seizing government buildings; they captured the prefecture in the Old Port on 21 August and arrested the prefect. Anxious German sappers began setting off their demolition charges in the harbor. But de Montsabert's troops easily entered the city and kept pushing toward the center. It took only a few hours on 23 August for Algerian *tirailleurs* (infantry) to reach the center of the city, to the excited delight of residents. However, getting to the waterfront proved easier than actually crushing German resistance. German troops held out in strongly defended buildings for another four days until General Hans Schaeffer surrendered Marseille on 28 August. Although the French had liberated the city, the Germans still held some of the surrounding hills, from which they lobbed artillery shells into the newly liberated port. The Allies found themselves with two ports and 28,000 German prisoners they had not planned on capturing for many weeks. They had expected a long, hard fight for Marseille and to find a miserable and hungry population. The people of Marseille were neither. Nevertheless, the Allies had a boatload of food waiting offshore, which they brought into the port on 26 August while fighting still raged in pockets and shells fell intermittently.[2]

While German soldiers held out in blockhouses in the harbor area, French and US Army engineers surveyed the damaged port and discussed the best way to get it up and running again. Everyone was pleasantly surprised that the Germans had not caused more damage to the ports in southern France. Although they had sunk a number of ships in the various harbors—including all five tugboats normally used to service Marseille—none of the harbors had been effectively blocked or rendered useless. When the last German soldiers filed out of the blockhouses and the last sailors left their ships on 28 August, the remaining demolition charges were rendered harmless, and the entire port was open for traffic. The Americans proposed to dynamite a dike separating two harbors in the north end of the port; this was approved by French engineers of the Bureau des Ponts et Chaussées, which was in charge of the technical direction of the port. French and Allied engineers consulted about the best way to clear the port, which quays to bring into service first, and how many cranes and other equipment would be needed to get the port functioning. It did not take long.[3]

The government of Charles de Gaulle had no intention of wresting the port from the Nazis just to hand it over to the Americans. French officials were dispatched to take charge of the port right away, even while fighting continued in warehouses and strongpoints around the harbor. The Gaullist government appointed a French naval officer, Captain Sticca, as commander of the port, and he had the final word on all questions. French military staff officers flew in from Algiers on 28 August to take command—if not control—of the port and set up meetings to talk to all responsible parties. PC chief engineer G. Le Bel arrived to assume technical direction of the port on 23 August, the same day North African infantry streamed into the city to take possession of it, in the name of General de Lattre, from FFI rebels. M. Peltier arrived soon after to serve as civilian director of the port. Both Peltier and Le Bel reported to Captain Sticca, but in practice, they were given wide discretion to operate the port, along with Allied military specialists, as they thought best; Sticca acted as liaison between Allied military commanders and the provisional government. Within the first twenty-four hours, Sticca met with German military leaders to talk about surrender, while Peltier met with representatives of the dockworkers' union to discuss the manpower needed to get the docks operating again. General de Lattre assumed control of the city from the FFI only with difficulty. As they were prone to do, the FFI raced around the city in expropriated vehicles, arresting people they suspected of collaboration, and generally acting as if they were in charge. French army officers took a dim view of this, and for de Gaulle's visit to the city on 15 September, they staged an enormous military parade as much to intimidate the FFI as to show off for the president. Soon after liberation, Le Bel established a good working relationship with his American counterparts as well as commanders of French army and navy units, the dockworkers' union, and Gaullist government officials. Events moved quickly, and Le Bel's energy and supportive attitude helped overcome many obstacles to getting the port up and running.[4]

The Germans did to Marseille what they had done to Cherbourg: the harbor was clogged with seventy-five sunken ships, cranes and quayside railroad equipment were demolished and dumped into the harbor, and all the tugboats were sunk. Thousands of mines and booby traps had been planted, as well as underwater mines sown throughout the harbor. Warehouses and other buildings had been razed. As early as 25 August, while Germans troops and the Vichy Milice (paramilitary police) were still holding out, a ship full of food intended for the civilian population of Marseille waited outside the harbor for clearance to enter. No quays were available to unload it, but the cargo could have been unloaded onto lighters, if any of these barges could be found. For the next week, French and US Army engineers met daily to discuss what to do next, what could be repaired most easily, and what was most important. Le Bel concentrated first on erecting temporary bridges to move supplies out of the harbor and out of Marseille. US Army engineers looked to the French to supply as much material, tools, and labor as possible so that scarce army supplies and labor could be used elsewhere. Because so many issues required immediate attention, Le Bel urged Captain Sticca to set up a central office manned twenty-four hours a day with officers capable of making decisions and issuing orders. It took US Army and Navy engineers three weeks to clear enough wreckage clogging the port to restore minimal service. Until the quays were repaired sufficiently, lighters ferried supplies from ships anchored in the harbor to shore; the beaches and small harbor of Saint-Tropez continued to receive military stores for the battle. The first ships were unloaded directly onto the quays on 15 September. For the rest of the month, US forces were able to unload 113,500 metric tons of supplies, as well as almost 33,000 vehicles. The smaller port of Toulon, which had also been sabotaged, handled 12,500 metric tons and 23,600 vehicles.[5]

Le Bel realized early on that, in the chaos that reigned in the port in September 1944, he would be unable to prevent the Americans from seizing properties and supplies on the quays, such as coal, copper, and cables. He therefore set about trying to assure payment for any goods taken by the Americans. But because of disputes over what constituted "war booty," compensation was sometimes hard to pry from them. Le Bel tried to protect some goods, such as rope in a warehouse on the docks, as property of the French government before the Americans discovered it was there. In most cases, all Le Bel could do was solicit bills for requisitioned goods from local businesses and hope for settlement someday. Some requisitioned items were obviously not war booty, such as hoses taken from a church and a barge full of coal that the Americans acknowledged belonged to the French but claimed they needed right away; the promised compensation never materialized. He faced similar problems, but on a vastly smaller scale, with the FFI, who were seen driving off with two commercial trucks. Such difficulties with the Americans made it all the more urgent to get an office of the Aid to Allied Forces (AFA), in charge of all Lend-Lease matters, up and running in Marseille.[6]

Despite French efforts to reestablish control over the port and bring order to its operations, the Americans made it clear that the port was being run for the benefit of the Allied war effort and that all other matters were secondary. As soon as they were on the ground in the south of France, the Allied military wanted French civil authorities to take care of everything they could handle, leaving the military free to fight the Germans. De Gaulle's provisional government in Paris saw fit not to contest the Allied pretense of controlling Marseille. As in North Africa and Cherbourg, de Gaulle's government claimed ultimate authority but wisely did not attempt to assert it. The American military commander of the port, Colonel Robert Clarkson, did not challenge the provisional government's authority, even though he declared that the port was reserved exclusively for support of the war effort. Theoretically, the French controlled most of what occurred on the docks, but the Allies controlled what happened in the water. Allied naval officers had the exclusive right to allow ships to enter the port. Only the Old Port (today the preserve of yachts and pleasure boats), run by the French navy, escaped Allied naval control. Because the Germans had sunk all the tugboats in the harbor, the Allies had to supply their own tugs to push supply ships into berths or anchorage. The French had no tugs of their own until the Allies agreed in January 1945 to rent navy tugs for civilian use. The Allies chartered lighters directly from civilian companies to transfer supplies from anchored ships to the docks. As was the case with most such deals, after September 1944 these contracts were taken over by French government administrators, who handled payments and served as intermediaries to fix any problems. Still, Allied navies shed control when they could: as early as 19 August, they handed off questions related to fishing from Saint-Tropez to the French. A "fishing zone" was created to keep fishing boats from interfering with Allied ships. Local FFI claimed the right to approve all "passes" to fish, and the French navy regulated where fishing could take place. Nevertheless, questions of jurisdiction inevitably cropped up, such as when the Americans tried to take charge of drawbridges in the port area. Because these bridges were crucial to the port's operation, this was not unreasonable, but the port employees who answered to Le Bel were already thoroughly familiar with the drawbridge mechanisms. Le Bel suggested to the Americans that his men remain at their posts and answer to him.[7]

Because the Germans sabotaged the rail network in the south, knocking it out of commission for at least a few weeks, the Allies had to rely on trucks to move military supplies off the docks and to the front. But the port of Marseille was designed and built to rely on railroads, and it was difficult to move big US Army trucks through the narrow, often crooked streets. By November, cargo unloaded on the quays filled 800 trucks per day. Despite German sabotage to the docks, the Allies were soon unloading more cargo than could be transported by trucks to the front. A shortage of transport and warehouses caused the available wharf space to fill up with mountains of cargo waiting to be transported to the front and forced ships full of cargo to wait offshore. On 12 September nineteen British and American ships were sitting in the harbor either being unloaded or waiting to unload. Thus, the initial problem was not lack of dock space but lack of inland transportation. Even the beaches of Saint-Tropez quickly filled with supplies that were brought ashore by ducks and landing craft but left the beaches slowly. It was too dangerous to allow stocks of ammunition to accumulate in the port area, so a giant dump was created outside of Marseille at Rognac; it covered thirty acres, and stacks of ammunition boxes lined the roads leading into town. Fortunately, French crews were able to repair the train tracks and run trains to move supplies along the coast and up the Rhône valley at a fairly early date. French engineers and temporarily unemployed railroad workers helped repair bridges damaged or destroyed by both Allied and German aircraft. German demolition teams did not have time to demolish the refineries, pipeline, and storage facilities at Port-de-Bouc, twenty-five miles west of Marseille, so these important facilities fell into Allied hands in almost perfect working order. This allowed fuel to be diverted from Marseille to Port-de-Bouc, which became the main supply base for petroleum, oil, and lubricants for the armies pushing up the Rhône valley. As in Normandy, army engineers built a pipeline to feed gasoline directly up the Rhône valley to Lyon and, by December, to Dijon.[8]

With ships in the harbors and docks receiving cargo, the Allies ran into another stumbling block: a shortage of labor. The Germans had drafted large numbers of skilled men to work in Germany, and many thousands of able-bodied young men had joined the *maquis* to avoid labor conscription. The Americans and French had to scramble to fill the void. The Americans were forced to rely on GIs and sailors to unload ships, and they scoured the Marseille region for willing hands, even if they had no experience as dockworkers. Le Bel also set about scrounging for laborers, landing first on 120 employees from a bombed-out pasta factory who had proved themselves good civil defense workers during air raids. He found unemployed sailors, underutilized French navy personnel, retired dockworkers, and tugboat operators without tugboats who could work on the docks and in lighters. Most were not used to this sort of work, and some of the dockworkers complained that these men were unfit or too slow and ought to be let go. It soon turned out that southern France was awash in displaced people who could help the Allies at ports and at the growing supply dump in Rognac. When the Germans overran France in 1940, they did not remove captured Senegalese, North African, and Indochinese soldiers and sailors to POW camps in Germany but put them to work in France. Most were turned over to the Todt Organization to build fortifications in the north; however, many thousands were discovered in the south, and they, along with displaced Poles and Italians, were recruited to work for the US supply services. The Allies had service battalions, made up of Italians, that could be moved into the area fairly quickly from Italy. By the end of September, 7,000 Italian service troops were on hand to handle supplies arriving by sea. Italian and eventually German POWs were brought in to help out, along with French soldiers and FFI who were more or less conscripted into the work, as well as thousands of mostly black American troops. These men did not necessarily get along well. The French resented both the Italian and German POWs and did not want to work alongside them—much less eat with them. Senegalese soldiers saw themselves as warriors, not laborers, and they resented being forced to perform what they considered demeaning work. Because of their pride as fighters, the Senegalese looked down on black American troops, who did not carry arms or speak French. The French were responsible for paying everyone who was not a POW or an American soldier, and early delays in payment caused already shaky morale to sink lower. Unhappy workers not only performed badly but also often failed to show up for work at all. Le Bel complained to one company contracted to raise the sunken floating crane "Goliath" that work was proceeding too slowly and no workers should have a day off until Goliath was raised. These solutions to the labor shortage were not ideal. As one contractor working to repair the docks under the supervision of Americans engineers reported to Le Bel in early October: "You requested a report on progress: I report there is no progress to report yet."[9]

Dealing with French labor had been challenging for the US Army in northern France, and the port of Marseille proved no different. Problems abounded, yet with deft handling by agile American officers, operations could go smoothly. Two officers in particular were singled out by both French administrators and French port workers as being especially sympathetic and effective. Civil affairs officers Major Marcus and Colonel Lex worked closely and cooperatively with the French to iron out difficulties and find a modus vivendi that was acceptable to both French workers and the US military. Much of Lex's assignment involved making small concessions to coax more out of the French workers. For instance, they wanted to select their own foreman rather than having one appointed by the Americans; this seemed reasonable to Lex, who agreed to the request. He also met their demands on wages and hours, which were not exorbitant, and he agreed to reconstruct a small shelter for garbage workers that had been torn down by the army for some obscure reason. A union delegation from Menton left a meeting with Lex "satisfied." The colonel listened to complaints and agreed to look into them, which went far to smooth ruffled feathers. Major Marcus often intervened to resolve difficulties between French dockworkers and US guards or naval personnel overseeing the unloading of ships. He won high praise from the dockworkers' union and port officials for his efforts to improve the lot of French workers and ensure that they and their families had access to more goods to improve their lives. This earned him a rare nomination for the Ordre du Mérite Maritime, awarded to those who rendered notable contributions to French maritime services (he did not receive it).[10]

Much of Major Marcus's time was spent trying to prevent US military personnel from treating French dockworkers like the enemy. MPs and sailors were quick to resort to brute force and threats, which usually did not produce the desired result. Marcus then had to intervene to settle disputes aggravated by this inelegant handling by the US military. Much of this friction was probably caused by the inability to communicate, as few French or Americans could speak the other's language. Unable to use words, young men with guns too often resorted to threats and intimidation. Marcus spoke French, and he was a practical man who saw that threats backfired more often than they led to compliance. He also knew that, organized into unions, French workers wielded a powerful weapon that was more effective than guns and clubs: the strike. French workers were quick to stop work to achieve their ends. In February 1945 what started as an argument between the timekeeper on the docks and American guards turned into fisticuffs, leading to the Frenchman's arrest. When French dockworkers failed to see the justice of this action, they stopped all work on the quays. This led the MPs to call the French port police, who drew their pistols and threatened the striking workers with arrest. Nothing good came of this, even after the arrest of two more dockworkers and a shop steward. Major Marcus intervened and got work started again. On another occasion, a strike was called when, for unknown reasons, a US guard shot a French truck driver on the docks, sending him to the hospital. When the man's union chief tried to visit him in the hospital, he was physically prevented from entering the room and given no explanation. Work on the docks resumed only after Marcus promised that the US guard and his sergeant would be arrested for the shooting. Major Marcus could not be everywhere, so sometimes disputes erupted and fights broke out. When an American guard on the Joliette docks ordered French stevedores to stop unloading the cargo from an American ship directly onto the quay and wait for trucks to arrive, the foreman replied that they were just following instructions. The American soldier punched the foreman. An American lieutenant intervened, and when the foreman attempted to tell him what was going on, the guard slapped the foreman twice in the face. Other US soldiers, attracted to the commotion, appeared to be drunk, according to the foreman. At that point, all work on the Joliette docks stopped until the soldiers were sent away, the offending guard was escorted off the docks by MPs, and the lieutenant promised the stevedores they could do their jobs in peace. The workers complained that this sort of insult occurred too often and had to stop.[11]

Fortunately, Le Bel and Marcus had help. The French military and civil administration appointed liaison officers to work directly with their American counterparts in Marseille (Service de Relations avec l'Extérieure) to see that problems were addressed before they grew into bigger troubles. The teams of French and Americans looked into complaints by French workers (I found no examples of complaints by Americans) and tried to be evenhanded. The Americans were quick to fire workers for accidents, holding them responsible for mishaps that were not their fault. The Service de Relations usually sided with the French and tried to get the workers reinstated, such as truck drivers on the docks, who worked under difficult circumstances and really could not avoid minor accidents. One driver failed to see how he could have prevented his truck from getting a flat tire when the tires were so worn; he was rehired. The United States agreed that dockworkers who had to work in bad weather should be provided with appropriate clothing, and those who had been dismissed for refusing to work without adequate clothing were rehired. Complaints by warehouse workers at the rail yards that they had too little time to eat lunch were dismissed as exaggerated. However, the US military accepted a union proposal to allow rail-yard workers more say in the handling of trains in the yards. French protests at a proposal to reduce truck loading teams from ten men to six were dismissed as unwarranted. The Service de Relations agreed to undertake a study to determine whether wages for all sorts of work in Marseille were reasonable. Good relations between the US military and French workers were largely due to the Americans' willingness to listen to French workers and take them seriously. Close coordination between US and French officials—port, police, municipal, and provisional government bureaucrats—resulted in a reliably functioning port.[12]

Professional liaison officers assigned by the US Army and US Navy performed outstandingly, but their masterful achievements were undermined again and again by the loutish behavior of (usually) lower-level US military personnel, often guards, MPs, or noncommissioned officers. French workers at a gasoline depot outside of Marseille protested that the American chief sergeant mistreated them and threatened them with his revolver, often while he was drunk. MPs arrested two Frenchmen who had dropped and broken a box aboard the SS *James Manning*, which led the shop steward to protest their detention and demand their release. When his complaint was ignored, he ordered all the men to stop unloading the ship, and they complied. Two American officers intervened and secured the release of the arrested men, but they also informed the commander of the port that such work stoppages over minor incidents were becoming a problem, and disputes had to be resolved without workers resorting to strikes. The commander agreed and wrote a letter to the ship-servicing company, which accomplished little. In another incident, an American lieutenant berated and manhandled a shop steward who was supervising the unloading of the SS *Gutun* in October 1944, shouting that the work was proceeding too slowly and the Frenchmen did not know how to operate a simple windlass. The steward warned the lieutenant that the windlass was broken, but when the officer tried to use it anyway, he dumped a net full of cargo onto the dock. The stevedores tried to retake control of the unloading and asked another US officer to intervene, but he declined to get involved, provoking another work stoppage on the docks. French workers were virtually powerless against GIs—who were often armed and quick to resort to violence. A French crew loading beer onto a railcar was interrupted by a group of GIs who started appropriating cases of beer for themselves. When the foreman objected and threatened to fetch the MPs, the GIs beat him, getting away with forty-five cases of beer. The French could do little more than protest after the fact. It is hard not to conclude that US soldiers' abusive treatment of French workers was responsible for most of the problems.[13]

Despite the best efforts of port administrators and American civil affairs officers, incidents continued to occur. On 29 October a group of MPs armed with submachine guns charged into the office of some barge operators and began a thorough search for items unknown, ordering everyone in the office to stay where they were. The MPs remained until 10:00 p.m. and refused to allow the port workers to respond to calls for service from ships entering the harbor, leaving the ships blowing their whistles and bewildered by the lack of response. Perhaps worse was the case of the *Eissero*, a tugboat that remained half sunk in the harbor in late November. It was boarded by American engineers and a party of German POWs, who dismantled and carted away three pumps. French civilian guards had been stationed on the boat twenty-four hours a day to prevent exactly this type of event from occurring. They protested the seizures but were roughly treated by the Americans, in full view of the Germans. Such episodes humiliated the French and helped erode the reservoir of goodwill that had existed since August.[14]

French workers also complained about their pay, but these complaints were addressed to French authorities. Wages for French workers were set and paid by the French government, which was then reimbursed by the US military. The rates were low by American standards: 10 francs (20 cents) per hour for a laborer, and 14.3 francs (28 cents) for a skilled worker such as a carpenter. Skilled workers performing dangerous work, such as underwater divers (*scaphandriers*), were more highly rewarded at 38 francs (76 cents) per hour; their helpers were paid handsomely as well, even though their work was less dangerous: 17 to 20 francs (34 to 40 cents) per hour. The benefits for workers legislated by the Popular Front government in the 1930s (health insurance, unemployment insurance, vacation pay, family allowance, prenatal bonus, retirement, and so forth) were still in effect in 1944, as were the charges to employers, which added 50 percent to labor costs. Unloading ships in Marseille was very labor intensive because of the lack of machinery. The US military provided the only cranes available on the docks, bringing in cranes that were mounted on treads. The use of lighters to shuttle cargo from anchored ships to the quays was a slow process and required the loading and unloading of all goods twice. Because of the slow turnaround in discharging ships, the United States demanded that the port remain open and operating twenty-four hours a day, seven days a week, whether there were ships that required unloading or not. This policy mandated overtime pay for many workers, who often had little or nothing to do. The United States willingly ran up the bills for all this labor, but the French office that handled payments (AFA) balked at these excessive—perhaps padded—charges. The chief engineer for the port pointed out to the AFA in Paris that as inefficient as the Marseille operation was, it was still cheaper than labor costs in New York City. During the month of December 1944, the port of Marseille billed the AFA 68.75 million francs ($1.375 million); 55.2 million francs ($1.1 million) went to pay dockworkers' wages, which the Americans probably considered a bargain.[15]

Trying to get the most out of these workers, the US military agreed to provide civilians with many benefits that only the Americans had access to, such as food, clothing, footwear, and even temporary housing. The United States had learned in North Africa that giving the locals free clothing and footwear was a strong incentive for them to work for the army. In 1944 the need in France was just as urgent as it had been in North Africa, and many people were making do with old or improvised clothing and shoes. Some of those who worked for the United States in Marseille and the surrounding region had no access to amenities such as cafés, restaurants, or housing, so the United States agreed to feed and house them. This policy was not adopted for everyone; it was applied on an ad hoc basis as situations arose that justified it. At first, in September 1944, the US Army recognized the hardships imposed on workers required to keep docks in the distant northern part of the port operating twenty-four hours a day, so the Americans agreed to provide free food for the dockworkers and lighter crews. Soon the Americans expanded that to include supplemental rations and, in many cases, free breakfasts and dinners for up to 800 dockworkers elsewhere who had little access to eating establishments. In November 1944 the port authorities asked the United States to supply two meals a day for 4,000 workers and complained about the housing provided for 150 of them. The United States agreed to feed all these workers only until 1 January, after which the French port administration would have to take care of them—something it failed to do because the French did not have access to the food supplies the US military did.[16]

In early September Le Bel appealed to the gendarmes of Marseille: "I call to your attention that crowds of people of the quartier have been methodically pillaging the contents of warehouses located at [address]. Please see that the contents are safeguarded." Marseille had a long history of highly active criminal gangs that gleefully exploited the flow of goods from Allied ships. Their networks for the disposal of stolen property contributed to the rampant pilfering and black marketeering by American soldiers with access to these valuable goods. Perhaps as much as 20 percent of all US supplies unloaded in Marseille found its way onto the black market. This posed a significant problem because Marseille became the principal port for supplying Allied forces in France. Gasoline was especially susceptible to pilfering, and huge stocks in Port-de-Bouc were diverted from military to civilian use. As a result, US military units literally ran out of gas in their rush up the Rhône valley. The Americans mounted guards, who treated the French warily, but the diversions continued because of the willing participation of many GIs. In one case, American service troops agreed to sell three tons of soap to a black-market dealer in Marseille, but when they could not locate that much soap, they substituted boxes of dynamite. Organized gangs operated on the docks of Marseille, pilfering whatever they could in alarmingly large amounts. The president of the Chamber of Commerce observed that the people of Marseille had adopted lax morals under the German occupation and continued to exercise the same after the Americans arrived. To lie, cheat, and steal had been virtues under the occupation, and that *mode de vie* faded only slowly. Living off the black market had become a way of life, and that continued to be true after the Allies' arrival because shortages of essential goods kept the black markets alive and thriving. Selling goods stolen from the Allies kept many families fed, and this would not have been possible without the connivance of large numbers of American supply troops, who also made a good living off the pilfering. Shortages plagued the south of France long after Germany surrendered, and once the cornucopia of Allied supplies ran out in late 1945, shelves in stores remained empty, provoking a loud protest movement by the hungry inhabitants.[17]

The monopolization of the port by the US military interfered with civilian use of the docks. Marseille had been one of the most important trade ports on the Mediterranean Sea, and although trade diminished during the war, it did not stop. Only with the Allied takeover of the port did civilian commerce almost cease. The Americans set aside some quays to receive civilian cargo, but only at the convenience of the military; in addition, the cargo had to be cleared from the docks immediately because there was no warehouse space allotted for it. If the cargo could not be unloaded directly onto trucks—and often there were none available—the cargo could not be offloaded at all, and the ships could not sit at the quays waiting for trucks. In one case, stevedores unloaded cargo from a ship from Corsica directly onto a quay in February 1945, and the MPs forced them to put it all back and have the ship turn around and sail back to Corsica. This incident fueled the demand to have some docks reserved exclusively for civilian cargo, which the Allies finally agreed to the following month. Dock space did not come with warehouse space, however. Also, the section of harbor set aside for civilian use was still partially blocked by sunken ships, and the Allies had no plans to remove them anytime soon. An agreement in March 1945 to make more provisions for civilian life and commerce in the port area by releasing requisitioned properties and moving military units out of the city may have represented a step forward, but it also meant that the French would have to solve their own problems, without US military help.[18]

Although the Allies started to return the port to French control in the spring of 1945, while the war still raged in Germany and Marseille was still needed as a supply channel, it was a slow process. When the rush of military supplies entering the port dwindled, the amount of equipment and men leaving the port grew to a torrent. Much of the material the Allies had brought in left again via the same port, which also served as the principal transit point for French forces heading to the Far East or back to Africa. For most of the summer of 1945, the harbor facilities remained in Allied military hands. Not until September 1945 did the Allies hand back many of the buildings and wharves that had been occupied by the US military. The giant depot in Rognac was returned to the French in January 1946. The Allies' departure was almost as chaotic as their arrival. Quays set aside for the French were suddenly filled with US material waiting to be loaded onto US ships, and warehouses that were supposed to be empty remained full of Allied supplies. There were thousands of details to attend to but only a small number of French officials and Allied officers available to do so. Many things went right: the Americans agreed to dismantle a fence that prevented access to some buildings turned over to the French; surplus wooden crates and skids were donated to the city of Marseille for fuel to heat schools and hospitals. However, wrangling over money—who owed how much to whom, and for what—ratcheted up between French administrators and American officers. The Americans had given the French some temporary barracks built in the harbor area, but how much should the French pay for them? When GIs mistakenly burned down some temporary buildings that had already been turned over to the French but not yet painted by the French to indicate they had taken possession, the French wanted compensation for the destroyed buildings. When the US Army relinquished possession of a student dormitory at the University of Marseille, it sent a team to dispose of any leftover debris, and whatever the team found in the rooms was burned as rubbish. Unfortunately, the students had already moved back in, and the "rubbish" was their belongings. Then there was the question of who was going to pay for the damages caused by both American and British sailors who had used hand grenades and dynamite to "fish" in the harbor. Pleas to make them stop had gone unheeded, and by July 1945 the explosives had damaged buoys, lights, lamps, and two boats. French officials were understandably concerned about important items such as tugboats and cranes, which the United States had promised to declare "surplus" and sell to the French. Too many of these items ended up disappearing either in flames or in ships' hulls, placed there by GIs who were just following orders.[19]

There also remained the touchy question of payment of the charges imposed on the Allies by the French government, such as import taxes and taxes on ships' use of French waterways. The Americans refused to pay such levies; the British followed suit but were willing to negotiate some compensation for the use of port facilities, such as pilot fees. The French raised the issue with the US State Department. The Americans had paid plenty for services rendered, such as pilot fees, but they saw no reason to pay taxes or government-imposed duties and did not do so. Recorded receipts from the Allies for June 1945 equaled *Neant* (none). In May 1945 the provisional government in Paris threw in the towel and created an account to pay the taxes due from the Allies (United States, United Kingdom, and Canada). Payment for damages, rents, utilities, and the like became uncertain when Lend-Lease ended on 1 September 1945. Until then, French companies could expect compensation from the French government (AFA), which in turn was paid by the Allies, but who was going to pay the electric company after 1 September? Many such questions poured in from nervous French vendors providing goods and services to the Allies. Despite all these uncertainties, the Marseille Chamber of Commerce was delighted to supply the champagne at the 5 April 1946 ceremony restoring the port to the French. Port director Couteaud marveled at what had been accomplished over the past twenty months and underlined the importance of working together to win the war. He also delivered some good news: The US government had agreed to leave behind all the machinery necessary to run the port. Payment would be worked out later.[20]

Once the Marseille Chamber of Commerce regained control of the port after 1 April 1946, the Allied military contracted directly with the Chamber of Commerce for the use of port facilities, just as any shipping or import company would have done. Although the Chamber of Commerce was in charge of the docks after 1 April, the formal agreement to that effect was not signed until 13 August 1946. The Chamber of Commerce had no hand in negotiating the contract, which was written entirely by officials from the Ministry of Public Works in Paris and expired on 30 June 1946, months before it was even signed! The United States agreed to turn over quantities of goods, such as oil and gasoline, on the assumption that these would eventually be declared surplus. Some French administrators were nervous about using machinery and material that was still technically US Army property, and they were assured that if the Americans asked for any machinery (winches, cranes, trucks, locomotives) back, it would be returned to them, and Paris would negotiate any repair expenses if necessary. Officials in Paris seemed confident that the Americans would not ask for the items back. Indeed, in May 1946 the Americans signed an accord in Washington promising to honor all bills incurred by the US military since the end of Lend-Lease. Both sides obsessed over damages caused to French property by GIs and compensation due to civilian victims of attacks by GIs. This remained a sore point with the French long after most GIs had sailed away from French shores.[21]

With victory looming in May 1945, Brigadier General Wayne Allen, in charge of procurement in France, gave a speech in Marseille that summarized the Franco-American working relationship of the past year. He thanked the French for all their help and observed that Allied procurement in France had gone smoothly and greatly aided in achieving victory. French factories had reconditioned engines for tanks, retread tires for trucks, and much else. He praised French workers' cooperation, noting that, from stevedores to railroad workers, from mechanical to clerical workers, they had all performed excellently. Colonel Jacques Lévy in Paris had done much to ensure that this system worked well, and despite minor differences of opinion and different methods of doing things, relations were always cordial and problems were worked out amicably. Just a week before, the American commander of the port, Colonel Robert Clarkson, had issued an open letter in English and French to all units involved in port operations, praising their excellent work and acknowledging the cooperation of all who had helped make the port of Marseille the most important Allied supply center in Europe. He marveled at the speed with which the port had been brought into operation and the continuing efficiencies that made the turnaround time for supply ships at Marseille the lowest of all the major ports, including Antwerp. This made life easier for the Allied military and for everyone in the supply chain, reaching all the way back to the United States. These observations fairly represented the view of the Franco-American working relationship among those at the top level of the US military. These sentiments were echoed by French port director Couteaud a year later, when the port was returned to French control. He rhapsodized about the spirit of cooperation that had animated all those involved to make the port such a successful operation. He quoted a speech by Theodore Roosevelt delivered at the Sorbonne in 1910 and posted on the wall of the US port commander, eulogizing the man of action "who spends himself in a worthy cause." He did not complete the quote, but it would have been apt: "the man who is actually in the arena, whose face is marred by dust and sweat and blood; who strives valiantly; who errs, who comes short again and again, because there is no effort without error and shortcoming; but who does actually strive to do the deeds; who knows great enthusiasms, the great devotions; who spends himself in a worthy cause; who at the best knows in the end the triumph of high achievement, and who at the worst, if he fails, at least fails while daring greatly, so that his place shall never be with those cold and timid souls who neither know victory nor defeat."[22]

5

Displaced Persons

The handling of displaced persons (DPs) revealed both cooperation and confrontation between the Americans and the French government. France, like the rest of Nazi-occupied Europe, was awash in civilians who had been forcibly removed from their homes by the Germans and sent to labor in foreign lands. Most of them ended up in Germany, but as noted, many hundreds of thousands of foreigners were sent to work in France. These foreign workers were overwhelmingly Polish or Russian, but they also included Hungarians, Italians, Czechs, Dutch, and Germans. After liberation, housing and feeding these displaced people became a bone of contention between the Americans and the French soon after Commissioner Coulet arrived in Normandy. Although agreements were worked out between the Allies, new irritants arose over the handling of DPs that outlasted the war. Fortunately, there was no question about what to do with French DPs found in Germany, and the US Army returned them to France as quickly as possible. The French government freely expressed its gratitude to the Americans for the assistance rendered, and the repatriation of French DPs from Germany counted as one of the successes of Franco-American cooperation. According to historian Michael Marrus, despite some difficulties, identifying and caring for DPs in France by both the Allies and the French proceeded more smoothly than almost anywhere else in war-torn Europe. Close coordination between the French and SHAEF accounted for much of the success in handling DPs in France.[1]

Before D-Day, Allied intelligence estimated that France contained 2.7 million foreigners from twenty countries who would be classified as DPs. Additionally, 2.4 million French were thought to have been displaced outside of France—many of them forcibly. Preinvasion plans called for Allied civil affairs officers to assume responsibility for all DPs, regardless of nationality, until they could be turned over to French authorities. This did not work out very well. Civil affairs personnel did what they could for DPs, but they were overwhelmed with other tasks and did not wish to add caring for DPs to their headaches. As long as fighting persisted in a region, the US Army wanted all DPs to stay where they were, rather than using transport and personnel to move them. The Allies expected most DPs in France to be French, and they assumed the French would care for them. Many French had fled cities made unsafe by Allied bombs; others had been forcibly evacuated from coastal areas by the Germans. US intelligence estimated that around 260,000 French had been expelled from Alsace and Lorraine, and the Nazis had expelled about 700,000 French from thirteen departments entirely or partially located in the "forbidden zone" (including annexed regions) of northeastern France. An unknown number of French citizens were displaced for various reasons during the course of the war; French historian Jean-Luc Leleu posits that one-third of the population moved at least once during the war years. The French expelled from the eastern provinces were replaced by an estimated 125,000 Russians, Poles, Italians, and other captive peoples, all of whom were considered DPs when they fell into Allied hands. The ultimate fate of 75,000 Spaniards loyal to the fallen Republic who still languished in camps in southern France remained an open question.[2]

SHAEF set up an office within the Civil Affairs section to act as liaison with the French government to handle DP questions. Although plans drawn up before D-Day called for the French to take responsibility for all DPs within France, regardless of nationality, it was clear that French authorities were in no position to care for hundreds of thousands of DPs. Even after most of France had been liberated by January 1945, the French had no food to feed them, no places to house them, and no means to move them; hence, much of the burden of caring for the DPs fell on the Allies, even if the armies stipulated that they had no de jure responsibility for them. Many hundreds of thousands of French DPs had no homes to return to because of Allied bombing, which argued strongly in favor of the Allies helping to care for them. The Americans made food, blankets, tents, and medical supplies available, but they relied on the French to run the DP camps. Civil Affairs reported in September that the French were overseeing scattered DP camps and doing a credible job. In October 1944 more French DPs arrived daily in centers not far from the Atlantic coast, as the German forces holed up in Saint-Nazaire, La Rochelle, La Pallice, and other oceanside fortresses allowed the remaining civilians to leave. SHAEF asked Allied air forces not to bomb the German-held pockets until French civilians had evacuated. In December the Germans agreed to a cease-fire so that the civilians left in Saint-Nazaire could be cleared out. The United States provided 50 tons of clothing for the refugees, which proved inadequate. After SHAEF received an urgent plea for more, another 100 tons of clothing was sent. This had to suffice for all the refugees sheltered in Brittany, including the many tens of thousands who were still unable to return to Brest.[3]

By December 1944, France was awash in DPs from all over Europe, and the problem of where to put all these refugees became acute. Chaos reigned in Paris: too many authorities—French, American, and British—were claiming priority in requisitioning facilities where DPs might be housed. The Allies had assumed responsibility for caring for DPs from Europe, but these DPs' needs were competing with those of French citizens without housing, who were quickly becoming the exclusive responsibility of the French provisional government. Minister for Inter-Allied Affairs François Coulet, Minister of War André Diethelm, and Minister for Prisoners, Deportees, and Refugees (PDR) Henri Frenay worked out among themselves how responsibility would be apportioned, but this division of labor would work only if the Allies allocated the necessary resources. The French established twenty-one reception centers located reasonably close to the eastern borders to receive and temporarily house and feed the 2 million French POWs, STO workers (French workers drafted to work in Germany), and deportees who were expected home in early 1945. Unhappily, many of the designated facilities, such as the Hotel de Gare and the professional school in Jeumont (on the Belgian border), had already been requisitioned by the US Army. Internally displaced French, such as the estimated 300,000 expelled from the Moselle by the Nazis, would also need places to stay until their home situations were straightened out. The US Army still occupied all the barracks and many other buildings in the Moselle in the spring of 1945, and until it cleared out, French returnees would have to find somewhere else to stay. To complicate matters, the US Army employed almost all the available workers who were needed to build, alter, and repair buildings for the returning French to live. And even if the French government found workers to perform the necessary jobs, how would it feed them? The United States shipped food to France by sea, and the US Army then trucked it in for its French workers, but there was no extra food available for other French civilians in the spring of 1945. To add to their problems, the PDR minister agreed in principle that non-German orphans in Germany should be brought to France for care.[4]

French DPs Return from Germany

When Allied armies overran Germany in the spring of 1945, they came across millions of non-Germans stranded by the war. Overwhelmingly, these people had been conscripted to work in German industry or on German farms to make up for the manpower shortage caused by the war. Millions of others were POWs held by the Germans, many of whom also worked in German factories or on farms. All DPs were expected to fill out a three-page form identifying who they were and where they came from. By mid-April, of the nearly 1.9 million DPs crowded into camps in liberated Germany, 163,000 were known to be French. The American military wanted to move them out of Germany and return them to France as quickly as possible, and by 17 April, 120,000 had been sent back to France. French DPs proved to be the easiest to repatriate, yet their numbers grew with each passing week as more DPs of all nationalities were discovered in Germany. By VE Day, the number of DPs had swollen to millions, including 230,000 French in the American sector alone. More DPs trickled over from the Soviet sector and added to the tally in the US zone; by 10 May, an additional 7,000 French had been identified, bringing the total number of French DPs still in Germany to 482,000. Over the next nine days, 110,000 of them were sent back to France, almost all by American airplanes. It actually proved easier to transport people by air than by ground, as few rail lines in Germany were functioning and the roads were crowded with military traffic. The US Army figured it flew 5,000 French DPs and POWs to France per day aboard returning supply planes. SHAEF and French authorities worked out a plan to exploit Swiss rail lines to transport people back to France via Switzerland—the International Red Cross had used this route even while the war still raged. An unknown number of French DPs walked home from Germany and never visited a reception center, thus eluding both French and American officials tasked with identifying them. Around 125,000 were thought to have "self-repatriated," getting home by any means available to them. One such Frenchman was writer and resistance fighter Robert Antelme, who was picked up at the Dachau concentration camp by friends. One of those friends, François Mitterand, had received news in Paris that Antelme was in Dachau and in very poor health. In fact, Antelme was one of about 18,000 French camp inmates judged too sick to move. Mitterand and the others barrowed a car, drove to Munich, fetched the typhus-infected Antelme, and drove him back to Paris. By the end of May, 1,453,000 French had been repatriated from Germany, 912,000 since 1 May; of these, 119,000 were flown in US airplanes, 22,000 on a single day. By 6 July, 1.5 million had been repatriated, and only 13,000 French DPs remained in the US zone in Germany. The return of French citizens to France, coordinated or carried out directly by the US Army, was swift and relatively uncomplicated.[5]

Not all French DPs wanted to return home as soon as possible. Agnès Humbert, a member of a resistance group operating out of the Musée de l'Homme in Paris, had been arrested and deported to Germany, where she labored under horrific conditions in a chemical plant. A German speaker of sorts, she remained in Germany to help care for DPs and to help American counterintelligence identify Nazis. Humbert stayed in Hesse, taking charge of a town full of DPs and acting as the vice-mayor and liaison with the US Army. She supervised relief efforts for the endless procession of DPs, including Germans, trudging through the town of Wanfried. She also tried, without success, to convince the Americans that the woods were full of die-hard Wehrmacht who should be rooted out and rounded up. In mid-June 1945 she became a DP herself and was driven back to Paris in a US Army truck with a French driver.[6]

The speed with which French DPs were returned to France in the spring of 1945 produced its own problems. It proved easier to transport French DPs from Germany to France than to find places for them to stay once they arrived. When the French who had been evicted from Alsace-Lorraine by the Nazis returned in 1945, many of them had no homes to return to. The war damage in Lorraine had been immense, wrecking tens of thousands of houses. Many people tried to live in their homes regardless of the damage, but they required a lot of day-to-day assistance. Metz was inundated by refugees—DPs and returnees—in addition to housing thousands of US troops occupying every available living space. French officials were at their wits' end trying to find places for people to live—American soldiers, returning French, Lorrainers bombed out of their houses, and foreign DPs stranded by the receding Nazi tide. The many barracks in the fortress city offered a lot of living space, if only the American and French armies would decide they no longer needed them as the war came to a close.[7]

Competition for living quarters between the US military and the French people was greatly aggravated by the number of dispossessed French in need of housing. The French wanted to set up reception camps at the borders for returnees, but this would have required the Americans to give up their many camps in these regions, which they were reluctant to do. Quarters designated as reception centers in Lorraine were still occupied by American airmen with nowhere else to go. The French were frustrated that the US Army Air Force, for example, retained possession of most of the large buildings in Maubeuge, in the Nord, while returning French POWs had nowhere to go. SHAEF personnel recognized the seriousness of the problem and agreed that the army had to surrender space to the returning French, but they were flummoxed at the task of finding somewhere to put the Americans. The US military still claimed enormous amounts of requisitioned space that was often only partially utilized. The French government wanted to know why only 200

US soldiers were billeted in a barracks in Charleville that could hold 2,000 returning French POWs. When the Americans quit requisitioned schools in Charleville-Mézières so that French returnees could be housed there, French officials were shocked by the condition of the properties: American troops had burned 200 beds for fuel, 600 blankets were missing, and the soldiers had eaten all the food stockpiled in the schools' pantries. French newspapers gave vent to such grievances, spreading resentment about the returnees' reception, even if they had been whisked out of Germany on American planes and trucks. There were reports of French citizens being held at the border because there was no place for them in France, causing "clashes" with American troops. The newspaper *L'Aurore* picked up this story and began referring to "our American 'friends'" in a less than friendly manner. Many among the French political left—rarely friendly toward the United States on principle—argued that the Americans aggravated the problems facing DPs and returnees. Marguerite Duras, a writer and member of the PCF, critiqued Gaullist bureaucrats just as severely as the Americans for their indifferent treatment (according to Duras) of returning POWs and concentration camp inmates; she expected the government to requisition apartments (from Parisian bourgeois) for returnees, as it had done for US troops. In contrast to Duras's impression, when US Army Captain Robert S. Gerdy saw trucks full of returning French POWs being unloaded near a Parisian train station just before VE Day, he admired the kindness with which they were treated by the French and decided to help. He lent a hand carrying their small, pathetic bundles of possessions and received thanks from the returning POWs and from the other French helping out.[8]

The American Red Cross (ARC) took an active interest in helping people stranded in DP camps, regardless of nationality. The organization collected donated clothing and other useful materials to distribute to people in need. In December 1944 the ARC was still handing out clothing in Normandy, 70 tons in Cherbourg and 30 tons in Caen, and it had set up quarters in northeastern France, liberated in September, to do the same. In January 1945 it provided 20 tons of clothing to the French National Welfare Coordinating Committee for distribution in the Paris region alone. Huge quantities of goods had been amassed in the United States and Britain (800,000 garments), awaiting space on ships to be transported to France. Room was found for 1,000 tons of powdered and condensed milk, as well as 5 million quarts of fresh milk to benefit French children. By June 1945, the ARC had opened seven distribution centers serving every region of France. Even though large numbers of Red Cross volunteers had moved into Germany to help care for the populations of the concentration camps—where the need was dire—many still labored in France, with Paris serving as the nerve center of activity. Because Paris was the reception center for French returnees from concentration camps, the ARC was kept busy finding clothes, food, and medicine for them. France's Atlantic coast remained an active war zone until the German surrender in May 1945, and the need there remained great into the summer. The ARC gave away 67,000 items of clothing in May in the region of Saint-Nazaire alone. Later in 1945 the ARC was able to turn its attention to areas in less dire straits, such as Saint-Etienne, where it delivered 22,000 articles of clothing, 2,500 hospital gowns, 300 layettes, and 20 cases of soap. In December 1945 the ARC sent another five truckloads of powdered milk, intended for children, and lots of warm clothing. The distribution in Saint-Etienne was handled by a committee composed of the ARC, the Croix Rouge, Entr'aide française (see below), the director of public health, and delegates from Protestant, Catholic, and Jewish charities. These various groups worked well together, and the prefect of the Loire reported that the population greatly appreciated the aid.[9]

As an international voluntary organization dedicated to providing evenhanded and impartial aid during wartime, the ARC worked through other independent and voluntary organizations whenever possible and avoided distributing relief through government agencies. Thus, the ARC established a good working relationship with the French Croix Rouge, which was desperately short of everything and leaned heavily on its British and American counterparts for support. Croix Rouge workers themselves needed clothing, especially women's shoes. However, while the fighting raged, the ARC relied on the US Army to distribute donated clothing to people in dire need in areas close to the front lines. The ARC had yet to establish a presence in the French southwest, where only a handful of Allied intelligence and civil affairs officers wandered around in jeeps checking on the FFI, which seemed to have the area under more or less benevolent control. Without any real US presence in the southwest, the ARC handed over donated items directly to French government officials to distribute as needed, contrary to ARC regulations. As the provisional government gained confidence, it asserted its authority and created a government agency, Entr'aide française, to take over the distribution of relief goods. Entr'aide française supplanted the various Vichy-era social aid and public welfare organizations, and it became the only organization allowed to distribute relief aid. Entr'aide française proved prickly to work with as early as January 1945 because its functionaries did not see the French umbrella aid organization as an equal partner with the ARC or any other group; it was the sole hand controlling aid in France. The ARC used

Entr'aide warehouses in Paris to store its donated goods, but it had great difficulty getting access to the materials once they came under Entr'aide's control. Requests that designated ARC donations in Entr'aide warehouses be sent to certain locations were ignored, and Entr'aide disposed of the donated items as it saw fit. The ARC protested and asked SHAEF to intercede in January 1945. SHAEF agreed that the ARC should maintain its own warehouses, and the army offered to provide trucks and personnel to move ARC goods. SHAEF balked, however, at ARC's suggestion that it should no longer sit with Entr'aide on the committee coordinating aid in Paris; SHAEF suggested that as long as the US Army was participating in aiding the needy in France, ARC should retain its seat on the committee.[10]

A storm erupted between the American Red Cross on one side and the French government on the other when the ARC protested to the prefect in the Yonne that it was against Red Cross policy to hand anything over to the government for the benefit of citizens; aid was to be distributed strictly through volunteer channels. Although the ARC was willing to accept Entr'aide as an independent voluntary association, it was not willing to let Entr'aide monopolize the distribution of clothing to the exclusion of its partners in the Croix Rouge, a view seconded by the Croix Rouge. Nor was the ARC going to allow the French government to dictate how it operated, and it threatened to stop all deliveries to the Yonne unless government policy changed. At Christmastime 1945 the ARC donated toys and candy for orphans in Auxerre and other towns of the Yonne, with the distribution actually carried out by the departmental Inspection du Service d'Enfance, a government organ. The Croix Rouge sent the Yonne prefect a long list of clothing for women and children—23 cubic meters worth—to be delivered to Auxerre by the ARC in the spring of 1946, including 113 dresses for little girls, 89 woolen pajamas for children, 240 short pants for young boys, 65 pairs of small overalls, 425 woolen outfits for infants younger than two years old, and so on. This was in addition to the hundreds of items already sent by the ARC and distributed by the departmental children's services agency to hospitals, nursing homes, and orphanages in the Yonne in the winter of 1945–1946. Inquiries by the prefect revealed that in 1945 the ARC had donated thousands of articles of clothing for women, children, infants, and men (men seemed to receive mostly shoes and socks), with the vast majority of clothing destined for children and babies. His response to the ARC's protests was to agree that the Croix Rouge could distribute items for infants, but Entr'aide would handle everything else. The prefect in Auxerre was not going to let the American Red Cross call the shots, even if it was providing free clothing to French children.

In this case, the Gaullist government was more interested in demonstrating and exercising control, and it was willing to compromise the welfare of those in need to do so.[11]

Foreign DPs in France

In addition to accommodating French DPs and returning POWs, the French—assisted by the Allies—had to care for the hordes of foreigners stranded in France. The Germans had forcibly relocated tens of thousands to France to labor on the massive war-related construction projects and to serve as domestic servants to Germans stationed in France or colonizing its eastern provinces. The newly established provisional government was still finding its feet in the fall of 1944 and was forced to rely on the Americans for help. The US Army employed many thousands of foreign DPs from friendly countries such as Poland who could not return home while the war still raged. Challenges posed by DPs from countries overrun by the Soviet Union's forces continued to nettle the French long after the fighting ended because they had no agreement with the Soviets about how to repatriate DPs from central and eastern Europe. With few other facilities available, the French herded Poles, Russians, and Yugoslavs into old barracks near Verdun when they could find no other place to put them. The DPs complained they were being treated like enemy POWs, with guards posted around the camps and tight controls on their movements. The American Red Cross took an interest in the 1,000 Russian women and children housed in a camp in Briey and provided volunteers to help run the camp. However, as winter approached, the DPs were in desperate need of warm clothing, which the ARC was unable to provide, despite promises from its counterparts in the United States that supplies were on the way. The US Army was willing to help out when it could, but Civil Affairs resolved in October that the fate of foreign DPs in France was for the French to decide. The US Army still had charge of around 125,000 DPs in army-run camps in the fall of 1945, with Poles accounting for the majority, and Hungarians and Italians making up most of the rest.[12]

Poles formed the largest contingent of foreign DPs in France, and the US Army was looking after 75,000 in October 1945. Many had been sent to Lorraine to work as agricultural laborers on "Reichland" farms that had been seized from French farmers. When many of the German settlers fled with the Wehrmacht, the Poles were left behind to fend for themselves. As French farmers arrived to reclaim their farms, they often found Polish families—men, women, and children—living there. The French farmers, not surprisingly, wanted the Poles expelled, which they were, but where were they to go? It was hard enough to find places for the displaced French in Lorraine in the spring of 1945. French authorities in the Ardennes proposed placing the Poles under the supervision of the Forest Service, the Agricultural Service, or the Ponts et Chaussées, which could put them to work. However, left to their own devices, some of the estimated 300 Poles in Nancy took to thievery, provoking so many complaints to the police that the prefect felt compelled to round them up and hold them in a secure camp until they could be returned to Poland. The roundup did not go smoothly everywhere, and some Poles resisted the French police. When gendarmes proved insufficient to the task, FFI units were called in, and they were reportedly pretty rough. A delegate from the Polish Red Cross protested the arrests and demanded that all the Poles be released, but the French refused. When the Polish Red Cross official insisted, he too was arrested and placed in the camp with the others. The Americans had put hundreds of Poles on trains in France destined for either repatriation in Poland or camps in Germany, but the majority jumped off the trains before they left France. The French tried to convince the Americans to gather them up, but the Americans replied that the Poles had ceased to be their problem the moment they left the camps and boarded the trains. The French also tried to get the Americans to turn over files from the camps to at least help identify the evaders, without success. Then the French asked the Polish consulate to intervene, but it, too, refused, responding that the Poles roaming the countryside were a problem for the French to deal with. French police tried to detain them, but the courts declared that in the absence of serious charges, they had to be released.[13]

So many of the DPs in camps in northern France were Polish that they were renamed Camp Sikorski, Camp Varsovie, Camp Pulaski, and the like. An inspection of a DP camp at Charleville in December 1944 found 711 Poles crammed into barracks that were much too small. They included 266 women and 277 children who were sharing 500 beds and only 200 blankets. Both the kitchen and the infirmary were deemed "entirely inadequate"; there was no mess hall and no eating utensils. The inspectors—a mixed delegation that included an ARC representative—also found the building infested with lice and other bugs, although it is easy to imagine that the DPs brought the pests with them. The cluster of buildings was shared by 200 GIs from the Army Corps of Engineers and a unit of gendarmes, which no doubt underlined for the inspectors that US requisitions contributed to the DPs' cramped conditions. Many of the Polish DPs were brought together in large camps in the Marne and employed by the US Army for various jobs at the many camps, supply depots, and maintenance facilities constructed by the Americans around SHAEF headquarters in Reims. As US Army camps in the Marne emptied of American soldiers, the American authorities filled them with DPs, who took over many of the tasks previously performed by GIs. However, as the US Army presence waned in the Marne, the 50,000 Polish DPs had less work to do, and the Americans left the administration of the camps largely to the DPs themselves. According to the French, the camps soon descended into dens of gangsters. Poles entrusted to guard surplus American supplies—which, by 1946, had become French property—looted the warehouses at will. Polish women who had sexually serviced American troops in the Marne took to thievery and prostitution with other Poles and French after the Americans left. Poles from the camps marauded the surrounded towns and countryside, pillaging, raping, and even murdering. French police, the prefect claimed, were outmanned and outgunned. The Poles came from a variety of backgrounds, but those who had suffered the worst indignities in Nazi Germany, he mused, had abandoned all civilized codes and reverted to the law of the jungle. Agnès Humbert developed a skeptical view of Polish DPs during her stint as the reigning authority in Wanfried, Germany, after its liberation in April 1945. When most of the SS guards fled, she took charge of the camp, which contained a large number of Polish prisoners. They smashed everything and mercilessly beat their former warders in a fever of revenge. "Everything is destroyed, defiled, smashed beyond use," she wrote. "I don't even raise a hand to stop this senseless vandalism. These are primitive people, I tell myself, venting their primitive instincts." The DP camp where she ended up in Kassel, Germany, was populated by Poles and offered nonstop bedlam.[14]

As troublesome as the Polish DPs were, they were no match for the Russians. Like the Poles, Russian DPs could not be repatriated until Germany was defeated, so the French and the Americans had to find someplace to put them. Some of the Russians who had served in the Wehrmacht were segregated from both German POWs and Russian DPs. The US Army employed 600 Russian POWs in the kitchens and mess tents at the massive ordnance base in Le Mans in January 1945. After the German surrender in May 1945, Russian POWs were petrified of being returned to the USSR, and French guards in the Rhône had a difficult time keeping 500 from escaping to avoid being sent back. The escapees turned to crime and made life miserable for the French, who wanted the Russians gone. The Germans left behind an unknown number of Russian conscript laborers in France. Many of them had joined bands of FFI and fought for the liberation of France, but unlike French *maquis,* the Russians could not be drafted into the French army. In October 1944 an FTP commander installed ninety Russian FFI fighters in a large barracks in the center of Nancy, without orders from anyone. When the local FFI commander, Gilbert Grandval, attempted to get them out, the

Russians refused to leave. Learning that the Soviet ambassador had ordered all Russian FFI to join an autonomous combat team answering to Russian Colonel Lishuevsky, Grandval passed along these instructions for the Russians to report to a camp being set up elsewhere in the Meurthe-et-Moselle. Only orders from the Red Army succeeded in getting the Russians out of the Nancy barracks. Two hundred Russian POWs had been used by the Germans to mine coal in Ronchin—a suburb of Lille—until it was liberated by FFI and British troops in early September 1944, and they were left in a camp until the Allies could find a use for them. The Russians somehow got their hands on weapons and led an armed protest in November, demanding back wages never paid by the Germans. Gendarmes intervened, and after an exchange of gunfire, they were disarmed by the Russians and taken captive; a French MP eventually negotiated their release. The armed Russians then marched on the center of Lille, where they were again met by gendarmes, who managed to stop them without shooting. Agents of the French Deuxième Bureau (intelligence) persuaded the Russians to leave quietly and promised to take a serious look into their demands. The lesson to be learned from this incident, according to the British intelligence officer who reported it, was the dangerous weakness of French forces of order in the Nord and the delicate situation that existed in a region with strong Communist sympathies and still-armed bands. Just when it appeared that US Army units would have to help the French army and the FFI disarm a group of determined Russians in the Ardennes in October, their commander agreed to disarm if they were transported to Lille to join their comrades.[15]

At a large internment camp inherited from Vichy at Bourg-Lastic, in the Puy-de Dôme, a group of Russians, including 500 ex-members of the FFI, were gathered for safekeeping in December 1944. Almost immediately, chaos erupted in the surrounding towns and countryside as foraging Russians stole, robbed, and assaulted French residents. A farmer was shot when he tried to defend his farm from a marauding band of thirty Russians. The gendarme captain in charge of the camp telephoned his headquarters in Clermont-Ferrand to alert his superiors that he had lost control and needed reinforcements. Twenty gendarmes were sent to the camp in response, but the Russians refused to let them enter. The population around Bourg-Lastic threatened to arm themselves and form a militia to defend their farms if the French government did not regain control. When a convoy of trucks carrying Russians passed through Clermont-Ferrand on its way to the camp, the Russians forced the trucks to stop and staged a protest against their internment. When some of the Russians turned out to be armed, French soldiers were called to quell the demonstration and disarm the Russians. Thefts and pillaging continued on farms around the camp during the following days. One farm was stripped of its kitchen utensils, bedding, and 200 kilos of potatoes. At another farm, one Russian was killed and another wounded when a farmer opened fire on the plunderers. True to their word, local farmers formed a self-defense unit to patrol the area and threatened to shoot any Russians they found outside the camp. Finally, fifty more gendarmes arrived, and order was restored at the compound; 300 Russians were removed to another camp near Clermont-Ferrand. That, however, was not the end of troubles provoked by Russian DPs. Police in Saint-Amand-Montron, not far away in the Cher, complained of a reign of thievery unleashed by the 700 Russians housed at a camp there. Days after the agitation in Clermont-Ferrand, forty Russians marched on the police station in Saint-Amand-Montron in an effort to liberate two of their comrades who had been jailed for stealing. Reinforcements were rushed to Saint-Amand-Montron to face off against the Russians, who eventually returned to their camp. The two thieves were whisked away to a larger, more secure jail in Bourges.[16]

Meanwhile, in Châlons-sur-Marne, the US Army was preparing to take over the massive Forgeot barracks that had been used to house Russian DPs. When army officers came to inspect the barracks, they were shocked by what they found: the Russians had taken almost everything from the buildings and wrecked whatever was left. The army had told Russian Commandant Kovalev that the Russians could take their blankets with them, but they also took the beds; the mattress covers, after dumping all the straw onto the floors; all the supplies and equipment from the infirmary and the kitchens; and the light fixtures, including the lightbulbs. The three pianos the city of Châlons had loaned to the DPs were likewise missing. The floors were covered with broken glass and human excrement. This was characterized by the inspecting US Army officer as "pure vandalism and sabotage." During an investigation of the incident by the French Ministry of PDR, the Russian delegate in charge of repatriating Soviet citizens from the west, General V. N. Dragun, claimed that all the items removed from the barracks belonged to the Soviet Union. This breathtaking pronouncement was believed by neither the French nor the Americans, but they were in no position to do anything about it without provoking an international incident, which both governments wanted to avoid. Even while the Russian DPs were behaving so badly, the US Army delivered to them musical instruments donated by the American YMCA and 2,500 Russian-language books gathered by the American Red Cross.[17]

Other camps containing Russians and controlled by Red Army officers continued to operate in France for much of 1945, and as long as they did, reports of serious incidents continued to pour in. A fifteen-year-old girl was brutally raped by a "Russian soldier" in Ecrouves, west of Nancy. Her mother entered the house as the Russian was strangling the girl. She smashed him on the head with an iron casserole, and he staggered out to the street, where he was held by neighbors until police arrived. Two Russians residing in a Soviet-administered camp at Casseneuil in the Lot-et-Garonne, southeast of Bordeaux, left the camp and murdered a Polish couple in March 1945. Two months later, other Russians from the camp stabbed and seriously wounded an Italian wearing an American uniform. French police arrested the Russians but then turned them over to the camp commandant to an unknown fate. Mayhem caused by Russian DPs did not completely cease until the last DP was repatriated to the USSR in September 1945—52,000 Soviets were repatriated in August alone. The camp in Meaux was finally emptied of Russians in September, to the great relief of the local population and the prefect, who claimed that "grave and frequent incidents" continued until they were gone.[18]

There also remained the problem of what to do with German civilians stranded in France by the war. There were an estimated 150,000 Germans—including women and children—in Alsace-Lorraine in December 1944. Strasbourg alone held nearly 50,000; Mulhouse another 50,000. The prefect of Moselle wanted all Germans abandoned in Alsace-Lorraine sequestered in secure facilities, and in December 1944 the roundup began: 4,500 Germans were herded into one camp in the Moselle, 4,000 into another; 6,000 were held near Strasbourg. The available camps were not sufficient to hold all those marked for "evacuation," but the French figured that as Germans were sent back to Germany, space would open up for more Germans designated for removal. In the meantime, officials scrambled to find places to put them all. One thousand could be housed in the citadel of Verdun if a means could be found to get them there. Minister Tixier thought perhaps they could be concentrated near Poitiers or sent to camps near the Spanish border, which Vichy and the Third Republic had used for detainees—mostly Spanish Republicans. But neither the American nor the French army was willing to provide trucks or railway space to move them. German civilians were not found only in the east: 800 were being held in Rennes, 800 at Montreuil Bellay near the Loire valley, and 700 at Fort Barraux near Grenoble, among others housed elsewhere. The government would have preferred to hand the responsibility for them to Entr'aide française or the Croix Rouge, but neither organization was capable of assuming responsibility for so many. Minister Tixier mused that perhaps the FFI could be profitably employed here. General de Gaulle wanted the settlers gathered together and kept someplace secure; he suggested the citadel of Metz. US Third Army had established camps near Malmédy, in the Meuse, and Thionville, in the Moselle, for German civilians who fell into

American hands in September 1944, and it wanted the French to take them over as soon as possible. General Patton preferred to move these detainees away from the German border and, ideally, into the interior of France. But as it turned out, his concern was not for security: he wanted the buildings used to hold the Germans to house US soldiers. Third Army declared that because the Germans had not been found guilty of any crimes, they should be released. The French army officer confronted with this demand rejected it as of no concern of the Americans; it was an exclusively French affair. The French were in charge and had the authority to settle all questions of the DPs' fate.[19]

Trying to come up with a common policy on the treatment of German nationals in France proved to be complicated. A number of different French authorities had an interest in the issue. Both the commissioner in Strasbourg and Raymond Haas-Picard—in charge of the Interior Ministry's relations with the Allies—wanted to fix one policy for France that the Americans—meaning General Patton—could agree with. Minister Tixier was alarmed to learn in January 1945 that the Americans still held an unknown number of German civilians mixed in with DPs of other nationalities in camps in Normandy. He wanted them sorted out, handed over to the French, and removed from Normandy as quickly as possible because he believed they posed a security threat. One policy was ultimately agreed on: all German nationals in France were the responsibility of the French, and the US Army would hand them over, except for those of special interest to the United States. The Americans then started to identify all German civilians in their custody and deliver them to the French. In May 1945 the Americans identified 800, including some women, in camps scattered around southern France; after screening to ensure that they were not war criminals, they were turned over to the French, who proposed to use them as agricultural laborers until they could be repatriated. Most often, camps and their inhabitants, such as the one in Vittel, Vosges, were simply turned over to the French to administer, with the hope that someone would be able to read the English-language records left behind by the Americans.[20]

Both the French government and the US Army agreed that questions and problems related to DPs were for the French to answer and solve. However, the US Army was generally cooperative in helping the French whenever and wherever it could. The US-led repatriation of French DPs and POWs from Germany revealed that close collaboration could work to the benefit of all concerned. The principal irritant was the massive US Army presence in France, which made finding housing for the French returnees more difficult. There was no easy solution to this problem, which was recognized by both French and American authorities. The same problem pertained to finding housing for foreign DPs in France: GIs took up space that could have been used for DPs awaiting repatriation. Relying on the American and British Red Cross to alleviate the material needs of DPs of all nationalities seemed like a good idea to the Allies and even to Red Cross officials, but they ran into prickly Gaullist ideas about sovereignty and control. The starchy government reaction to Red Cross largesse was typical of the new Gaullist regime, reflecting de Gaulle's personality and mirrored in his appointments. De Gaulle remained intensely sensitive to questions of legitimacy, and he reacted to every intrusion on French governmental prerogative as if it questioned the very legality of his regime. In fact, the legality of his regime was very much open to question, but its acceptance was not. The French population and political establishment—including the PCF—accepted de Gaulle's leadership without hesitation. The idea that the American Red Cross making decisions about who should distribute children's clothing endangered the authority of the French government was pure paranoia.

6

Axis Prisoners of War

The large numbers of Axis prisoners who fell into American hands in France and then Germany only soured French attitudes toward the American military and offered almost no prospect of improvement as the war ground on and then concluded. American treatment of captured Axis soldiers became an irritant in Franco-American relations early in the battle for France because the Americans followed the Geneva Convention rules of war that required them to adequately feed, clothe, and care for all captured enemy soldiers. The Americans also hewed to the rules about the kind of work POWs could be compelled to perform, and they eagerly exploited the labor possibilities of the Axis prisoners. In doing so, however, American officers appeared to be treating the enemies leniently, causing great resentment among the French population. After the war ended, the United States housed hundreds of thousands of POWs in France, even though many French had inadequate shelter. The US military also looked to France to help feed all these Axis prisoners, while French had little enough food for themselves. The French government also saw the POWs as an excellent source of labor—especially for dangerous work—and argued for months with US authorities about the number of POWs to be turned over to French responsibility and the conditions of their maintenance. The French and Americans found one area to agree on: all Frenchmen serving in Axis military uniforms and captured by the Americans should be turned over to the French government for disposition.

Liberated French civilians, who lived with minimal food and insufficient shelter, were furious when they saw German POWs enjoying both. They complained to French officials, who in turn protested to the Americans: if there were not enough food to feed everyone, why should POWs get the share that rightfully belonged to French civilians? SHAEF's plan for handling this problem was to use captured German food to feed prisoners. However, much if not most of that food had been grown and processed in France, and even if the German army had paid for it, the French saw it as rightfully theirs. If the French people had to scrounge for food, they saw little reason to release

German stores captured by the FFI to the Americans so that they could feed the Germans. The subprefect in Vendôme (close to Orléans) complained bitterly first to American officers and then to his own government that food supplies that had been carefully protected during the fighting in August were being used to feed POWs in October. The issue of feeding POWs according to Geneva Convention rules became aggravated in 1945 because the food situation in France was even worse than it had been during the German occupation. This came as a surprise, as everyone had expected the Americans to make food more plentiful. Most French were severely disappointed that the Americans did not send more food to France, especially because they believed the Americans had the ability to do so. Although the food shortage in France in the summer of 1945 was not as severe as both French and American authorities had feared, there was still a shortfall. Urban dwellers without direct access to farms subsisted on around 1,800 calories a day, which was not enough to maintain the weight of an active adult. The French wanted the Americans to supply all food eaten by POWs in France, regardless of custody. They also wanted the United States to provide food for refugees and displaced persons. When French authorities demanded that the United States supply clothes and blankets for POWs held by French forces in the French occupation zone in Germany, the Americans refused outright.[1]

Feeding the growing horde of German POWs moving into France as the German armies collapsed posed a real dilemma for General Eisenhower and his staff. SHAEF had planned on feeding POWs with food captured in Germany; however, such food was in short supply. Food seized from German supplies in Alsace had been used to feed the local civilian population as part of the compromise on "booty" worked out earlier, given the dearth of food in eastern France. But as SHAEF looked around for ways to feed the captives, it resorted to requisitioning food that had already been handed over to French authorities. The French reaction was predictable: outrage. FFI fighters on the Atlantic coast already resented the inadequate support they received from their American allies, but they especially resented that POWs working for the Americans got better food than they did. Similarly, civilian refugees driven from their homes in Morbihan, Brittany, by the fighting were incensed that POWs received better shelter and food than they did. Many refugees lived in appalling conditions, which got worse as winter approached. Local French newspapers took note and fanned the flames. The repatriated prisoners of the canton of Melle, Deux-Sèvres, formally protested the good treatment accorded German POWs by the US Army. They recognized that the United States was acting in accordance with the Geneva Convention, but the Germans did not honor the treaty, so why should the Americans? Making matters worse, the Americans were feeding German POWs luxury imports that were unavailable to the French and should have gone to French children: canned milk, chocolate, sugar, and oranges.[2]

French resentment of the Americans' lenient treatment of POWs increased with time. As early as July 1944, the Americans were using Axis prisoners to perform menial tasks in Normandy: clearing debris, disposing of garbage, cleaning streets. By February 1945, 73,000 Axis POWs labored for the US Army in the Cotentin Peninsula alone, supplementing 46,000 US service troops. Most of these POWs worked around Cherbourg, which was home to 30,000 French—some of whom were French soldiers and sailors. Thus, the POWs vastly outnumbered not only the Americans but also the French civilians living and working around Cherbourg. French civilians complained bitterly about having to hear German POWs singing their songs in the streets as they passed to and from work, reminding them of the "sad days" of the occupation. Under the rules of the Geneva Convention, POWs did not work for free, but they did work for cheap. Because the US Army paid them, POWs had money to spend, which they did in French stores. Attitudes toward the Americans in Cherbourg were already deteriorating in January 1945 when US Army personnel organized a free distribution of clothing for French in need; the recipients were aghast to discover that the worn-out clothes came directly from German POWs who had just received new uniforms from the Americans. Some of the shirts and jackets still bore the white "PW" painted on the backs. German POWs hired to work on the docks in Marseille were greatly resented by the French who also worked there. French employees at the train station in Marseille insisted that if the German POWs had to work there, at least they should eat separately from the French. American officers in charge agreed to this accommodation. Making the Germans' presence even more irritating was that the Americans were often very friendly toward their prisoners—friendlier than they were toward the French. This may have been because the Germans were friendly to their captors—friendlier than the French were, especially as the Americans' presence began to grate on their French hosts. Americans often found German soldiers highly compatible and easy to get along with. Indeed, many French noted that the cultural similarities between Germans and Americans made them more like each other than like the French. Americans were ordered to stop giving POWs candy, cigarettes, and other supplies. "No fraternization with German POWs" was added to the list of do's and don'ts for US Navy personnel visiting Marseille. Nevertheless, in April 1945 a poll revealed that 80 percent of French felt that the Americans were too lenient with German POWs.[3]

French bitterness increased with the repatriation of French POWs from

Germany in the spring of 1945. Since 1940, the Germans had used the 1.5 million French POWs as bargaining chips to pry concessions and cooperation from the French. The captured French soldiers were subjected to brutal and abusive treatment by their Nazi guardians. While the same held true for American and British POWs in German custody—and this affected the views of SHAEF and especially George Marshall on the treatment of German POWs—the French people had lived with this sword of Damocles hanging over their heads for five years. The ex-prisoners of Deux-Sèvres revealed that they had survived in the stalags only because of packages sent to them by their families and friends, while the Germans helped themselves to the produce of France. French families sent parcels to their husbands, fathers, and sons through the Red Cross, often at a steep price to their own welfare because no one had enough to eat, and food for POWs meant less food for children. This was a matter of extreme anguish for all French families with loved ones imprisoned in Germany; the POWs who pleaded for food were almost entirely ignorant of the shortages and privations back home in France. Thus, the ill treatment of French POWs—many of whom returned in 1945 in poor health and psychologically damaged—increased French bitterness over the seemingly good treatment of German POWs.[4]

In spring 1945, as SHAEF looked for more locations to open POW camps, French public opinion toward the American forces was turning cooler. The mayor of Tholonet, Bouches-du-Rhône, complained that the POW camp in his commune (as well as the army hospital) used up all the town's water. During the dry summer of 1945, farmers had no water for their crops and animals. Furthermore, the sewage from the camp was befouling the local river. The people of Mézières, Ardennes, were dismayed to learn that a "temporary" billeting of US troops had evolved into something more permanent; then the US Army requisitioned more buildings and land for a POW camp, which demanded even larger amounts of local fuelwood. Requisitioning more land and facilities for the benefit of well-fed and well-looked-after German POWs also angered the residents of the department of Aisne. The people around Cherbourg had had enough of POW camps by January 1945, as the camps grew bigger and consumed more land. Norman farmers were dismayed to learn that their farms were being taken over to house more German POWs, and they wanted to know why the best farmland was being used for POW camps when less desirable land remained available. Few French could see any benefit from having a POW camp nearby.[5]

The demand that German POWs conduct land mine–clearing operations in France became an oft-repeated motif among both French officials and the populace. Land mines posed a grave problem in the liberated zone, making it impossible to harvest crops in some areas and endangering people who returned to their damaged towns containing hidden mines. The deadly battle zone of the Meurthe-et-Moselle provides abundant evidence of the mortal danger posed by hidden mines. The Forest Service placed the vast woods next to Nancy off-limits because of the large number of mines planted on its paths. It had to do the same in the forest near Lunéville because of the number of injuries and deaths reported there and the lack of people trained to remove the mines. A fifty-five-year-old forest worker west of Metz had his foot blown off by a hidden mine while he was clearing trees toppled by retreating Germans to block the roads, but he had the good fortune to encounter some American soldiers in a jeep who drove him to a military hospital in Verdun. A farmer looking for potatoes in a field in Rechicourt, Meurthe-et-Moselle, found mines instead; he survived the experience, but his eighteen-year-old neighbor did not. The boy and his brother were searching for a cow when the teenager stepped on a mine, killing him instantly. A forty-nine-year-old miner was killed and a twenty-six-year-old accountant was injured when the miner stepped on a mine near Briey while they were foraging for food. A forty-nine-year-old glass worker in Baccarat, the father of five children, was killed in his own yard by an undiscovered mine. The subprefect in Lunéville complained that people could not resume their lives so long as land mines continued to make the communes so dangerous. People rooting in the fields for beets and potatoes were in constant danger of being blown up. He noted that in two months, sixteen people had been killed by mines and fourteen injured in his jurisdiction alone. Two months later, that toll had risen to fifty dead and forty-eight injured. Around Blâmont—east of Lunéville—many cow carcasses in an advanced state of decomposition, as well as German soldiers' bodies, still lay out in the open as late as February 1945 because hidden mines made it too dangerous to bury them. The subprefect complained that these rotting animal carcasses and dead soldiers posed a health hazard. In April 1945 the bodies of twenty FFI remained unburied in Neufmaison because the region was still plagued by hidden land mines. The village of Lientry was totally abandoned because it was too infested with mines to live in. Farmers all around Lunéville feared to work their fields because of mines, so the ground was not prepared for planting in the spring of 1945.[6]

The number of mines and unexploded ordnance to be discovered and removed was staggering, and this task required many months to accomplish. A 136-acre park on the outskirts of Nancy, the Parc de Brabois, was not cleared of mines and unexploded ordnance until mid-September 1945. The French military team that cleared it reported that it had unearthed 13 anti-tank mines, 299 antipersonnel mines, 112 artillery shells, 98 mortars, 43 grenades, and 1 aviation bomb. During all of 1945, the same team, led by retired artillery officer Henri Gille, cleared hazards from 110 villages around Nancy and disarmed 34,920 mines, 21,800 shells, 15,520 grenades, and 42 aviation bombs. They also cleared 170 antitank mines along one segment of National Route 4, which connected Paris to Strasbourg. Although Gille—a "66 percent invalid" of the First World War—declared himself proud to perform this service for his country, he no doubt would have preferred, as did most of his compatriots, that German POWs do the work.[7]

In summer 1944 the Allies had insufficient trained personnel to devote to the task of finding and digging out land mines. Initially, the French government sought Allied assistance from London to train their own people to perform this dangerous task. However, such training took about a month and would not provide sufficient personnel quickly enough to meet the urgent need. In some cases, in view of the severe danger posed to civilians, untrained FFI undertook this work voluntarily. Regardless of the Gaullist regime's desire to find useful ways of putting the FFI to work, the provisional government discouraged them from doing this. Eventually, the French government took to requisitioning men to demine the farm fields to get them back into production. The conscripted men wanted assurances that if they were injured, the government would award them pensions. The subprefect in Lunéville wanted to know why German POWs were not tasked with finding and eliminating the mines. Even if this transgressed the Geneva Convention, did not the Germans' failure to follow it release the French from the obligation to do so? Returned French POWs protested that the Germans had used them after June 1940 to do this dangerous work and had forced political prisoners to dig out unexploded bombs. They therefore demanded that German POWs be employed for these same hazardous jobs in France, and so did the Liberation Committee of Meurthe-et-Moselle. On a single day, 12 April 1945, six demining workers were killed in Pont-à-Mousson, bringing the total killed performing this dangerous job to twelve in just one canton. Two of those workers had seventeen children between them, provoking outrage among the local population, who clamored even louder for German POWs to undertake this work.[8]

The disaster at Pont-à-Mousson did the trick: German POWs were brought in to supplement the French workers demining the Meurthe-et-Moselle, and they quickly made up half the contingent searching for mines. Despite the addition of POWs, French workers continued to perform this treacherous work, and in May and June 1945 both French civilians and German POWs were killed and maimed by mines. By late June, the canton of Lunéville counted fifty-seven dead and fifty-eight injured by mines. On a single day in September 1945, thirteen German POWs were injured and one was killed when an undetected mine exploded.[9]

Meanwhile, the French were just as irritated by the Americans' lax treatment of Italian POWs as they were about the Germans. The French population of Algeria was outraged by the liberal treatment of the 112,000 Italian POWs held there by the British and Americans. French officials protested that the "arrogant" and "insolent and sometimes violent" Italians were allowed almost complete liberty and were treated more like allies than enemies, "that is to say, much better than the civil population." The rations provided by the Allies were so generous, the French complained, that the Italians diverted the surplus to the black market. According to the authorities in Algeria, the populace complained that the Italians openly insulted France and the French, and they angered the Arabs with their slights and rudeness; the Italians harassed women and committed crimes, including the murder of a French civilian and an Arab soldier. French army officers protested that Italian POWs in Algeria were dressed as MPs and used to direct traffic. A grave incident occurred near Rouen in August 1945 when an Italian POW in an American uniform stabbed and killed an Arab in a French army uniform. North Africans serving in the French army sought revenge and started hunting Italians. They found at least three, who were wounded in knife attacks by the North African soldiers.[10]

The south of France was especially crowded with Italian POWs put to work by the Allies because of the shortage of French workers to undertake all the tasks required by the war. As early as 26 September 1944 the Americans were convinced that French workers were insufficient in both number and vigor. Dissatisfaction at the pace of unloading ships in Marseille led the United States to bring in 28,700 Italian POWs to work on the docks, and the Americans came to rely on the labor of these Italian prisoners. French officials were appalled, but they could only negotiate terms to minimize the affront to French workers. When the French dockworkers' union protested layoffs in the fall of 1945 while POWs were kept on as stevedores, this failed to move the American officers in charge. When the French insisted that the POWs not be employed as truck drivers, the Americans asked whether the French could produce 1,000 drivers. The French had to concede that they could not, so the Americans agreed to use the Italian drivers only in escorted and guarded truck convoys. Residents of La Ciotat were already angry over liberties granted to Italian POWs by their American overseers, but when an Italian POW stabbed a French soldier, local French officials predicted trouble if the Italians were not reined in. The commissioner of the Republic in Dijon, Jean Marin, reported to Minister Tixier that the townspeople were very upset that the Americans allowed Italian POWs to wander around freely, identified only by an armband. Even as the Allies—including France—accepted Italy as a cobelligerent (although there was no alliance between the Italian monarchy and the Allies, Italian troops fought alongside Allied troops against the Germans in Italy), the French people still harbored great resentment against the Italians, who had behaved so treacherously in 1940. Yet the Americans treated Italian POWs like allies and even employed them as MPs. In Marseille, Italian POWs served as guards at depots and truck parking lots, and in Nice and Martigues, they actually patrolled the streets. The use of Italians as MPs in southern France was at the top of a list of complaints by French mayors when they met with American commanders in July 1945. The French were extremely upset that the Italians, who had so recently strutted about town as conquerors, now returned as the forces of order imposed by the Americans. The southern littoral of France contained a large native population of Italian heritage, as well as hundreds of thousands of Italian immigrants who, for the most part, got along well with the French with longer roots, so prejudice against ethnic Italians probably played little part in the public disquiet over the presence of Italians in uniform. Paradoxically, the French, too, relied on the labor of Italian POWs, mostly as farmworkers, until as late as November 1945.[11]

The problems created by putting German POWs to work only got worse with the end of the war and the flood of German POWs into camps in France. The French maintained that they needed POWs for the harvest in 1945. In an unexpected turnaround, the Americans denied the request in Aisne, arguing that the French could not adequately guard them. Thus, the Americans kept thousands of POWs working on roads in Oise instead of converting them into farmworkers. In August 1945 Eisenhower agreed to transfer to French custody 1.3 million German POWs so that they could repair war damage; 50,000 would be shipped from Norway right away. Various POW camps in France run by the American military would also be handed over to French control. In addition, the Americans proposed that their operation using German POWs to assemble boxcars in Marseille would be turned over to the French. When the Americans transferred 350,000 POWs in September, they informed the French that they were now responsible for supplying the POWs with food and clothes. That same month, the International Red Cross Committee (IRCC) issued a damning report claiming that 200,000 ill-fed and ill-clad German POWs suffered from malnutrition and poor health in French POW camps because of inadequate care by French authorities. In view of the report, Eisenhower declined to turn over any more POWs and informed the French that if they could not properly care for the POWs, they should return them to American custody. French officials were livid. They claimed the Red Cross report had been written by a German-speaking Swiss whose sympathy lay with Germany. Furthermore, most of the sick and malnourished POWs had been in that condition when the French received them from the Americans. If they were poorly clad, it was because the Americans had handed them over without any replacement clothes. Because the French declined to pay for food and clothes for the POWs, the United States agreed to give food and clothes to the IRCC, which in turn would distribute these items to the POWs in French camps.[12]

Eisenhower agreed to take back any POWs the French claimed were in ill health or unable to work. Meeting with the IRCC and Americans, the French agreed to a joint inspection of all POWs, and those who could not be rehabilitated in French camps would be returned to American custody. This inspection identified 100,000 POWs who should be returned to the Americans. In response to this finding, POW camps slated to be turned over to the French remained under US jurisdiction, even while their German inmates continued to repair war damage in France, as was the case in Sens and Joigny. The French were slow to turn over the POWs: by mid-November, only 17,000 had been returned; by mid-December, the tally reached 57,000, and the French had another 25,000 ready to leave their camps; they still held 90,000 prisoners incapable of effective work. Facing a labor shortage caused by the reverse flow of POWs, the French demanded 200,000 more POWs by March 1946 and another 500,000 afterward. When Eisenhower testily replied that the French should not request more POWs if they could not feed and clothe the ones they already had, French authorities responded that the Americans should turn over only healthy Germans capable of work, and they wanted 100,000 a month transferred. The POW fracas soured relations and made the situation worse. When the French demanded clothes, shoes, and blankets for the POWs turned over to them, the Americans told the French that they could buy the supplies if they wanted them. None of the supplies for POWs was covered by Lend-Lease, which ended on 1 September 1945 in any event. The French reaction was a proposal to solicit clothes and supplies from the German population of the French-occupied zone in Germany. All this wrangling was reported in French newspapers and further inflamed French public opinion, which was turning against the Americans as elections approached. In view of the crisis in French coal production, Eisenhower agreed to make a special exception and hand over another 20,000 POWs to work in French coal mines. The French appreciated the assistance but asked that no SS be among them, as they feared sabotage. To compensate for the lack of German POWs, the French continued to use 37,000 Polish DPs still languishing in camps in France. When Polish DPs failed to provide enough workers to dig French coal, the French asked to recruit miners from DP camps in the American zone in Germany.[13]

As fewer American soldiers remained in France to perform necessary functions, the United States resorted to using DPs to serve as guards at POW camps. In September the United States hired 500 Dutch DPs to guard 18,400 German POWs performing various jobs in the Greater Paris region. Polish DPs brought in from Germany—laborers who had been forcibly conscripted by the Germans during the war—proved to be unreliable guards. Those guarding POWs in Saint-Julien, Aube, and Mourmelon and Brimont in the Marne dove into the black markets in Troyes and Reims, along with Polish immigrants living there, and worked with the Germans to establish a lively underground trade. French police claimed that Polish guards at Saint-Julien rented American uniforms to the POWs so they could leave the camps and stroll about freely in the evening. Some Poles acted as couriers for the Germans, taking messages back to Germany and returning with parcels and money. Around Reims, the center of five POW camps, Polish guards were accused of unleashing a crime wave that included burglary, robbery, and murder. The French blamed German escapes on Polish DPs being used as guards, and they claimed that networks of Germans, Yugoslavs, and Poles collaborated to help the escapees because the Americans were too few and too lax to do anything about it. When appeals to the US Army failed to effect change, the Ministry of the Interior asked the US ambassador to intervene, without result. The local Association of Deportees and Ex-prisoners was incensed that a war criminal—"a torturer of Dachau"—was among those allowed to escape.[14]

In fall 1945 German POWs remained on the job in various places in France that were still under US authority. Many still labored on the docks, even as the amount of work required by the US military diminished. As the workload got lighter, US authorities laid off French workers and kept on the less expensive POWs, producing the predictable howls from French unions, local authorities, and newspapers. As the number of GIs in France decreased, the US Army employed more German POWs as truck drivers, even though this aggravated the French. Civil Affairs offices closed all over France on Bastille Day 1945, leaving local French officials with no US Army liaisons to complain to, so they protested to their own government. French chief of staff General Alphonse Juin took the matter up with the US Mission in Paris that replaced SHAEF, demanding that Germans be removed from behind the wheels. The prefect of Marne had convinced the US Army to remove German POWs from the streets of Reims, only to have them careening around departmental roads in big trucks. The prefect complained that German drivers had been involved in several hit-and-run accidents, greatly irritating the locals. After the Association of Ex-POWs and Deportees of the Marne registered an energetic protest with the prefect, he feared they would take matters into their own hands and violence could ensue. Officials in Troyes were convinced that German truck drivers were transporting prisoners who had escaped from the large American-run POW camp in Mailly, which held 40,000 men of many nationalities, including SS troopers. The worst affront for the French was the employment of German guards in November 1945 at a US Army hospital in Nancy; it employed fifty-two French citizens who had to work under the watchful eyes of the Germans. This proved intolerable to the French. The Americans promised to replace the Germans with American MPs as soon as possible and with French police soon afterward—as MPs were leaving France in droves at the time.[15]

In April 1946 the Americans started transferring the last of the POW camps in France to French authority, but the process dragged out into the summer, and then the French were saddled with Polish guards. At least this meant the French were free to employ German POWs as they saw fit, so the POWs were put to work cleaning buildings and chopping firewood in Troyes. As per the Geneva Convention, the POWs were paid for their work; the French even gave them a raise from 112 to 200 francs per day at the beginning of 1947 and then to 250 francs at the beginning of 1948. POWs were still laboring for the office of the prefect in Troyes as late as September 1948, long after they had ceased to be an irritant in Franco-American affairs.[16]

The French government was especially eager to retrieve its own citizens from among the POWs captured by the Allies. French citizens caught in German uniform fell into three categories: citizens of annexed eastern provinces drafted into the Wehrmacht, those drafted into the SS, and those who had voluntarily joined the SS. The French government wanted all French citizens held by the Americans turned over to French custody; however, it was especially interested in members of the SS. The Americans agreed to the transfer, but it turned out to be more complicated than imagined. The US policy toward Frenchmen caught in German uniforms was to interview them and determine whether they were willing to join the French army or labor service. If so, they were turned over to the French army; if not, they were held as POWs to be turned over to the French at the end of hostilities. This offended Charles de Gaulle, who demanded in October 1944 that all French citizens held by the Allies be turned over to French authorities regardless of their wishes. The French policy was to interview all those who had left the

German army, whether by desertion or by capture, to determine "their attitude on national point of view." Those who were physically capable of service were enrolled in the French army; those "of a certain age" were enrolled in the reserves; ex-officers of the French army were recommissioned at their old rank. Any who had advanced in rank above sergeant or accepted German medals would be given a three-month probationary period to determine their fate. Those who refused to join would be sent to labor service; those who refused to serve France in any capacity would be sent to labor in North Africa—transport permitting—and stripped of their citizenship. If married, their families would be shipped to North Africa as well, and they would all be forever barred from entering France or any of its possessions. If possible, they would be exiled to Germany. Minister Tixier demurred on sending them to Germany; if there were many of them, they might agitate for the return of Alsace and Lorraine to Germany![17]

By January 1945, the Americans had handed over to French authorities 1,200 Alsatians or Lorrainers captured as POWs who were slated to be incorporated into the French army as soon as the French could find uniforms for them. Until then, the men continued to wear their German uniforms, causing great discomfort whenever they ventured out among the French population. When the Americans made a greater effort to find French citizens among Axis POWs, they discovered another 1,500 and segregated them in camps at Chalon-sur-Saône and Marseille. After vetting, they were released to French custody, except for those recuperating in American-run hospitals. All this gnashing of teeth over turncoat French was much ado about nothing: interviews of POWs in US camps were conducted by French officers who had complete control over the interrogations, and not one POW from Alsace-Lorraine declined to be released to French authority. French citizens who had volunteered to fight in the SS were a different matter, and some of them did indeed decline to be released to the French. Both the British and the Americans declared the same policy of keeping custody of POWs who did not want to be released, but the numbers in both cases were small: the British held fifty, and the Americans held another fifty. French authorities became alarmed when they heard rumors that the Americans intended to send these prisoners to "work brigades" in the United States. The French proposed to deal with them as they had dealt with members of the Vichy Milice: put them before a judge and charge them with treason. Despite stories to the contrary, SHAEF proclaimed that no French held as POWs by the United States would "escape French justice."[18]

The US Army found itself as the custodian of thousands of French civilians swept up in the final chaos of the Nazi collapse in Germany and northern

Italy. US Army counterintelligence assumed that many of them were actually French volunteers in the SS who had shed their uniforms for safer civilian garb. An unknown number of French volunteers in the SS Charlemagne Division deserted in May 1945, shed their uniforms, and disappeared into the masses of DPs wandering Germany. In the spring of 1945, around 10,000 Milice and their families who had fled France in late 1944 remained stranded in Germany, and few wanted to be caught and remanded to French justice. Some French DPs claimed to be other nationalities, and some foreigners pretended to be French. Sorting out the French from everybody else and the real civilians from deserters and SS seeking to escape involved a good deal of detective work. All these people were sent to US-administered camps in the south of France until they could be properly identified and their fates determined. The Americans compiled lists of French citizens held in the camps, which mixed ex-SS troopers and Milice who had fled France with "civilians" picked up by the Americans in Italy or Germany. The Americans agreed to allow the French to determine who these people really were and what should become of them, with the hope that the French would assume responsibility for all civilians, regardless of nationality. In March 1945, well before the Nazi collapse, the US Army held forty French in a detention center in Bouches-du-Rhône known as Camp 404, reserved for suspect foreign civilians. The last remnants of the French SS who were swept up in northern Italy landed there, along with hundreds of members of the Milice who had tried unsuccessfully to get away in Italy. The US Army picked up scores of French in northern Italy trying to make it to Switzerland; many others were caught near Bolzano, fleeing Austria and hoping to find refuge in Italy. As the Americans rounded these people up, they discovered members of various French pro-Nazi organizations, French fascist groups, the Parti populaire française (PPF, a pro-Nazi political party), the Milice, the notorious French Gestapo, and the Georges Max Gallon Group, which had had infiltrated resistance circles and denounced numerous leaders. The biggest fish was probably Jean Luchaire, who had been in charge of pro-Nazi propaganda in the Occupied Zone and tried to pass himself off as Italian. They were all transferred to Camp 404 before being handed over to the French. The vast majority of French collaborators, however, did not end up in American hands; they were caught by the French themselves, within France, in the wake of the liberation. Orders went out to arrest all Milice and anyone who adhered to the tenets of any of the collaborationist political groups (PPF being high on the list); American cooperation was explicitly requested. By the end of the war, Camp 404 held hundreds of men and women, all of whom had to be sorted out; anyone who turned out to be French, whether civilian or military, was turned over to French authorities. Any foreigner determined not to be "suspect" was delivered to the French and placed in a DP camp. The Americans decided, for example, that all 119 people determined to be Hungarian were harmless workers conscripted by the Germans and should be placed in DP camps under French control.[19]

In the end, not many French POWs were handed over to the French because the Americans did not capture many. Most French who served in the German military fought on the eastern front, and their whereabouts remained unknown. Families of missing Frenchmen besieged prefects with queries about their fate. Many were convinced these men were still alive and being held captive, but where were they? The prefect of Moselle was skeptical and demanded that the French military send a delegation to Germany to search for Alsatians and Lorrainers in US POW camps. French officers were already scouring American camps, and such a search would have yielded no additional information. For their part, the Soviets refused to allow any French officers access to any POW camps. In fact, the American handling of the French POW issue was exemplary compared with that of the Soviets. Stalin made a big show in August 1944 of releasing 1,500 French who had been taken prisoner on the eastern front and shipping them to Algiers, where they were incorporated into the reviving French army. However, that was a unique event. De Gaulle saw no more French POWs held by the Soviets until 1945, when Stalin started to release them slowly. Refused access to their nationals in Soviet custody, the French demanded a census of detainees, which the Soviets declined to perform. Instead, the Soviets proposed that the French send a list of people they were looking for, and the Soviets would tell them if they were in Soviet custody. Foreign Minister Georges Bidault obligingly asked prefects in the eastern departments to provide him with such lists. Various branches of the French government were awash in letters from families to be forwarded to their presumably still-alive men, wherever they might be. The Soviets refused to receive the letters. The prefect of Haute-Marne reported that 22,978 men from his department had been enrolled in the Wehrmacht, and by mid-August, only 2,859 had returned (although he believed the actual number of returnees was greater). Where were the other 20,000? By September 1945, Alsatians and Lorrainers started trickling back home and reported that others were still alive and being held by the Soviets. In October 180,000 families in Alsace and Lorraine waited for news about their missing men. No doubt, most of these men were dead and buried nameless in mass graves in the east. As late as October, ten turned up in the custody of the French police in Marseille. In September 1945 the Americans were scouring lists to find any French citizens still in US custody, regardless of how they got there. As the

Americans left France, they were no longer involved in the quest to find the missing Frenchmen.[20]

It is difficult to imagine how introducing Axis POWs into France could have improved Franco-American relations. The POWs surely presented more problems than benefits to both countries, even if they also offered the potential for exploitation. In fact, the POWs were exploited by both the French and the Americans, largely for different purposes. Both used them to clear rubble and fix roads, but French attitudes toward German soldiers were understandably more bitter than those of the Americans. The Germans were responsible for killing and maiming hundreds of thousands of GIs, but the American military understood that this is what soldiers do. Even the French harbored little ill will against the common German soldiers who had, after all, behaved "correctly" for most of their four-year sojourn in France. Nevertheless, the German military was responsible for four years of French humiliation, which most French bore heavily. Thus, it is not surprising that the French thought German POWs should perform the dangerous demining operations, which, had to be undertaken by someone. Nor is it surprising that, once the French believed they had finally seen the back of the German army, they would object to German POWs merrily marching through French towns or driving big US trucks on French roads. That Germans were back in France, eating French food and enjoying French firewood, was bad enough, but that American GIs actually liked the Germans stuck in the craws of most French. They wanted nothing to do with the Germans by 1945, and they were not very happy about having to put up with Americans either. There was really no way for technical experts or American civil affairs officers to smooth over irritations caused by the presence of Axis POWs in France. Any difficulties born of the situation had to be solved at the top—that is, by Generals Eisenhower and Marshall, who had little time or patience to devote to the problem. Thus, these issues—aside from those pertaining to French nationals—remained largely unresolved and irritating until the US Army left France in 1946.

7

Black Markets and War Booty

Disruptions of French markets caused by the war inevitably led to scarcities, which, for enterprising people like the French and the Americans, offered opportunities for profit. The Germans probably profited the most from illicit trading in France, but huge numbers of French were drawn to the black market as a way to acquire the necessities of life, which were in short supply. Scarcities under the German occupation did not disappear upon liberation; indeed, some items became harder to find. There was actually less food available because the means to move it to markets were first disrupted and then co-opted by the US military. Thus, when the Allies arrived in France, well-established black markets adapted to new supplies and new opportunities. Both the provisional government of General de Gaulle and the US military wanted to suppress illegal markets in France—each for its own reasons—and thus cooperated in a nearly impossible venture that proved to be distasteful for most of those involved. Determining who was entitled to war booty, in contrast, pitted the French government squarely against the Americans, who laid claim to anything captured from the Germans that the French could not prove was legally theirs. This policy eroded relations between the two powers, and disputes were never resolved to either party's satisfaction. Mutual interests bred cooperation, as clashing interests provoked discord.

Cooperation: Black Markets

Most of the black marketeering in France during the war was just the normal bartering carried on at a local level by farmers and nearby villagers. Such unofficial markets had always existed in France, although their importance had greatly diminished by the twentieth century. During the German occupation, their importance rebounded, and these unofficial markets grew larger and involved vastly more people. Often this was the only source for townspeople to obtain eggs, cheese, milk, and butter. The majority of sales were made directly by the producer to the consumer, with little participation by middlemen. However, some retail merchants made unrecorded purchases from farmers they trusted and then sold these items to regular customers they also trusted. People bartered goods and services in private exchanges as well: Camembert cheese in return for cigarettes, or a sausage for a haircut. Vichy actively discouraged French police from interfering in this clandestine commerce. Some observers have commented on the loosening of morals and the ethical degradation that were encouraged by dealing on the black market. However, trust and integrity were at the center of these exchanges, even more so than under normal circumstances, and the ethical adjustments demanded by the situation did not erode the personal morality of those involved. Still, some exhausted refugees from Normandy in 1944 reported being charged exorbitant prices for food by farmers they encountered along their miserable route; one claimed a farmer charged him 1 franc for a glass of water. Farmers and villagers considered trading scarce goods as normal, so there was no real shame attached to the black market in the countryside. In larger towns, such traders were viewed as shady small-time criminals, and shopkeepers became widely unpopular as they offered less and less for sale and enforced strict limits on rationed goods. Black markets could not exist without the cooperation or at least a blind eye from the many officials who were in a position to stop them. Railroad workers, police, customs officials, market administrators, rationing officers, and the like all had to cooperate to some degree for the markets to function effectively.[1]

French police surveyed train stations early in the occupation, looking for suspicious people who might be transporting illicit goods. They caught mostly small-time smugglers who were briefly detained, had their goods confiscated, and had to pay small fines; however, such arrests decreased after 1942, as the police became more accommodating. Xavier de Guerpel was conscripted to serve as a railroad guard in his home region in Calvados in 1942, and he described heart-wrenching, "nightmare" scenes of young Parisians who had been sent with the precious little money their families had to scrounge for food in the Norman countryside. He got used to seeing crowds of Parisians heading home, carrying bags of foodstuffs at the train station in Vire. In September the station was routinely packed with people waiting for the one daily train to Paris, clutching their sacks of butter, eggs, fowl, lard, cheese, and vegetables. De Guerpel and the other "guards" made no effort to stop these rationed goods from leaving Calvados; they felt pity for the people crammed onto the blacked-out quays. When the train finally arrived—late again—no one got off, and there was little room to get aboard, resulting in a desperate scramble to get inside with their packages. Teenagers often wore backpacks stuffed with their precious provisions, making it easier to claw their way onto the train cars. The stations attracted shady characters, swindlers, and crooks who preyed on the innocent teenagers. More than once, de Guerpel witnessed a naïve girl, burdened with full bags, "assisted" by someone who offered to pass the bags to her once she got on board, only to have the "helper" disappear into the crowd with her provisions. He saw a fourteen-year-old girl on the platform sobbing because she had been unable to gain a foothold on the train and now had to wait twenty-four hours for the next one, and he knew the anguish her family would feel when she failed to show up with their food. Much of the illicit movement of goods relied on SNCF workers turning a blind eye or actively participating in the distribution of black-market goods. The disruption of transportation caused by the Allied invasion effectively upset the black markets and ended Normandy's role as a food source for hungry Parisians. Trains from Normandy stopped after 6 June 1944, and many Parisians went hungry.[2]

Some goods were more commonly diverted to the black market than others. Allied intelligence estimated that under the German occupation, about half of all milk, meat, fats, and oils ended up on the black market, but only about 10 percent of bread flour and wine and about one-sixth of sugar. Black-market butter sold for five to nine times the official price, whereas potato and milk prices were inflated to only two to three times the official price. Under-the-counter cigarettes could bring fifteen times the official price. Coffee was almost unobtainable, but when available, it sold officially for 60 francs ($1.20) per kilo; black-market coffee could command 2,500 francs ($50) per kilo. Regions of France where there were many farms and not so many town dwellers usually had an abundance of food, but densely populated regions with fewer farms, like Lorraine, relied heavily on black markets for fresh food. Otherwise, fresh produce was almost unobtainable. Bread became scarcer as the occupation continued, and one kilogram of bread on the black market eventually commanded more than five times its official price of 5 francs (10 cents).[3]

The Germans made no effort to shut down this illicit trade. In fact, they encouraged and participated in black markets as a means to reap more benefits from their occupation, forcing many French to rely on these underground sources for basic supplies. The Todt Organization relied heavily on black markets to procure food and fuel for its workers, often diverting construction materials to helpful farmers as payment. The Gestapo took advantage of black marketeers and confiscated goods after making only a down payment, but this practice did not encourage repeat business. The Wehrmacht, in contrast, was more interested in establishing reliable and steady sources of goods. Wehrmacht procurement officers bought goods wherever they could be found at whatever price could be negotiated. The German army frequently requisitioned goods at official prices and then resold them on the black market at a great profit. It actually ran the black market in coal in northern France, charging four to five times the official price. Occupation troops would seize illicit goods from people on the streets of Nancy if they could not prove they had acquired the items legally. Procurement on the black market was forbidden in 1943 by order of Hermann Goering, but enterprising Germans continued to patronize it anyway. When a meat merchant in Les Halles was caught by French authorities in March 1943 with almost two-thirds of a ton of meat without the proper paperwork, he claimed he had bought it at the behest of the SS, which intervened on the merchant's behalf.[4]

French police began to crack down on illicit trading in late 1943, with a measure of popular approval so long as they left small traders and minor offenders alone. The public generally applauded when big-time gangsters were apprehended. Four were tried and sentenced to death by Vichy judges in Paris after the Allied invasion. Attempts to quash the black market in food at its source—farms—was accepted as futile, as more or less all farmers participated in it, and townspeople depended on it for food. Once de Gaulle's provisional government was operational, it cracked down on the black markets, disrupting people's means of acquiring the necessities of life or, in some cases, the luxuries that made life more pleasant. With transportation networks severely disrupted and the fall harvest hampered by a lack of horses, trucks, and fuel to run machinery, the people in northern France relied on the black market more than ever to acquire life's necessities.[5]

The black market for luxury goods was a different matter. There, middlemen, often drawn from the interwar gangster underworld, predominated. The occupation also opened up avenues of opportunity for forgers and low-level officials in a position to procure permits and licenses. In this respect, the occupation bred corruption that could masquerade as patriotism. Of course, German officials also sold these documents, such as permits to operate a motor vehicle, to anyone with the right amount of cash. The liberation put an end to much of this corruption, or at least to the patriotic masquerade.[6]

The Allied experience with black markets in Italy heavily influenced Allied policies in France. Italian black markets grew more important in liberated zones than they had been under the fascist regime. Italian authorities actually looked to the Allies to stomp out the black markets, which to some extent they tried to do, with almost no success. Inflation of the lira, high exchange rates, unrealistic official prices, and scarce goods all worked together to pump up black markets in Italy, which largely replaced official markets in many liberated regions. American military officials grew increasingly pessimistic about the ability to shut down this illicit trade and questioned the wisdom of doing so. Their Italian experience had convinced civil affairs officers that the United States should dump the whole problem into the lap of the French. Only members of the Psychological Warfare Division urged the US Army to help clamp down on illicit markets. One civil affairs supply officer argued that shutting down black markets in France would be an impossible task and would breed resentment among the French. He claimed that black markets were an inevitable consequence of wage and price controls and that illicit trade should be minimized, not eliminated.[7]

The US Army had a profound interest in keeping GIs from participating in the black market, both to preserve good relations with French authorities trying to stamp it out and to stop the diversion of military supplies, such as gasoline and cigarettes, to French civilians. An artificially high exchange rate of 50 francs to the dollar encouraged trafficking in currency and goods among Allied troops in France. Troops complained that prices in France were too high, leading many to buy goods under the counter and to change currency on the black market. The US Army was concerned about its own supplies, not about enforcing French rationing laws; the existence of illicit markets for stolen goods encouraged felonious GIs to steal US Army property and sell it for personal gain. One Quartermaster (QM) Corps officer argued that normal security measures would prevent supplies from being pilfered, and the army had no need to intervene in the French black market. GIs were forbidden to purchase rationed items in France in any event, which meant that if they wanted to buy food, they had to do it illicitly. Legal alcohol was generally available to GIs, except when outlets were closed to them, usually following some kind of trouble. GIs resold cigarettes purchased at canteens at a great profit. Even soldiers who did not smoke, such as WAC Frances DeBra, bought cartons of cigarettes at the PX to use for barter. DeBra was too timid to flirt with the black market and just gave her cigarettes away as favors, but she was well aware that others profited from them. Gasoline brought high prices on the black market, and many soldiers in the Transportation Corps were in a position to supply it. Parisian police complained to Civil Affairs that when they attempted to break up an open market in US Army supplies being conducted by GIs with French civilians at the base of the Eiffel Tower, the French police officers had been beaten up and driven away. Thereafter, French police refused to interfere with US Army personnel who were overtly engaged in illegal activity, deeming it too dangerous. American MPs intervened and broke up the market at the Eiffel Tower, driving it underground somewhere else. To uncover GIs who were profiting by selling army supplies, postal order remittances were closely monitored for unusually large sums being mailed back to the United States. Some staff at SHAEF endorsed a plan to sell French silk scarves and perfume as souvenirs at the PX to soak up the GIs' extra money and keep them from competing with civilians in buying food and drink. To undermine the black market in cigarettes in Paris, General Robert McClure, chief of the Psychological Warfare Division, ordered cigarettes diverted from QM supplies to civilian outlets, more or less legally.[8]

American soldiers began feeding the black markets in French North Africa shortly after they arrived. Quartermaster troops noticed shortages in shipments from railcars in North Africa and suspected that the GIs in charge of the supplies were responsible for the missing consignments. Some trains moved supplies on open flatcars without guards, making them susceptible to looting by anyone at any time. Yet assigning guards did not stop the pilfering, as the guards were just as likely as anyone else to help themselves to PX supplies, which had the greatest propensity to disappear in North Africa. Investigators for the inspector general noted that trains and yards guarded by British soldiers experienced no problems; only American trains with American guards reported missing supplies. Questioning of the guards revealed that boxes of PX goods were being freely removed from railcars, and the guards failed to prevent it because US Army officers were directing the removals![9]

An investigation into disappearing hospital supplies in North Africa turned up similar results. When alarming numbers of sheets, pillowcases, mattress covers, clothing, and towels disappeared from hospitals in Casablanca and from hospital trains running between Algeria and Morocco, the quartermaster was initially inclined to blame Arab workers in the laundry. However, closer investigation revealed that the worst offenders were US officers who helped themselves to linens from the hospitals' supply closets. GI patients also traded their hospital gowns and linens to local civilians for wine or money. An expanded investigation revealed that the problem was worse than initially feared and led back to the railroads. The US Army tallied almost 7,500 missing sheets from its hospital trains, costing the army $6,750 but fetching an estimated $150,000 on the black market. This markup explained the GIs' motive to the inspector general, who discovered that GIs were throwing boxes of linens off trains to civilian confederates at designated sites; 94 sheets, 20 bath towels, and 71 mattress covers disappeared from a single train. The army assumed that another 1,000 missing pillowcases and 1,000 missing towels had been diverted by GIs to the black market in Morocco. Investigators uncovered only one case of Arabs stealing linens and clothing from a laundry. It turned out that the thieves were not employees of the laundry, which had no security to prevent anyone from walking in and taking whatever they wanted.[10]

Most black-market sales in liberated France were probably small time, as they had been during the German occupation. Individual GIs in rear-echelon positions became friendly with French civilians and got involved in small-time dealings in US government property. In these cases, neither the GIs selling army goods nor the French buying them were professionals who made a living at it; most were just opportunists who saw a chance to make a profit. When two civilians in Troyes were arrested and found to be in possession of thirty packs of American cigarettes and some chocolate, they claimed they had traded a bottle of cognac and 1,000 francs ($20) to some GIs for the goods, which they did not intend to resell. The two had never been in trouble before, and the local police were inclined to believe them. Sergeant Leland Lynch and Private Joseph Bielaski, who operated a refrigerator truck for the QM Corps, were arrested for selling eleven cartons of cigarettes (300 francs each), five cartons of chocolate bars (200 francs each), and a box of cigars (800 francs) to the proprietor of a hotel and restaurant in Conflans-sur-Seine in September 1944. Third Army investigators concluded that this was a one-time event for the two GIs and not part of a regular business. A staff sergeant in the QM Corps admitted to MPs that he sold eight cans of peaches to a café owner in Coutainville, Manche, for 7,900 francs ($158), which seemed a tad expensive. A search of the café turned up 122 pounds of sugar and 24 cartons of cigarettes, along with the peaches. The staff sergeant, who claimed he needed the money because his wife was sick, was busted to private and forfeited some pay but escaped the stockade. Two privates caught selling uniforms and K rations to a French civilian in St. Rémy-lès-Chevreuse for 400 francs ($8) were court-martialed, while another private accused of trading cigarettes for an apple—claiming he was just "trying to be friendly"—was reprimanded and confined to post for seven days. Six enlisted men convicted of pilfering large quantities of cigarettes in Versailles were sentenced to fifteen to twenty-five years in prison, which reveals the different attitudes toward large-scale and small-time diversions.[11]

It is difficult to discern how much US property was lost to small-scale pilfering versus large-scale organized theft. An investigation into disappearing cigarettes in northern France concluded that they were probably pilfered in small quantities all along the route from the ships in Cherbourg to PX employees in Paris. Paperwork on the shipments was so spotty that it was impossible to say where they went. Train cars arrived in Paris with missing seals and missing cigarettes, but guards in the yards thought the culprits were just as likely to be French civilians, perhaps railroad workers, as GIs. Posting guards on the trains reduced the problem. A lieutenant at the PX in Paris said his deliveries routinely showed up light, and then his employees stole more, but he was unable to pinpoint the source of the thefts. Almost certainly, all these filched cigarettes were funneled to the civilian black market in exchange for drink. Beginning in September 1944 the US Army requisitioned the French railroads from Cherbourg to Chartres and then to Versailles and Paris, using them almost exclusively to move supplies for the army. As First and Third Armies paused in eastern France in the fall, front-line soldiers complained more loudly and more frequently about the shortage of cigarettes. In mid-September John Savard's 38th Infantry Regiment was assigned to guard railroad cars carrying supplies from Normandy to the front. The trains faced bottlenecks along the way that forced them to stand motionless for hours, during which time they were repeatedly raided by parties unknown and looted of their valuable contents. Often the looting was carried out by French gangs working with cooperative GIs. Savard's new assignment was to ride in an improvised caboose and jump out and patrol the railcars during any stop. Posting armed guards on the trains proved effective in curbing the pilfering from standing trains, at least.[12]

Officers in charge of the US Army depot in Paris reported that trains arriving from Chartres had been seriously looted of shoes, cigarettes, food rations, and PX supplies, which inspired the Criminal Investigation Department (CID) of 21st Army Group to question the troops manning and maintaining the trains. One sergeant who confessed to the minor pilfering of food rations, cigarettes, and coffee claimed that the $700 worth of war bonds and postal orders he had remitted to his family in the United States came from gambling winnings. He admitted diverting twenty pounds of coffee to a French civilian for $80—a steep fall in black-market prices from the days of the German occupation, when coffee sold for $28 per pound. The CID investigators then turned their attention to the Matelots repair shops next to Versailles Palace, where repair crews regularly broke into boxcars and stole whatever they could find. Cigarettes proved to be the most valuable loot; they were easily sold to French workers in the yards, who resold them on the black market. A fireman on supply trains running between Normandy and Paris confessed to regularly receiving stolen cartons of cigarettes from other train workers and reselling them to French civilians. A carton brought 500 francs ($10), or 50 francs ($1) per pack. Black-market American cigarettes were easily available in Paris bars for 130 francs ($2.60) per pack, providing a nice profit to French black marketeers. Train repairmen also sold chocolate bars to French workers for 40 francs (80 cents) each—a fortune for a chocolate bar in 1944. One trainman barracked in Paris dabbled in fencing stolen US cigarettes but specialized in French pistols, which he bought from civilians and resold to other soldiers. He sent $550 in money orders to his wife in Mississippi, and like others, he claimed he had won it gambling. Another fireman on a locomotive explained that trainmen pilfered from boxcars while the trains were halted, waiting for bottlenecks to clear. On one occasion, the fireman strolled back to a car packed with rations only to find other train workers already there, helping themselves to cigarettes. He, too, resold German Lugar pistols he bought from soldiers, and he sent $400 in money orders home to Tennessee. MP raids on five depots rounded up 300 soldiers suspected of stealing PX goods from trains. Ultimately, 190 enlisted men and 8 officers were charged with systematically looting supplies from trains. One captain was convicted of pilfering and selling chocolate, razor blades, chewing gum, cigarettes, and boots. However, the Judge Advocate's office was understaffed and could not prosecute so many cases. Therefore, in view of the shortage of riflemen at the front in Germany, the commander of COMZ, General Pleas B. Rogers, agreed to allow any soldier who confessed his crimes to join a special disciplinary combat unit to redeem himself; 178 men were convicted, and 87 pled guilty. A special battalion formed of railroad troops convicted of looting reached the front in Germany just in time for VE Day, so they were sent to the Pacific theater instead.[13]

As noted, many French had become used to flouting the law and living by their wits during the German occupation, so it should come as little surprise that they continued to do so after their liberation. The provisional government made a real effort to stamp out black markets and depended on the police to do it. Many police—and many French in general—believed that members of the FFI were deeply involved in the black markets. A combined French and American police patrol searching for miscreants and contraband in the Bouches-du-Rhône discovered a truck registered to the FFI containing 315,000 packs of American cigarettes. The commander of the FFI for Avignon was also in the truck, and the MPs turned him over to French police. This no doubt delighted the French police, who frequently charged that the ranks of the FFI were heavily populated by brigands and other shady characters. The FFI countered that the police and the courts were still run by the same collaborationists who had served the Germans and Vichy—a charge they could not direct against American MPs. Janet Flanner asserts that the closing down of black markets by the French authorities after the liberation spawned a new, more sinister black market. Violent gangs of *mauvais maquis*, who were more gangster than guerrilla, had sprung up in the countryside and the suburbs, where they ambushed trucks and hijacked whole trains full of food. Such accusations against the FFI were widespread in France. They were disliked by many farmers, whose filched produce had fed thousands of *maquis* during the occupation; after the liberation, many of the same FFI "requisitioned" food from those same farmers. Many FFI busied themselves after the liberation roaming the countryside in search of black marketeers, even though it was widely assumed that most farmers had profited from black-market sales during the occupation. The commissioner in Châlons-sur-Marne worried that the vast opportunities for profit offered by GIs who were eager to trade with enterprising French would have a corrupting influence on French society after the war. The commissioner was mistaken: corruption was already widespread.[14]

Efforts by French police to suppress the black market often uncovered US government property in the wrong hands. The Marseille docks provided rich hunting grounds for police searching for contraband, but it could turn up anywhere American forces were found. A sweep by French police of a port services company in Marseille resulted in the arrest of twenty-four employees in possession of contraband, all presumably acquired from stores of Allied goods. Whether it had been stolen by the employees or bought from thieving GIs made little difference to French police, as it was illegal for French civilians to possess Allied military goods. The raid turned up five cartons of cigarettes, eight rubber soles, seven leather soles, a pair of sport shoes, three towels, fifteen bars of soap, seven packs of chewing gum, thirteen boxes of powdered milk, and other illicit goods. The police did not consider this an extraordinarily large haul; it was probably fairly typical for a day of petty trading or pilfering on the Marseille docks. Police records in the Seine-Inférieure reveal that dockworkers in Rouen, Le Havre, and Dieppe were deeply involved in looting Allied supplies coming ashore. In just one week in November 1944, 105 French citizens—overwhelmingly dockworkers—were arrested for theft or for being in possession of Allied military supplies. It is entirely possible that most of the pilfered goods were taken for personal use or for family members. Many of those arrested possessed only a single pair of US Army shoes; one man had shoes and socks, another had just leather soles, another had a pair of trousers and a hat, and another had a shirt and a pair of gloves. A French soldier in Rouen was handed over to French police for being in possession of American chocolate, and a dockworker was caught with cigarettes. A welder in Le Havre was picked up for being in possession of "a quantity of butter," which may have been destined for the black market. A sixteen-year-old boy who was arrested for possessing two pairs of US Army shoes told police he had bought them from American soldiers; that the French police kept the shoes but let the boy go suggests they believed him. Shoe soles made of leather or rubber were valuable commodities in France, as they were otherwise unavailable. Even fashionable women in Paris wore shoes with clunky wooden soles in the summer of 1945 owing to a lack of leather.[15]

Many French acquired US Army supplies for personal use, but much of the material was undoubtedly destined to be sold at black-market outlets. French police in Troyes caught three civilians syphoning gasoline from a US Army truck into a stolen gas can in November 1944. They had another full can in their possession. Police in Auxerre conducted periodic searches of the homes of "shady characters" in an attempt to shut down the black market there. One house frequented by GIs "smelled strongly of gasoline" when it was searched. While searching the house of a French employee of the US Army and a suspected black marketeer, police found a Colt pistol and various US Army items; a search of a second house in the suspected ring turned up thirty kilos of coffee. French police developed suspicions about a storekeeper from Grand Quevilly, near Rouen, who was arrested for possession of cigarettes, tobacco, and foodstuffs of Allied origin. Two restaurateurs arrested in Le Havre provided clues as to the destination of stolen food. Illegal brothels were frequently cited by French police as good places to buy black-market merchandise. Like so many criminal enterprises, bordellos bred other illegal acts. The prefect in Rouen reported that US service troops in his department had diverted "a considerable quantity of stolen goods to the black market" and used the proceeds to hire prostitutes. Three women arrested in Le Havre for possessing Allied goods were suspected of being clandestine prostitutes. Police in Auxerre complained that unregistered *maisons de tolerance* also served as black-market outlets, with a lively trade in cigarettes, chocolate, soap, and clothing.[16]

Both the US Army and French authorities tried numerous tactics to quash illicit trade. They launched periodic publicity campaigns alerting military personnel and civilians that it was illegal for the latter to possess US Army supplies. The posted regulations greeting GIs and sailors arriving in Marseille were unambiguous: "No soldier or sailor may make a present of goods originating from the US military to any French civilian. No bartering or trading is allowed." This posed a problem, as GIs frequently gave packs of cigarettes and even pieces of their uniforms, such as caps, to civilian friends or in return for gracious hospitality. French civilians who worked closely with GIs, such as a cook working for *Stars and Stripes* in Reims, were frequently given cigarettes, candy, and canned milk as perks of the job, even though it was against regulations; many thousands of French civilians no doubt benefited from these small gifts. GIs regularly sold American cigarettes to French friends or gave them away as gifts. When French police launched periodic expeditions to find contraband, they were commonly told that the goods had been honestly acquired and given in good faith. When a French cook employed at an American air base in the Yonne was found to be in the possession of US Army food, an American lieutenant and an interpreter showed up at the French police station to vouch for the cook, who swore that he had been given the food as a reward for services rendered. Of course, there was no way for the police to separate truth from fiction, so all contraband was subject to confiscation, regardless of how it was acquired. Xavier de Guerpel, whose farm had hosted a British regiment in August 1944, had traded large amounts of fresh vegetables and milk for British cigarettes, biscuits, soap, and tea. This type of direct bartering would have fallen within requisition regulations at the time, as his farm was directly on the front line, and French officials could not be expected to act as procurement officers. However, de Guerpel still had some of the tea and soap long after the British tanks and artillery had departed.[17]

Ham-fisted attempts by both the Americans and the French to quash the black market frequently created new problems. MPs provoked outrage when they launched a campaign in Marseille to confiscate cigarettes found on French civilians—or, worse, soldiers—on the streets. The commissioner in Nancy protested "energetically" to the US commander in his region when MPs searched civilians' houses for US Army property without notifying the French police or having them present. Although the searches did turn up some illegal items, principally food, the civilians protested that the MPs mistreated them, broke furniture and household items, and stole their possessions. The prefect in Châlons-sur-Marne lodged the same complaints about searches in the Marne. The CID was uncertain whether MPs had the right to confiscate any items from French civilians, so these sweeps were generally conducted jointly with the French police. The prefect in the Manche became greatly alarmed when he received notice of the roundup of US Army uniforms by French police and MPs because so many men in his department wore pieces of uniforms cast off and abandoned by GIs in the summer of 1944. Farmers in particular were in need of these clothes; many had lost much of their own clothing, and replacements were hard to come by. Even Assistant Minister of the Interior for Allied Relations Raymond Haas-Picard warned Minister of the Interior Adrien Tixier that this roundup was going to impose great hardships on the civilian population of the Manche. A French civilian in Auxerre was forced to surrender his USAAF bomber jacket in August 1945; he told MPs he had bought the jacket from a paratrooper in the 13th Airborne Division for 300 francs and was surprised to learn that he was not allowed to possess it. Likewise, a teenage boy had to surrender his Airborne sweater and jacket to MPs on the streets of Sens in October. Sweeps by MPs and French police turned up a lot of French children wearing khaki because GIs often gave away articles of clothing to French kids eager to have them. All were subject to confiscation, which led to many pathetic scenes on

French streets that were disheartening for everyone involved, including police and MPs, who found their task distasteful. Such confiscations did not reflect well on them, especially as the French police were already suspect for cooperating too readily with German authorities during the occupation. The commissioner in Dijon warned the Americans that if they used "Nazi methods," they risked losing all French sympathy.[18]

The Allied liberation severely disrupted the black markets, which had become pervasive and necessary under the German occupation. With the collapse of the transport system in the summer of 1944, many staples could not be found even on the black market at any price. Butter, milk, meat, and eggs had disappeared from both shops and the black markets in Paris by the spring of 1945. Five thousand outraged Frenchwomen staged a noisy protest in front of the Hôtel de Ville in Paris demanding government action to get food onto Parisian tables. Similar items disappeared from both shops and illicit markets in the Pas-de-Calais in the fall of 1944. Butter, which was unavailable in shops in the Pas-de-Calais, commanded 150 to 200 francs ($3 to $4) per kilo on the black market, if it could be found at all. Meat also disappeared from butcher shops and could be had in back alleys for about the same price as butter. People in the south of France complained that their situation was even worse than that in Paris in March 1945; they had no potatoes or bread in their shops. Milk was not making it to the market in Alsace because farmers were using it to make butter and cheese or to feed their piglets.[19]

The black market for alcohol tended to be regional: in most regions it was abundant—despite the larcenous behavior of the German army—and freely available at market prices (still set by the French government). Alcohol was not supplied by the US Army, but the French happily provided it to GIs. A SHAEF report in December 1944 noted that no black market existed for champagne or cognac because they were so plentiful and available for 125 francs ($2.50) per bottle. When soldiers' access to legal alcoholic beverages was restricted, they patronized the black market. Wine, cider, and beer were available in practically unlimited quantities and were rationed by neither Vichy nor the provisional government; the lack of transport was the only impediment to their availability. An enterprising US Army captain set up a racket buying cognac in Bordeaux for 190 francs (just under $4) per bottle and reselling it in Brussels for 390 francs (just under $8)—a tidy profit. He reportedly cleared $60,000 per month until the MPs caught up with him. He was given a twelve-year prison sentence. A café proprietor in Nancy had 180 bottles of cognac confiscated by the police because he could not produce a receipt to prove he had acquired them legally. Once the police began poking around, they found 28 more bottles that he claimed he had bought from

American soldiers; he was allowed to return those bottles, presumably getting his money back. Police records of black-market activity frequently cite wine acquired and sold illicitly, but US soldiers were rarely identified as the source. The GIs involved in the cases cited above may have been isolated incidents.[20]

GIs more commonly provided the demand for illicit alcohol, rather than the supply. When that demand surpassed the ability of French purveyors to supply it, this provided an unfortunate boon to enterprising but not always skillful home distillers. Ten GIs died in Nancy and two were left near death in a hospital after drinking "poisoned schnapps." The inspector general followed up on an idea that the liquor may have been sabotaged and left behind by the departing Germans, but that turned out not to be the case. An investigation by French police revealed that it was bootleg and not very artfully made crème de prunelle (a liqueur made from sloe berries) that proved deadly. Police discovered bootleg alcohol being sold in eleven cafés that should not have been serving distilled liquor at all. An ex–New York police detective put on the case told *Star and Stripes* that a few drinks of the stuff would not hurt anyone, but too much could kill you. French police turned up "Pernod," which turned out to be methyl alcohol, and pinned the whole affair on a "well known racketeer" in Nancy. In this case, nine GIs died, four were left blind, four remained in the hospital (ultimate fate unknown), and another four recovered after brief hospital stays. GIs were warned to stick to beer and wine.[21]

The diversion of gasoline was another serious problem. So much was syphoned off during transit that the US Army estimated that only two-thirds of the gasoline imported into France actually fueled army vehicles. The army was so alarmed that it beseeched French police to arrest any Americans involved in the illegal sale of army supplies, especially gasoline. Military authorities assumed that the wholesale loss of gasoline experienced in the south of France was orchestrated by French criminal gangs operating out of Marseille and Nice with the assistance of cooperative GIs, who likely traded gasoline for alcohol. Gendarmes in Romilly-sur-Seine found eight ten-liter cans full of gasoline in a café on 30 September 1944. The forty-seven-year-old owner, who had no criminal record, told the gendarmes that some GIs had paid for their drinks with gasoline when it turned out they had no money. The gas cans and the gas were confiscated by the police. The CID believed that most of the missing gasoline was either siphoned from army vehicles or tapped directly from the pipeline that carried fuel from Marseille to Alsace, and it asked for more French cooperation to catch the thieves. The first pipeline built by the Army Corps of Engineers from Normandy to eastern France was constantly springing mysterious leaks that the engineers assumed were caused by French civilians stealing small amounts of free gasoline. In December 1944 officers in charge of pipeline security worried about German agents carrying out sabotage, but they recognized that unauthorized siphoning was the greater threat. They urged French troops to take siphoning seriously and to treat it as sabotage warranting shoot-to-kill orders for anyone tampering with the pipeline. After the war in Europe ended, guards' instructions were amended to "shoot to wound," but their strict vigilance led to some killings and recriminations. In July and August 1945 French and American guards on patrol near Lyon shot at each other, assuming the others were thieves, leaving two gendarmes, a French soldier, and a municipal policeman dead in separate incidents. The Americans claimed the French police were tapping the pipeline rather than guarding it and noted the constant disappearance of large volumes of gasoline from the pipeline near Lyon. In a single week in July, one section of line guarded by the US Army company involved in the shootings lost an estimated 1,715 barrels to thieves. In addition, the pipeline lost about 45 barrels per day to seepage, and in the same week in July it lost another 3,750 barrels that could not be accounted for. The unit responsible for security estimated that thieves got away with 420 barrels of gasoline on a single day, 18 July. Despite obvious problems with thieves, the French remained upset that US Army guards used deadly force against French citizens, thieves or not (nor did the French believe the police were stealing gas).[22]

There also existed a black market in money. The overvaluation of the franc at 50 to a dollar (the rate had been changed in 1943 from 75 per dollar, after French protests in North Africa) encouraged both American GIs and British Tommies to sell Allied currencies on unofficial markets. GIs' complaints about the overvalued franc continued after the war was over, and an American captain complained to *Stars and Stripes* that the exchange rate made everything in France too expensive. The exchange rate encouraged GIs to use cheap cigarettes as money to make their pay go further. Money could also be changed illegally; in September 1944 a dollar brought 225 francs on the black markets in northern France. Both the Allies and the provisional government worried about inflation in France, and British officials in particular believed that adjusting the exchange rate would push up prices, perhaps leading to hyperinflation. They argued in the fall of 1944 that the rate should be left alone and that once the French economy recovered sufficiently, prices would readjust to reasonable levels. They made the same argument in the fall of 1945 but noted that the greatest contributor to inflation in France was the extraordinary amount of counterfeit bills circulation. French counterfeiters proved skilled at duplicating the Allied "supplemental francs" that had outraged de Gaulle. They continued to circulate as late as October 1945, by which time many of them were phony. The Bank of France implemented a campaign to retire all Allied-printed francs, but 500- and 1,000-franc notes kept turning up. SHAEF finance officers believed that numerous French gangsters were printing the notes, given their uneven quality; some were quite good, while others, which SHAEF believed were being printed in Marseille, were rather crude. Amazingly, counterfeit 5,000-franc notes were circulating, even though the Bank of France had not yet issued notes of that denomination. The large amount of counterfeit money in France might have actually been evidence that the government so feared inflation that it was starving the economy of currency. Still, it is hard to fault the Allies for their attempt to prevent inflation from adding to the burdens of provisional government.[23]

As the Americans prepared to pull out of France, the flow of army supplies onto the black market only increased. The region around Roye, Somme, hosted numerous American air bases, and their personnel stole enormous quantities of supplies and sold them to the French on the black market in the summer of 1945. US Army clothes, linens, shoes, and food were freely available in the towns and villages of the Somme. In May 1945, when PX supplies were being transferred from Paris to Germany, pilfering was so bad on the trains that Special Services sent many goods by plane, where no pilfering occurred. When the Red Cross shipped supplies intended for soldiers of the 82nd Airborne by train from Laon to Epinal in June 1945, the losses left Violet Kochendoerfer, the Red Cross volunteer in charge, "aghast": 925 pounds of lard, 500 pounds of coffee, and 780 pounds of sugar. One of the four trucks transferring the coffee and donut ingredients from the train station to a warehouse went astray en route; "all these supplies were like pure gold on the black market," Kochendoerfer observed. In a scene entirely appropriate to the film noir era, in 1946 CID investigators were on the heels of an American deserter calling himself "Lieutenant Hamilton." He had called on French investigators in Clermont-Ferrand and left with a thick file on the sale of surplus US Army materials that may have ended up on the black market. The CID investigators assumed that "Hamilton" had taken the files because they would have incriminated him and his French associates, but CID detectives from Marseille guessed that the files might have been "disappeared" by local police or possibly higher government authorities who were involved in the illegal dealings. Perhaps "Hamilton" was acting as their confederate to cover up their self-serving deeds, or perhaps there was no "Hamilton" at all. As during the German occupation, some level of official tolerance was usually required to keep a black market booming, and that was no doubt true during the American presence as well. The opportunity to profit from such forbearance was ever present and tempting.[24]

Both French officials and the US Army at all levels did what they could to suppress the black markets in France—with limited success. The diversion of army supplies was a serious problem for the Americans, who were bolstered by de Gaulle's real desire to shut down the illicit markets. However, American officers who warned that it was hopeless and foolish to quash the markets were probably right. The illicit sales could not have happened without the cooperation of many unscrupulous GIs and criminally inclined French—including some police—and catching the malefactors proved difficult. The diversion of cigarettes and particularly gasoline was a real crisis for the army, and corrective action aimed at large-scale thefts was the appropriate policy, even though it was only partially successful. Campaigns aimed at low-level traders looked a lot like harassment of French civilians, many of whom came into possession of US Army property quite innocently. French police and MPs detailed to take sweaters away from children knew they had a dirty job and expressed their distaste for it. They sometimes showed leniency toward French caught with small amounts of goods, but the gifts were confiscated nevertheless. Here, low-level cooperation mostly failed to achieve good results. Then again, when the MPs and police failed to do their jobs, this most likely went unreported, which would have been another kind of cooperation.

Conflict: *Butin* (Booty)

Both the French provisional government and the Allies wanted to stamp out the black markets if they could. That they had different motives did not prevent them from cooperating to achieve the same end. Controversies stirred up by abandoned or captured German property in France initially inspired little cooperation between the French and the US military because their interests collided. Repeated efforts in Paris to come to an agreement to share the booty often broke down upon implementation in the field. SHAEF claimed that all German booty was the property of the Allied armies, regardless of its origin or who had captured it. The issue of who had the right to dispose of goods left behind by departed or surrendered Germans arose early in Normandy, but in June and July 1944 the French were in no position to assert any claims on such goods. German supplies seized by Americans in Cherbourg were reserved for army use unless they could be spared for civilians. Civil affairs officers in Cherbourg developed a good relationship with their French counterparts and generally tried to pry loose captured supplies from the QM Corps for the benefit of French civilians, especially food and clothing. Problems arose during the breakout, when US Army units raced through regions and had no time to develop a rapport with French officials and especially liberation committees that tried to assert their authority. American commanders claimed that goods captured by the FFI from fleeing Germans were rightfully American possessions because the US military was the only recognized legal authority in areas just vacated by the Germans. The French saw it differently. When Patton's troops raced through Yonne and Aube, they left behind the FFI as the only authority; its members assumed they were in charge of German supply depots guarded by FFI volunteers. Disputes over food and fuel seized by the Americans assumed huge importance for the French government because of the dire circumstances of many of its people. The problem went beyond assertions of French sovereignty by prickly Gaullist officials: cold and hungry French citizens, disappointed at the fruits of liberation, viewed the *butin* as their sustenance. For the Americans, the problem was mainly a matter of logistics. Friction increased between French and American authorities once de Gaulle's government had established a sufficient presence in France to contest American seizures of German property. Conflicting policies on how booty was to be claimed caused both parties to put up posters in August outlining conflicting rules. The French were outraged that the Americans' posted notices directly contradicted French regulations on *butin,* but Commissioner for Inter-Allied Relations François Coulet recognized that he was powerless to do anything about it, and he ordered that the offending American notices not be molested.[25]

Food presented by far the biggest irritant in tussles over booty. The French strove to convince the Americans that any food claimed as *butin* belonged to them. They assumed, no doubt correctly, that almost all food left by the Germans was of French origin and had been sold to the Germans under duress. In any event, it hurt the Americans' image among the French populace to be seen seizing French food for themselves when civilians were so short of sustenance. The Americans settled this problem by "borrowing" captured foodstuffs and promising to replace it later if it turned out to rightfully belong to the French. Often captured food was not reported to anyone; it was simply eaten by the capturers, whether they were Americans, French troops, FFI, or civilians. The prefect in Troyes warned Civil Affairs that FFI guards were unable to adequately protect stocks of captured flour and bran from pilfering by civilians, and that being the case, he suggested the US Army turn the food over to Ravitaillement Général (General Supply). Civil Affairs replied that the issue lay outside its purview and kicked the question up to higher Allied authorities in Paris. The departmental liberation committee of Loir-et-Cher asserted that the FFI was ready to fight the Americans, just as it had fought the Germans, if SHAEF policy toward the public welfare did not change. French departmental officials took that threat seriously, as they did the FFI's claim on food, wood, and charcoal salvaged by its members. They pointed to several boxcars full of wheat claimed by the Americans that were in danger of spoiling due to exposure to the elements because of American carelessness and indifference—attitudes that angered the French, who could have used that wheat. An offer by a civil affairs officer to sell the load to the French only increased French anger. In September 1944 SHAEF gave army groups (such as General Omar Bradley's 12th Army Group) the flexibility to turn over captured supplies to Civil Affairs for use by civilian populations.[26]

Relinquishing captured food to the French posed a dilemma for SHAEF because the Americans had planned to feed German POWS with food stocks captured from the Germans. Friction also developed over food for animals, as SHAEF and the French bickered over captured fodder. The French wanted to use captured hay to feed French farm animals, and the Americans wanted to use it to stuff mattresses for German POWs. French authorities failed to see how hay that was obviously of French origin could be considered "war material," even if it had been discovered in a German depot. In 1944 the German army still relied heavily on horses for transport, and they required a lot of fodder. When the Americans overran Troyes, they found enormous supply dumps containing all sorts of material, including more than 2,200 tons of oats and barley intended for Wehrmacht horses and a huge amount of hay. However, the Americans failed to detail troops to guard the various depots, leaving that job to the French. American claims of ownership of captured property rang hollow so long as the FFI was left to guard the disputed goods. In the end, Civil Affairs told the prefect that his people should come and collect whatever food was fit for human consumption in the warehouses, but the hay was beyond his control. Service troops repeatedly helped themselves to stores of 3.5 tons of oats abandoned by the Germans, despite protests from the French official tasked with securing the oats for French use. Questions like these lingered without resolution until the end of the war, despite agreements signed in Paris. This kept relations between Civil Affairs and French officials off balance. After all, civil affairs officers were most likely to be sympathetic and helpful to the French, and if they could not resolve questions about the ownership of oats and hay, what hope remained for relations between French civilians and the US Army?[27]

French officials became irate when the US Army claimed possession of fleets of French vehicles that had been requisitioned by the Germans. The commissioner in Orléans was incensed that vehicles recuperated by the FFI had been claimed by the Americans, and he sought the intervention of Assistant Minister Haas-Picard. It galled the French that they were expected to buy back their own vehicles from the Americans. Dismayed that the Americans had seized all vehicles left behind by the Germans—most of which did not run—the prefect in Troyes proposed that the Americans keep any vehicle of British or American manufacture and the French keep any vehicle of French or German origin, thus guaranteeing that the French received almost all of them. At the very least, the Americans should sell to the French, for a modest amount, any vehicle that could not move for want of crucial parts. To thwart the Germans' attempt to seize French vehicles, many owners had used various subterfuges to immobilize them, such as hiding the batteries or removing the wheels.[28]

The US Army laid claim to anything captured from the Germans, and that included money, such as the 6,735 francs discovered in a German safe in Cherbourg, the 11,000 francs in the possession of a German POW who claimed he "found it," and the 10,000 francs found in an abandoned German vehicle. Sixteen wounded Germans captured in a hospital had 21,000 francs among them, and all of it went to the US Army. However, the 310 francs discovered in a drawer in the town hall of La Vacquerie was handed over to the French. Remarkably, many French voluntarily handed over currency to the Americans: 400,000 francs seized by the FFI in Soisson from the German wife of the head of the local Todt Organization, 105,000 francs taken from a German officer captured by the FFI, and 20,700 francs found in the office of a German firm in Troyes. Most of this probably occurred during the early, heady days of liberation.[29]

With de Gaulle established in Paris and much of France freed from the German yoke, the French provisional government and the Allies worked out an agreement in August to reduce friction. Abandoned war supplies, such as ammunition, weapons, and field kitchens, belonged to the Allied armies; everything else belonged to the French. Any food left behind that was clearly of French origin, even if it had been purchased by the German army, was to be considered French property. The French and Allies differed on the status of goods manufactured in France for the German military and abandoned in France: the French considered this property French; the Americans considered it German but agreed to a "liberal interpretation" on a case-by-case basis. The Americans also agreed that all war booty should be inventoried in the presence of French officials, who had the right to inspect depots containing booty under American control. This accord signed on 25 August helped smooth over problems provoked by *butin,* but it did not end them, as the provenance of captured goods could not always be established.[30]

Disputes over oats were precisely the sort of headache SHAEF had no time for, and it expected civil affairs officers to deal with these issues on the spot through negotiations with local French officials. However, as the GPRF became more confident of its legitimacy, local French officials had less flexibility to handle these sensitive questions. Moreover, many French officials were probably glad to pass such headaches on to higher authorities, just as some civil affairs officers were relieved to hand off prickly disputes to staff higher up the chain of command. Some civil affairs officers were more amenable to finding quick solutions to knotty problems than others. General George Patton was famous for being a stickler about appearances, but he was always willing to bend or break the rules when they got in his way. Thus, civil affairs officers under his command in Third Army were more willing to accommodate the French than were officers in other armies. When large quantities of clothes, blankets, and sheets were captured in German depots by Patton's troops in Saint-Julien (south of Troyes) and claimed as American war booty, French officials insisted that these items had been made in France and were needed for civilian use. The Americans resolved the problem by agreeing that material in the warehouses could be used to equip the FFI as part of the war effort. Patton set up an office in Nancy to handle all questions related to war booty. As was usually the case, items deemed useful to the Americans were kept by Third Army, and other supplies were used for Axis POWs; whatever was left over, Civil Affairs could dispose of as it saw fit. When the Americans took control of much of the port of Marseille, civil affairs officers developed a modus vivendi with their French counterparts who ran the port and worked out their own arrangements for the disposition of war booty. Stores of soda carbonate and cordage left behind in warehouses by the Germans were claimed by the French and put to use without any protest from the Americans. The question of who would take possession of the large stores of coal left behind in the city by the Germans was another matter. The Americans took all the coal, but they promised to compensate the French for their fair share. Some of the seized coal had actually belonged to a French company, which demanded compensation for this irregular requisition and received the backing of the French government.[31]

It usually took goodwill on all sides to resolve such disputes, especially when officers encountered unusual circumstances not foreseen in the agreements inked in Paris. Third Army ran into a problem when trying to dispose of coal in its possession in the Aube. The prefect wanted the coal turned over for civilian use, but Civil Affairs refused because, it claimed, the provisional government in Paris had assumed control over all questions related to coal, so this issue could not be handled at the local level. Yet it had been handled at the local level in Marseille that same week, suggesting that the individual personalities involved often determined the outcome. And therein, perhaps, lay part of the problem. De Gaulle sought to centralize authority to the greatest extent possible in Paris and have his direct appointees regulate relations with the Allies. He appointed a former member of his London staff, Raymond Haas-Picard, to the post of assistant minister of the interior for inter-Allied relations, tasked with solving problems that arose with the British and Americans. Haas-Picard was a hard-charging, get-things-done administrator, and like François Coulet (who was named commissioner for inter-Allied relations in September 1944), he tended to replicate de Gaulle's prickly personality and starchy obstinacy—traits that were not recommended for gaining the cooperation of SHAEF or Civil Affairs. French efforts to centralize decision making in Paris did not work out well when it came to resolving disputes over *butin.* Coulet presented SHAEF with a list of *butin* seized by the US Army that he argued should have been allotted to the French by right or because the French needed the items more than the Americans did: materials left in factories in Hagondange and Lunéville; food in Orléans, Montargis, and Vendôme; materials intended for the construction of French ships in the Chantiers Navale in Trait; and materials clearly stamped with the mark of the Ministry of Colonies. Haas-Picard argued that the French should be allowed to keep anything left behind in France by the Germans that was not clearly needed by the US military. Certainly, anything of French origin should be assigned to the French. These were not unreasonable suggestions. The question was: what booty would the Americans concede they did not need for the war effort? De Gaulle' drive to centralize decision making pushed local disputes onto the desks of SHAEF personnel, where they were definitely not welcome. De Gaulle's policy of resolving problems in Paris clashed directly with Eisenhower's practice of dealing with as many issues as possible at the local level.[32]

In December 1944 representatives of the Aid to Allied Forces (AFA) and the Allies arrived at a definitive accord on war booty that assigned a category to all captured material. Category A consisted of goods produced in France not by order of the Germans but nevertheless acquired by them; such goods were assigned to the French. Category B goods, produced in France for the Germans and considered German property, were allotted to the Allies if seized by Allied soldiers. Category C goods were produced in Germany or German-occupied territory and were considered Allied property if seized by the Allies. Anything that could not be clearly assigned to a category was considered French. All booty was subject to inspection by all parties with a valid order, and it was subject to Allied military requisition if deemed necessary to the conduct of the war, regardless of category. This may have been the "definitive agreement," but it left a lot open to interpretation, and it was not always honored by Allied units in possession of abandoned or captured material.[33]

Regardless of the December agreement, questions involving booty were often resolved through expediency or negotiation—exactly what the agreement intended to eliminate. In December 1944 the Americans turned over to French guards 234 depots in the Seine base section (Paris and the two surrounding departments, Seine-et-Oise and Seine-et-Marne), as well as the responsibility for inventorying the contents left behind by the Germans. This gave French authorities wide discretion to decide what should be declared French and what should be turned over to the Allies. As far as the French were concerned, everything should be divided up among the various French ministries, except for the captured armaments, which would probably be declared American and then turned over to the French army under Lend-Lease. It took until mid-December to inventory everything, by which time the French ministries had laid claim to almost everything in the depots, including 1.1 million bottles of cognac in Depot 104 turned over to General Supply. This was accomplished not by subterfuge but by agreement with SHAEF, which thought generosity was called for in view of the hardships facing those in Paris. Nevertheless, Commissioner Coulet had little faith in American intentions and recommended that the supplies in the depots be distributed as quickly as possible, not to meet a dire need but to prevent the Americans from reclaiming them. Under the circumstances, it would have been a public relations nightmare for the Americans to hold on to food and fuel that were desperately needed by Parisians. The French generally reacted badly to news of GIs seizing wood, food, and clothing of French origin as booty, especially when the US soldiers appeared to have everything they needed and a lot more. American inflexibility sometimes courted bad public relations. Before the Germans abandoned Givet—in a coal-mining district near the Belgian border—the German commander had been ordered to burn the 27,000 tons of coal stored there. Described locally as "not too bad a guy," he not only declined to destroy the coal but also suggested to local authorities that they move it to their own storage areas. Not seeing any need to do so, they did not move the coal, which was then seized by the Americans, placed under guard, and held as captured booty for American use, even as the weather turned freezing and the locals had no way to heat their homes.[34]

The French exhibited surprising honesty, given the opportunities for French authorities to simply take materials left behind by the Germans without clearing it with the Americans and the opportunities for French civilians to simply help themselves without bothering French officials. A man in Troyes turned over to the police some clothes the Germans had left behind at his house. It is understandable that people would want to get rid of broken telephones or filing cabinets—and especially ammunition—left in their houses, but they even reported cooking equipment, pots, casseroles, tables, chairs, beds, armoires, footstools, and other useful household items. The French police would cart these items away, declaring them *butin* to the AFA and subject to seizure by the Americans. The prefect in Troyes got together with the head of local AFA and went over long lists of inventories compiled by the Germans during their occupation, hoping to identify goods found in derequisitioned houses and hotels and determine who they belonged to. One astonished man wrote to the prefect that his house was full of someone else's belongings, but where were his? French efforts to obtain inventories of French goods held by the Americans in the Aube garnered only a few lists of charcoal and oats that the US Army had already turned over to the French.[35]

Disputes about French property did not stop at the French border or with the end of the war. A lot of French property had been looted by the Germans and taken back to Germany, where in 1945 the French made a concerted effort to locate and seize anything of French origin. They expected their allies to assist them in their respective zones of occupation, but the Americans were not always helpful. When the French discovered photographic equipment and projectors looted from the justice building in Strasbourg in the American zone, the Americans claimed the equipment for themselves as booty. The US Army did try to track down some French vehicles seized by the Germans, but the effort was neither vigorous nor very successful.[36]

The French civilian population and the officials responsible for their welfare soon experienced in their dealings with the French army all the frustrations they had endured with the Americans. In 1945, as the last remnants of French soil were liberated from the Germans by French units, the French army claimed as its own *pris de guerre* anything captured from the Germans. Stocks of coal overrun by the French army were claimed, even as civilians in eastern France shivered in their homes for want of fuel. Any item not considered useful to the French army was subject to sale to civil authorities, much as surplus US Army supplies were. The French army also claimed a large cache of tires discovered in Strasbourg in May 1945, even though civilian officials protested the dire need for tires for civilian use.[37]

By spring 1945, questions of war booty were largely moot, and the US Army was turning over to the AFA any German military equipment the Americans had no use for: helmets were destined for scrap metal, helmet liners and knee pads manufactured in France for German paratroopers were turned over to the French air force. The USAAF took possession of vast amounts of Luftwaffe equipment, especially furniture and office supplies, when the Americans overran German air bases in France. The Americans then used the bases for their own fighters and medium bombers to wage war in Germany, utilizing the captured equipment to operate the bases. By midspring 1945, many of those bases were too far from their targets in Germany to be of much value, so the Americans turned them, and all the booty attached to them, over to the French. The French planned to use some of the big air bases, such as those at Romilly and Mailly, for the French air force; redundant bases, with all their living facilities, workshops, dining halls, and such, were used to house returning French POWs, deportees, and other displaced persons. As the Americans no longer had any use for the pots and pans, bathtubs, mattresses, and the like that had been captured with the airfields, all this property was turned over to the commissioner in Dijon with no fuss.[38]

As the number of Axis POWs in Allied hands grew in the spring of 1945, the problem of feeding and clothing them became acute. The QM Corps, tasked with solving this problem, became increasingly possessive of captured supplies. The fundamental conflict of interest between the Americans and French over the issue of booty could not be resolved happily in anyone's favor. SHAEF stuck to its policy of reserving for Axis POWs as much captured material as possible, giving in to French demands only when it had to. Eisenhower showed less flexibility on these matters than he did on others because of the huge numbers of Axis POWs falling into Allied hands and SHAEF's inability to ship in adequate supplies to care for them. Only the end of the war and the Americans' departure from France really ended the disputes. By then, the Americans were only too happy to turn over captured supplies to the French. Determining whether the French had to pay for them was another question, but that would be left to the accountants in Paris and Washington to resolve. Like other problems generated by Axis POWs in France, disputes over booty were produced by policies formulated at the highest levels. Occasionally, these disputes could be resolved at the local level between civil affairs officers and French municipal officials, but for the most part, conflicting interests put the French and the Americans at loggerheads, and only if one side was willing to surrender its interest could the problem be settled.[39]

8

Problem GIs and the GI Problem

The French and Americans managed to get along well enough to win the war against Germany. However, some conflicts were unavoidable, such as disputes over the disposition of war booty or the treatment of Axis POWs. Other impositions, such as requisitions, inconvenienced the French, but for the most part, the civilian population understood the need for these vexations and tolerated them. One inconvenience foisted on the civilian population that was not at all understood or tolerated was the misbehavior of bored, drunken, or uncouth American soldiers. The vast majority of GIs undoubtedly behaved appropriately toward their French hosts, but discipline in the American citizens' army was lax compared with that in other armies in the contest, and Americans were less prone to self-restraint than other peoples, especially the French. Crimes committed by a small number of soldiers placed a cloud over the reputation of all. Persistent and pervasive brawling and petty crime—not to mention rape and murder—by even a small number of GIs wore down the French, and by late 1944 or early 1945, many were ready to roll up the welcome mat extended to their liberators.

French police reports revealed a monotonous repetition of the same crimes from late 1944 to the end of 1945: drunken GIs attacked French men and women alike and committed wanton vandalism and petty thefts. Less often, GIs engaged in armed robbery, rape, and murder. Those regions saturated by US soldiers—such as around Cherbourg, Le Havre, and Rouen—experienced elevated levels of crime and violence as long as the Americans remained. Supply depots in the Oise intermediate section, such as at Reims and Laon, experienced crime and violence perpetrated by GIs as long as the bases operated. From November 1944 to late 1945, French officials charged with monitoring public opinion reported that GI criminality was turning the populace against the Americans. Confrontations between French civilians and Americans soldiers in which both sides employed fists, knives, clubs, and even guns became more common as relations soured and public anger increased throughout 1945. As early as November 1944, General Paul-Louis

Legentilhomme of the military district around Rouen warned of a violent public backlash against the Americans. An August 1945 letter from the prefect in Châlons-sur-Marne to the US provost marshal in Reims warned that immediate and vigorous measures "to stop outrages by American soldiers" were needed to maintain "good Franco-American relations." Raymond Haas-Picard, the Interior Ministry's liaison with the Allies, warned in September 1945 that attacks by American soldiers fueled by alcohol continued to be an irritant to good relations: "The frequency of these attacks in several regions has rapidly altered very cordial relations to an atmosphere of fear, rancor, and suspicion."[1]

Most shockingly, American behavior contrasted badly with that of the German occupiers so recently evicted from France. It became commonplace for the French to characterize German comportment as "correct." For the most part, German soldiers had behaved politely toward the French—so long as there was no shooting going on. When the Germans first arrived in 1940 they had behaved like brutes, and when they left in 1944 they departed with astonishing savagery, but in between, they faced severe disciplinary action if they did not behave properly. The behavior of German troops who requisitioned the large farmhouse of Marie-Louise Osmont near Caen was often far from ideal, but she thought it compared favorably to that of the Allied soldiers who displaced them.[2]

The operating agreement among the Allies stipulated that Allied soldiers in France were subject to the military justice of their own countries. GIs accused of crimes in France were arrested by US Army MPs, investigated by the US Army Criminal Investigation Department (CID), and tried by judges of the Judge Advocate General (JAG). French police cooperated with Allied authorities but had no jurisdiction over GIs. French police were not allowed to use force against Allied soldiers except under extraordinary circumstances to protect lives or property; they had no power to arrest GIs but could detain them until MPs arrived to take custody of the accused. It took several months for US Army police functions—MPs, CID, and the Office of the Provost Marshal (OPM)—to work out a useful reporting system with French police. Until September or October 1944, there was no routinized procedure for gendarmes to notify MPs about offenses. Most frequently, gendarmes contacted civil affairs officers; these officers then contacted MPs, who took reports of infractions and passed them on to the OPM or the CID, the OPM's. investigative division. In the summer of 1944 the CID complained that it took five or six days for the French police to report crimes, probably because they did not know how to contact the CID. Such a time lag reduced the probability of a successful outcome in any investigation.[3]

By the fall of 1944, reporting mechanisms were in place, and the French government was functioning effectively enough to take note of crimes committed by GIs. Most transgressions by GIs during the summer of 1944 remained unreported because French law enforcement largely disappeared as battles raged and civilians had no means to report miscreants. Despite this lack of records from the front lines, GIs did indeed commit crimes against French civilians. In mid-August, while still in Normandy, OSS Colonel David Bruce noted in his diary, "[OSS officer] Charlie Vanderblue reports that in the Third Army area the French in certain respects entertain a very low opinion of our troops. He says that he has heard from a Judge Advocate of twelve rape cases in the area involving American soldiers. On my last visit I saw a little French girl of about twelve appeal to Joe O'Malley, when I was visiting Corps, to afford her and her family protection against some negro soldiers who had terrorized them for two days. Discipline in the American Army is far too lax except in the fighting divisions." As the front line moved into Lorraine, reports of incidents involving GIs began to arrive in French police stations and were passed along to Third Army officers. Two sergeants and a private were convicted of attacking and robbing several French civilians in the Meurthe-et-Moselle in late October and early November 1944 and of killing another with a pistol. They were court-martialed in January 1945 and sentenced to long terms of hard labor in federal prison. In early November, when Nancy was still on the front line, three GIs strong-armed their way into a house, ransacked the place, and raped a twenty-four-year-old woman. Police reported that the three attackers were black, strongly suggesting that they were not front-line infantrymen but service troops. Police suspected the same three soldiers of assaulting a sixteen-year-old girl later the same day, but she managed to fight them off. Otherwise, police reports from the Meurthe-et-Moselle in the fall of 1944 contained few accusations of malfeasance by GIs, suggesting that criminal behavior by front-line soldiers in France was not common.[4]

Soldiers' experience in the Second World War involved vast stretches of time with little to do, and bored soldiers found ways to cause mischief. Shortly after the liberation of Marseille, port engineers alerted chief engineer Le Bel that American soldiers had broken most of the mirrors for the lantern in the harbor lighthouse. Shiny mirrors and bored young soldiers with access to stones were a bad combination. Le Bel pointed out that German soldiers had broken only one mirror, whereas the Americans had broken seven or eight, and a functioning lighthouse was indispensable for the operation of the harbor. A woman south of Auxerre complained that Americans soldiers eating lunch by the side of the road near her farm had amused themselves by shooting birds on a telephone line, severing the line and disrupting her phone service. Bored GIs sometimes shot farm animals for sport. The AFA officer in Nancy objected to treating the shooting of a cow belonging to a widow with seven children as an "irregular requisition." When GIs shot her one and only cow, they deprived Mme. Balthazard of twenty liters of milk per day and her sole source of income. GIs looking for amusement were assumed to have shot and killed another cow two weeks earlier. Things could have been worse: American soldiers on a train used two railroad workers in Maubeuge for target practice in November 1945; the workers saved themselves by jumping down an embankment.[5]

Inebriated GIs

The most common offense by GIs was public drunkenness, which was often accompanied by riotous behavior. WAC secretary Betty Magnuson, stationed in Paris, asserted that she had seen more Americans drunk in Minnesota than she ever saw in Paris. While this may have been true, public drunkenness was not acceptable behavior in most of France, perhaps because almost all French drank alcohol regularly but rarely to excess. GIs were introduced to alcoholic cider in Normandy, but with its low alcohol content, it would take a lot of cider to get drunk. Many young GIs did not have the experience to know that they should not mix different types of liquor. After drinking cider, calvados, and cognac one evening in early October 1944 in Saint-Rémy les Chèvreuse (south of Versailles), an army private found himself in Paris, asking directions of a gendarme, several days later. Upon returning to his post at a supply company, he was arrested for being AWOL for four days and claimed to remember nothing about the missing time. He also asserted that before his arrival in France in September, he drank very little; this seems to have been the case with many GIs who acquired a taste for alcohol in France. A police commissioner in Sens suggested that some GIs who became sick after having five glasses of *eau de vie* mixed with red wine were probably not used to drinking and should not indulge so much. Nine noncommissioned officers (NCOs) drinking champagne and cognac in Troyes in January 1945 became loud and obnoxious, drawing the attention of an American captain, who was upset by their behavior. When a sergeant threatened to knock the captain's teeth out, he summoned the MPs. At his court-martial, the sergeant claimed to have had only a third of a bottle of champagne and two glasses of cognac—not a lot, but a bad combination for someone not used to it. Two American army officers trying to enjoy a drink in a café in Troyes in November 1944 were disturbed by a group of drunken GIs and had them escorted from the premises after one "puked all over the place." One of his comrades made an issue of the officers' complaints and pulled a knife, threatening first a barmaid and then a captain, who had the soldier arrested by MPs. A few weeks later, a group of thoroughly inebriated GIs made a nuisance of themselves and terrorized a female streetcar conductor in Troyes. A male conductor and an American chief warrant officer, who described the soldiers as "loud and profane," attempted to intervene, but it made no difference. The American NCO had the men arrested at the end of the line; at his court-martial, one of them said he remembered drinking that day but had no recollection of the events on the streetcar.[6]

Surveys conducted in France after the war revealed that 27 percent of the French respondents believed that Americans drank more than French did. In fact, Americans drank less. French adults, almost all of whom drank alcohol, consumed three times as much per capita (measured in pure alcohol) in the immediate postwar years as adult Americans. While almost half of Americans in the 1940s drank distilled liquor at least occasionally, around one-third did not drink alcohol at all. Only 17 percent of Americans reported that they were "regular drinkers." Beer was by far the preferred drink among American men; very few drank wine regularly, and many never drank wine at all. In one 1941 case study of drinking in a Maryland high school, 71 percent of boys reported never drinking at all. It is impossible to say whether the GIs who got in trouble in France were experienced or inexperienced drinkers, beyond the anecdotal evidence collected in courts-martial or French police records. Nevertheless, it is easy to imagine that some of the young GIs who ended up in police custody in France had little experience drinking before hitting the French bars.[7]

Few drunken-GI antics made it into police reports unless they resulted in bodily harm or property damage, which happened too often as far as the French were concerned. Many French police reports note that GIs involved in malfeasance were "taken with drink," "in a state of drunkenness," "inebriated," or "drunk." Haas-Picard, among others, was convinced that much GI misbehavior could be attributed to the effects of alcohol and suggested that limiting the sale of alcohol to GIs would help diminish "outrages." Police reports involving American paratroop units in the Yonne are full of references to drunken soldiers attacking people and committing crimes. Drunken sailors in Marseille tried to forcibly commandeer the boats of some Frenchmen who refused to take them to their ships late at night. MPs were summoned and took the sailors into custody. This was an all too common scenario: drunken Americans who threatened or hurt French citizens being taken away by MPs. One night in early June 1945, police in Laon reported that a dozen drunken

GIs broke the windows of a store, and others beat a French soldier on the street; when an agent of the Interior Ministry's Compagnies républicaines de sécurité (CRS) came to the soldier's aid, they kicked him in the groin. The next night, soused GIs beat a recently liberated French POW on the street.[8]

Drunken GIs with guns were a danger to everyone. One drunken GI discharged his rifle and put a bullet into the tire of the town's only firetruck in September 1944, at a time when replacement tires could not be had at any price. When fighting broke out among some GIs in a restaurant in Jouarre, Seine-et-Marne, one drunkard grabbed the .45-caliber pistol of another soldier (who had violated regulations by bringing the gun into the establishment) and shot the proprietress in the leg when she tried to stop the fight. At his court-martial, the private admitted he had consumed between seven and twelve drinks that evening and claimed he recalled nothing about the fight or about shooting the woman. When the owner of a café in Arcis-sur-Aube tried to throw a group of arguing GIs out of his establishment in October 1944, most left. Four, however, refused to go, and one of them shot the owner in the stomach with his rifle. An American lieutenant took the man to a military hospital, but he died soon after. In March 1945 three inebriated soldiers threatened to shoot a café proprietor in Laroche-Migennes for obscure reasons and threw some glasses around before storming out. The same GIs then invaded a nearby butcher shop and pushed past the butcher's wife to get upstairs to the living quarters. She summoned the French police, who called a nearby MP post, but the GIs had disappeared by the time the MPs showed up. It turned out the GIs had seen the butcher's daughter, wearing only a slip, in her window and wanted to introduce themselves. She was not harmed, and the MPs could not find the sociable GIs. One American soldier was killed and another wounded near Grenoble when a drunken GI opened fire on French gendarmes who were trying to question him in February 1945. Nearby Senegalese troops heard the shooting, mistook the Americans for German infiltrators, and shot them. Incidents continued after Germany surrendered. A drunken GI evicted from a dance in Auxerre in August 1945 was charged with murder after his .45 caliber pistol discharged and hit a sixty-year-old broom merchant, killing him. It was unclear whether the GI meant to shoot the Frenchman or his pistol fired accidentally, but the result was the same. In any event, it was unlawful for him to have the gun in his possession.[9]

French authorities worked with the Americans to curb excessive drinking by GIs, and when that did not work, they took unilateral measures. After a series of attacks and rapes by drunken GIs, all establishments serving alcohol in Cherbourg were placed off-limits to GIs. This policy proved ineffective because the GIs routinely entered by back doors and traded cigarettes for bottles of alcohol. The commissioner in the Aube distributed notices in 1945 reminding everyone that it was illegal to serve any alcoholic beverage except that made from wine and containing less than 18 percent alcohol (which is not very strong: cognac and Armagnac are 40 percent, and vermouth is around 16 percent). Establishments caught in violation would be closed. Considering the lack of action by American MPs, the prefect in Troyes invited mayors in the Aube in July 1945 to use their police forces more vigorously to curb incidents involving drunken GIs. The prefect cited numerous acts of violence by soldiers, including an attack on a fifty-year-old woman that sent her to the hospital and an armed assault on his own secretary, who had offended a drunken GI when she refused to walk with him. In the wake of a series of incidents in Sens (Yonne), the subprefect reached an agreement with the local American commander, Colonel Harper, that no more than 10 percent of his soldiers (about 350) would be allowed off base at one time, and MPs would escort any drunken GIs back to the base. For their part, the French ordered alcohol vendors not to serve drunken Americans and shuttered shady establishments. After the stabbing of a Frenchman by a GI, General Stuart Cutler wrote an open a letter to *Le Travailleur de l'Yonne,* apologizing for the incident and asking for French cooperation in curbing American drunkenness. He repeated General Maxwell Taylor's observation that if French civilians did not illegally sell alcohol to soldiers, the GIs would not get so drunk and commit such stupid, vicious crimes.[10]

Lecherous GIs

Young men also like to pursue women, and this gave GIs in France a bad reputation. Nicole Braux, a teenager in Nancy who eventually married a GI, had been warned by her mother to avoid American soldiers—British and Free French soldiers were all right and could be trusted, but not Americans. "To our sorrow," she wrote, "mother's warnings were true—young women often enough weren't safe among American soldiers. A number of GIs ignored their little instruction in how to behave among civilian populations. Practically every day we heard reports, and even read in newspaper accounts, about rapes, girls rescued from difficult situations, etc. This was our first disappointment. What we never feared during the German occupation now was a sad fact and difficult to accept. During the occupation, women never had concerns over sexual advances. A knitting needle now went back into my purse and beware to the soldier pressed too close!" When WAC Frances DeBra shared a tent in Valognes, Manche, with five other American women in September 1944, it was closely guarded by MPs at night; if any woman had to use the latrine during the night, she was escorted by MPs for her protection. When she was stationed in Paris, DeBra wrote to her parents that she never went out alone at night, which had not been an issue in London. She did not elaborate on the reason for her caution, but neither she nor WAC Betty Magnuson ever mentioned being scared by Frenchmen while in Paris. In March 1945 two young women in the Yonne went out on dates with two GIs, and the evening ended badly. One soldier held his date tight and tried to kiss her, even as she struggled to get away from him. When she bit and kicked him, he punched her in the mouth, threw her to the ground, and tried to rape her. She said, "OK, but not here," and led him away. She then started yelling for help, which was heard by some French workmen, who came running. The soldier fled, and the Frenchmen escorted her home. A Renseignements Généraux (RG) agent in Le Havre reported in November 1944 that women and young girls were afraid to go out on the streets after 7:00 p.m. because of the American soldiers who had recently taken up quarters in their town. Rumors abounded—evidently believed by the RG—that seven women had been killed in a two-week period and many had been raped by American soldiers. In April 1945 a GI shot dead a twenty-one-year-old French woman in Laon who refused to sleep with him.[11]

American soldiers occasioned many such complaints. In Joigny, two drunken GIs forced their attentions on two young French women, who appealed to two civilian men passing by for help. The GIs attacked the men, punching and kicking them, giving the women the opportunity to escape. French police were called, but the GIs had already fled, and they could not be identified. Sometimes other Americans stepped in when their fellow soldiers treated French women badly. When Warrant Officer Selig Kaplan told Lieutenant Dye to stop harassing a Frenchwoman in a café in Troyes in December 1944, Dye pulled rank and ordered Kaplan to mind his own business or he would be busted to private. A colonel intervened and ordered Dye to "knock it off" and leave both the woman and Kaplan alone. Kaplan's court-martial acquitted him of insubordination, suggesting that his actions to save the Frenchwoman from harassment were justified. Numerous witnesses to a fight among GIs in a bar in Jouarre testified that an inebriated soldier became angry when the barmaid, with whom he was infatuated, refused to pay attention to him. A fellow GI testified, "She didn't pay any attention to the rest of us either." The drunken soldier first pulled a knife and then waved a gun around, threatening to shoot the barmaid. When the other GIs in the bar tried to wrestle the .45-caliber gun away from him, he shot the barmaid's mother. A few days later, at another café in Troyes, an American captain intervened to stop two sergeants who were aggressively pursuing two Frenchwomen. The sergeants were accused of being loud and boorish and behaving outrageously, embarrassing the US Army. A French major testified at the court-martial of an American corporal that he had encountered the corporal and two Frenchwomen on a street in Melun one night in February 1945 and had heard one woman say in French, "I don't want to go with you." When the French officer told the corporal (in English) to leave the women alone, the corporal ignored him. The major then shoved the GI, who knocked the major to the ground and kicked him in the head several times, even though the Frenchman identified himself as an officer. At his court-martial, the corporal's commander testified, "He's the finest soldier who ever served under me." The corporal was nonetheless busted to private and lost three months' pay.[12]

Community dances—mixing alcohol, GIs, and women—offered many opportunities for GIs, drunk or not, to get into trouble. A woman in a village in the Aube complained to the prefect that inebriated GIs regularly showed up at Sunday dances, where they were rude to the local girls and picked fights with the local boys. An American Red Cross volunteer had difficulty finding Frenchwomen willing to attend a dance for soldiers of the 82nd Airborne in Epinal because French mothers refused to allow their daughters to attend unchaperoned. In September intoxicated GIs tried to force their way into a civilian dance being held to raise money for a local school in Châlons-sur-Marne. When they did not have the price of admission, the GIs tried to take tickets by force. Trouble escalated when a soldier tried to take money from the till; a fight erupted with the ticket taker, and the soldier pulled a knife. When the manager of the dance, M. Parizot, intervened, some of the GIs beat him, and one pulled a revolver. Parizot wrestled the pistol away from the GI but was knocked to the floor. When one of the GIs threatened him with a club, Parizot shot him dead. After the gendarmes and MPs arrived, Parizot was detained while the French police investigated the incident. Local prosecutors accepted his claim of self-defense and declined to indict him. The Americans opened their own investigation, but they had no power to prosecute a French citizen, regardless of their conclusions. The prosecutor pointed out in his report that a similar incident had occurred in the nearby village of Mourmelon-le-Grand in July, and relations had been tense between "certain elements of the American Army" and French civilians ever since. The public in Berre-L'Etang, near Marseille, was similarly outraged when an MP inexplicably shot and killed a French civilian at a dance the following week. The MP had been attempting to arrest a Yugoslav, when a French civilian interceded. The MP warned the Frenchman not to interfere, and Frenchman backed off, but the MP shot him anyway. The locals—including local police—were greatly shaken by the event and could not understand why the

MP had shot their countryman. At a dance in rural Sougères, in the Yonne, two GIs tried to force the band to stop playing because the music was not to their liking. When the musicians refused to stop, the GIs broke their violins, and a fight ensued. One soldier pulled out his pistol and fired into the crowd, killing one Frenchman and seriously wounding another. In late September a Frenchman who was walking a Frenchwoman home from a dance was set upon and beaten by some GIs.[13]

The American military adopted the unfortunate practice of sponsoring dances and inviting Frenchwomen to attend but excluding Frenchmen. This was not a good idea. A company of the 13th Airborne Division stationed in Joigny arranged to hold a dance at the Café des Voyageurs, starting at 7:30, but when no Frenchwomen showed up, the GIs decided to go out and recruit some. They accosted several women leaving the cinema at 8:15, causing them to flee. With no one to dance with, the GIs drank, got into fights with one another, and busted up the café, smashing glasses and windows. The US Army agreed to pay for the damages. The army continued to sponsor dances, with similar results. A dance in Migennes on 25 March degenerated into a brawl between white and black GIs; after MPs closed down the dance, both sides took to the streets with firearms. The 101st Airborne Division continued the practice, and over time, Frenchwomen warmed up to the GIs, attending their dances, going out on dates, and even celebrating a marriage between a local woman and an American soldier. The women liked listening to recordings of the latest swing music at army-sponsored dances, and besides, there was free food and drink. Young French girls learned how to jitterbug at these dances, which could not have pleased their conservative parents. A reader of *La Vie de l'Yonne* suggested that women of the area showed impaired judgement by consorting with the Americans. This view was seconded by the RG agent in Auxerre, who said, "They were not the choosiest and their reputations reflected it." He noted that many GIs promised marriage but almost none followed through, and he doubted they ever intended to.[14]

National and Race Relations

Bringing together large numbers of young, intoxicated soldiers could lead to tumultuous, even riotous, results. In early December 1944 a patriotic Frenchwomen's association in Saint Raphaël, near Cannes, sponsored an evening of entertainment for a Moroccan unit stationed there. Also in attendance were members of the FFI, civilians, and some GIs. A white GI got into an argument with a black GI, who was expelled from the hall. He soon returned with some of his black comrades armed with knives, razors, and pistols—

which were quickly put to use. A general riot ensued, pitting the Moroccans, the FFI, the white GIs, and French civilians against the black service troops. Numerous FFI and two Moroccan soldiers suffered serious knife wounds. The battle then moved outside, with both sides exchanging gunfire before the MPs and gendarmes arrived to reestablish order. One American was mortally wounded, and three others were rushed to a hospital. One Frenchwoman and a civilian man were also injured in the fracas. Just four days later, a brawl erupted between French civilians and US soldiers in the Cabaret Bagatelle in Marseille, after a drunken GI reportedly picked a fight with one of the Corsican patrons. Other Corsicans and GIs soon joined the fray. Some of the Americans produced pistols and started shooting, leaving two French civilians wounded. Such incidents repeatedly appeared in French police reports from the south: a "violent riot" between GIs and French civilians in Martigues in February with "shots fired"; a brawl between French sailors and US soldiers in Toulon in March. Meanwhile, the war still raged, and even after Germany surrendered, peace did not reign.[15]

Poor race relations among US soldiers contributed to these problems, especially when all or some of those involved had been drinking. Around 7:30 on the evening of 30 March, an army truck dropped off about a dozen white GIs at a hotel in Migennes. At the same time, around fifty black GIs who were *pris de boisson* (taken with drink) exited a nearby café. According to French police, the black GIs approached the white GIs menacingly, "looking as if they wanted [to take] the truck." After exchanging insults and threats, the white GIs retreated to the truck and drove away, firing shots as they left. The black soldiers then returned to their barracks, armed themselves, and went in search of the truck. When they failed to find it, they roamed the streets firing rifles at random, prompting shopkeepers to close their stores and civilians to get off the streets. By the time MPs arrived, all the GIs had gone back to their quarters. The police commissioner in Migennes pointed out that five days earlier, a fight had broken out between white and black GIs at a dance. After peace was restored at the dance, gunfire could be heard outside. According to French police in Frouard (north of Nancy), black and white GIs initially seemed to be getting along fine at a dance organized by the local Socialist Party in July 1945, even though everyone had been drinking. Then, a white GI insulted a black GI, and a general melee ensued. MPs and gendarmes arrived and emptied out the Salle de Fête of the Marie, but someone fired a shot outside, and the (outnumbered) white GIs disappeared. A brawl between black GIs and French civilians broke out at a gathering the next month in Longwy that left the local Communist Party secretary in the hospital.[16]

The *Maisons de Tolerance* Problem

The French were first mystified, then frustrated, and ultimately angry that SHAEF would not let GIs patronize licensed *maisons de tolerance* (brothels). This policy encouraged a thriving market for unauthorized prostitution that was difficult to police, encouraged the spread of venereal disease (VD), and abetted underground criminality. Even though brothels in Le Havre had been closed, prostitutes still plied their trade. Colonel Donald W. McGowan, the provost marshal responsible for military law in Normandy, told investigators for the inspector general that although he had followed SHAEF guidelines and closed all brothels to GIs, this policy was "not helpful." He was unwilling to criticize the policy, but he failed to endorse it when given a chance. The provost marshal for the upper Normandy base section agreed with his superior: the brothels should have been reopened and made available to US soldiers, if not for the sake of good order among the troops, then because there were insufficient CID personnel to investigate all the problems associated with the illicit sex trade. Despite such testimony, the investigators, Colonels Eddy and Turner, concluded that there was no evidence that closing the brothels increased the number of rapes committed by GIs in Normandy. It is hard to imagine what such evidence might have been, had they looked for it.[17]

Most French believed that the American policy of banning GIs from brothels deprived young men of regulated sexual outlets and encouraged them to seek satisfaction elsewhere: freelance (illegal) prostitutes and rape. The prefect in Nice, for one, complained that forbidding GIs to patronize licensed brothels on the Côte d'Azur only encouraged illicit prostitution and the spread of venereal disease. Without access to prostitutes, he suggested, GIs solicited sex from Frenchwomen who did not welcome the attention. Illegal bordellos attracted shady characters, strengthened gangsterism, offered a ready venue for black-market trading, and generally encouraged lawbreaking. Both the CID and the French police opened investigations into the goings-on at an underground brothel in Nancy after a black GI murdered a white GI there in January 1945. Commissioner Chailley-Bert approached General Patton in January 1945 and suggested that he allow his troops to visit licensed brothels; when Patton refused, the commissioner proposed to Minister Tixier that the issue be raised, yet again, with General Eisenhower.[18]

Placing brothels off-limits to GIs failed to keep them out of these establishments. Drunken GIs seeking prostitutes were hard to deter, especially if they were armed, which they often were. An American major refused to quit a brothel in November 1944 when ordered to do so first by an MP sergeant and then by a captain. In March 1945 French police investigating a commotion at a brothel in Joigny discovered twelve GIs inside, one of them waving a pistol around. Among these GIs were two MPs, one of whom was busy with a prostitute upstairs. The police noted that MPs had raided the house just the day before, rounding up a crowd of GIs who were not supposed to be there. Even though it was a licensed establishment, the police recommended that it be closed. Five GIs dressed as MPs tried to gain entrance to a bordello in Joigny, but they did not fool anyone. When hook did not work, the soldiers resorted to crook: they broke down the locked door and rushed upstairs, looking for women. The owner responded by firing his pistol into the ceiling, which inspired the GIs to draw their own weapons but also convinced them to leave, shooting at the house as they left. The proprietor returned fire.[19]

Unregistered bordellos in particular tended to attract trouble, such as the house of registered prostitute Blanche Malleck, which did a lively business with GIs in the Meurthe-et-Moselle. She also hosted card games that mixed GIs with French civilians of both sexes. When one private insisted that he had not gotten his money's worth from an encounter with a prostitute in Malleck's house, he took jewelry and cosmetics as compensation. He later returned to the house drunk, armed with a pistol, and demanded his money back. When he brandished his gun and punched two women, other GIs playing cards intervened. A Frenchman flagged down some MPs, who took custody of the miscreant. The private was sentenced to four months of hard labor in a stockade. Illegal streetwalkers and clandestine brothels servicing American soldiers occasioned many complaints from the citizenry of Marseille. Women complained that GIs aggressively solicited them on the streets, and drunken GIs in search of prostitutes often caused trouble at night. Soldiers "queued up" outside one bordello caused a commotion on the street; unlicensed streetwalkers waited in packs at the exit of bases housing black service troops, disturbing peaceable citizens. Because MPs were not authorized to arrest illegal prostitutes, they asked the police in Nancy to crack down on the illicit sex trade. The police agreed to make sweeps of bars, cafés, and hotels where unregistered prostitutes were known to congregate and have them examined by physicians. They also promised to step up medical exams for legal prostitutes to help check the spread of VD among American soldiers. MPs and French police agreed to cooperate in surveying hotels in Nancy, and those establishments with shady reputations were subjected to joint patrols. MPs agreed to detain any GIs found there, and the French agreed to hold any prostitutes found doing business with GIs.[20]

The French response to GIs cut off from sex ranged from annoyance to indulgence. An inspector with the Department of Forestry in Troyes wrote a letter to the prefect of the Aube in June 1945:

> Last night an American soldier, white and taken with drink, forced his way into my house and demanded "women," confusing our house with that next door *maison de tolerance* frequented by American soldiers. He tried to punch me and tried to force the door of two female renters in my house, a woman and her young daughter. MPs were summoned and he was taken away. I do not want to press charges. I am a veteran of WWI and served with Americans in Argonne and Saint Mihel and know what it is to be a young soldier. I sympathize with them and am not deeply irritated by this misadventure. Nevertheless, I think the Americans should be reminded that French people should be treated with respect. That if a foreign army came to their country and molested their daughters, wives, and sisters, they would oppose it vigorously. A house next to a *maison de tolerance* is not itself a *maison de tolerance.* I have to double lock myself in at 7 p.m. I would move but no other apartment is available in Troyes.

Another resident complained to the prefect:

> I have to protest against an intolerable situation. There are two prostitutes who live on our court. It was bad enough under the German occupation, when lines of Germans would wait for their turn, but it is even worse now. We have crowds of black American soldiers who urinate in the court and in our hallways, they enter into our apartments and look in our windows and bother all the young women. One exhibited himself in our court. I have a store and women cannot come here anymore. . . . I am deprived of all my rights. MPs could put all this right.

Days later, the prefect requested that the mayor of Troyes place the street off-limits to all US military personnel and that MPs enforce the closure.[21]

A curé in the Bouches-du-Rhône wrote to Commissioner Paul Haag in June 1945:

> Twelve days ago, a convent in my parish was assaulted in the middle of the night by fifteen white American soldiers who left only when the alarm bell was rung. We complained to the MPs but have heard nothing from them about it. Three nights ago three soldiers knocked on the doors for a long time. The same night shots were fired near the train station and a man was wounded. Why do we have to rely on foreign authorities to address problems in France? Why do not French authorities do something? We even have French aviators and colonial troops stationed here. We have the right to expect protection, security, and

> order. The population here lives in constant anxiety; women and children are afraid to go on the streets. Isolated farms are very exposed to danger. Women of bad character come here from Marseille to infest the areas around the American camp and even around the convent. We talk of self-defense.[22]

The commissioner wanted to know from the head of police in Marseille why he could not take back the streets.[23]

Rape by GIs

The French people were riled by robbery and murder, but they were particularly incensed when GIs committed rape. Their anger was intensified by the US Army's failure to apprehend and punish the perpetrators. The first reported rape occurred on 14 June 1944 on a farm close to Sainte-Mère-Eglise, where two Polish sisters were raped by four black service soldiers. Six days later, the wife of the mayor of Carentan reported that she had been raped by a black soldier. The first reports of rape in Cherbourg were received by Civil Affairs on 28 July—more than a month after the city surrendered—when gendarmes reported three rapes by black soldiers in nearby villages. Civil Affairs passed the report on to the OPM. However, until lines of communications were established—something that did not happen until many weeks after Cherbourg was liberated—CID could not investigate the accusations. Technical Sergeant Albert Small of CID complained that by the time he heard of the earliest cases, it was much too late to pursue them.[24]

There is no way to know what percentage of rapes were reported to the French police. The inspector general concluded, "It is probably true that some rape cases are not being reported to the police authorities because of the shame suffered by the victim and her family by the publicity." Subprefect Leviandier in Cherbourg believed there were many such cases in which the victim or her family was too ashamed to report a rape. Sergeant Small reported, "Several cases have been withdrawn because of the adverse publicity a rape will bring upon the family in the community." One French rape victim told Small to drop her complaint because if her common-law husband of twenty years found out about it, he would beat her; the CID did not pursue the case. In all cases, women filing complaints were interviewed by male police officers. A seventeen-year-old woman in Nancy was interviewed about her rape three times in as many days by three different police officers. After the third interview, she withdrew her complaint, claiming she had willingly had sex with four soldiers in a thick forest outside Nancy in the middle of the night and then walked the many miles back home early the next morning. She said she had invented the rape story because she feared her mother would disapprove of her having sex with GIs. Her original claim of abduction was more believable but problematic, which was why she had been interviewed three times. Because most rapes occurred in the countryside, where many people knew their neighbors' business, verifiable violent crimes occasionally came to light despite the victims' ambivalence. A French police official told the provost marshal that although families often did not want to report rapes, CID investigators sometimes followed up on statements from third parties and tried to learn what had happened. In a case of attempted rape in Nancy in April 1945, MPs caught the culprit, but the victim got away. Some Frenchmen intervened and held the would-be rapist for MPs, but the woman being accosted ran away, and no one knew who she was. With no one to make a formal complaint, the case against the GI was dropped. Sometimes the American response was phlegmatic, provoking anger among the French. A young Frenchwoman went directly to MPs after being raped by two black soldiers in Saint-Jean-de-Vignes, Soane-et-Loire, but they "refused to trouble themselves" with her. By the time she contacted French police, the culprits were long gone, and she was unable to identify them. News of this incident made it all the way to Raymond Hass-Picard at the Interior Ministry in Paris, who demanded that the US Army discipline the MPs involved.[25]

Lieutenant Colonel Edwin Lee Clarke, provost marshal for General George Patton's Third Army, alleged that rapes were almost always committed during rapid advances and that when troops were stationary, incidents of rape dropped to almost nothing. During the winter in Lorraine, there were almost no rapes. Once the offensive reached Germany, rapes occurred in record numbers. It is difficult to judge the accuracy of Clarke's statement, given the reporting problems already discussed; however, gendarme reports in the Yonne, Aube, and Meurthe-et-Moselle do not back up the provost marshal's assertion. According to the French, most rapes were committed behind the lines and in isolated settings. All the rapes around Cherbourg in the summer and fall of 1944 occurred on isolated farms in the countryside, and this may have been related to alcohol.[26]

Because the sale of alcohol was easier to control in towns, where there was a heavy police presence—both French police and MPs—soldiers often visited farms in the countryside, looking for drink. It was not illegal for farmers to sell them alcohol, even though the US Army forbade GIs to buy it. The prefect also banned the sale of alcohol to Americans, but many farmers sold it anyway because they were afraid *not* to. The head of the gendarmerie in Cherbourg, Captain Robert Bouluc, argued it was the US Army's responsibility to keep soldiers from demanding alcohol from farmers. On 5 November an eighteen-year-old girl was home alone at her farm in Fourcarville—near Utah Beach—when a black soldier came to the house asking to buy alcohol. She refused, and he left, but when she went outside to get some coal, he was still there and demanded alcohol again. Alarmed, she started to run, but he caught her, knocked her down, and hit her on the head with his helmet, which rendered her unconscious. He tried to rape her but was scared off when a car drove by. A man and woman in Touqueville were roused at 2:30 a.m. by three black soldiers demanding cognac. When the husband refused, they went away, only to return shortly thereafter and demand water. One of the soldiers pointed a rifle at the man, so his wife got up to get the water. The husband then struck the soldier, and the GIs dragged him outside and held him; they also dragged the wife outside, and all three men raped her. In another case, an eighteen-year-old woman was raped eighteen times by black soldiers, and her father was murdered. After two young girls were raped and the priest who had tried to protect them was murdered, the French commander of the military district that included Normandy, General Legentilhomme, wrote to War Minister André Diethelm in October 1944. He told the minister that Norman women were afraid to go out into their fields alone, and even the presence of a man did not protect them. The Normans, he wrote, were starting to not only fear but also hate Americans soldiers because of the murders and rapes they committed. In the Seine-Inférieure, a woman had been raped and killed after her husband was murdered. He continued, "Many times I have been astonished to hear people say, 'Germans, at least, were correct.'" During the German occupation, only two Germans were convicted of rape in Normandy, and both were publicly hanged. The general echoed a common opinion when he wrote that the Americans had erred in placing brothels off-limits to troops, and if they refused to bring in American women to meet the needs of their men, they should at least protect Frenchwomen. He demanded that US commanders take responsibility for their troops, and if they did not, Frenchmen would take up not only pitchforks but also rifles against the Americans.[27]

The French were convinced that black GIs were responsible for all rapes. Gendarme commander Bouluc insisted that all the rapes in his jurisdiction were committed by "colored soldiers." He testified that black servicemen committed the thirty-five rapes reported in September and the ten in October 1944. He argued, "The colored are more easily affected by alcohol—they have lower tolerance. They also get very noisy when drunk, which is no good.. . . I see all reports of rape in the Manche and I send them all to CA. I receive no information [back] about these cases." Yon Baniul, editor of *La Presse* of Cherbourg, asserted, "The colored men enter the houses, see the women, and want to rape them. They will kill the father or man of the house and then rape the women. It happens every day." The population of Marseille became very agitated after black soldiers in a jeep snatched a young girl off the street and tried to rape her. She was saved by the intervention of a French officer. Afterward, rumors circulated that 90 to 95 percent of black GIs suffered from second-degree syphilis, which they were passing to Frenchwomen. Even though Baniul, the subprefect, gendarme captain Dufossey, and General Legentilhomme insisted that *all* rapes had been committed by black GIs, information provided by the Americans showed otherwise. The issue attracted a good deal of interest from the US Army. Third Army Provost Marshal Clarke testified that two-thirds of rapes were committed by black GIs. A memo on the incidence of criminal behavior by black GIs presented to General Benjamin O. Davis, the highest ranking black officer in the US Army at the time, pointed out that of 152 rapes investigated by the CID in France in the summer of 1944, 14 of the accused were white. Of 43 rapes reported to the CID in Normandy from the beginning of September to mid-November, 35 were assumed to have been committed by black soldiers, as were 50 of 54 attempted rapes. In the Mediterranean theater of operations, black soldiers accounted for about 10 percent of all American troops (79,000 of 743,000) but 56 percent (15 of 27) of rape and sexual assault convictions from November 1942 to September 1944.[28]

Criminally Violent GIs

French sentiments were further inflamed by violent crimes committed by GIs against French citizens. A spate of attacks in the Cotentin Peninsula set much of the population on edge in the fall of 1944, especially after a young husband and wife, aged twenty-one and twenty-four, were murdered by soldiers near Barnville in mid-October. In November 1944 four GIs tried to break into a closed café in Garches, a suburb of Paris, and when that failed, they attacked a mother and daughter with knives and clubs, injuring both and tearing the daughter's clothing. A GI attacked two women in separate incidents in Nancy in March 1945, stabbing one woman in the right shoulder and the other in the chest after they resisted his advances. Both women were taken to hospitals and survived; the police had no suspect. Brutal attacks on French citizens were bad, but murder was worse, and it often occurred for trivial or unknown motives. Two Indochinese workers were killed by two unknown US soldiers in Marseille in February 1945. Four months later, two GIs searching for a particular prostitute in Laon shot and killed a thirty-eight-year-old mechanic for no apparent reason. They were arrested by gendarmes and turned over to MPs. The same week, three black American soldiers in Martigues stabbed a French soldier in the back and tried to rape his fiancée. The same soldiers later attacked an electric company collector and stole his satchel after shooting him in the back; he died at the hospital. When Fernand Cartier offered a ride to two GIs near Roissy, outside of Paris, on 9 February 1945, they forcibly took his luggage, shot him in the head, and stole his car; he survived. They then embarked on a crime spree—robbing a farmworker and a road-crew boss—that ended when they were apprehended by French police in Choisy-au-Boeuf and turned over to MPs in Meaux. They were in possession of 16,279 francs they had taken from various victims. Police in Versailles reported that two GIs robbed the Café de la Post on 22 February and made off with 12,000 francs, escaping by car.[29]

Criminality: France versus the United States

There is little doubt that crime rates in the United States were higher than in France in the 1930s. France, with a population of approximately 42 million, averaged 482 homicides per year during the mid to late 1930s, or 11.5 homicides per million population. During the same period, the United States, with a population of about 130 million, averaged 10,022 homicides per year, or 77 homicides per million population. It is difficult not to be struck by the vast difference: the murder rate in the United States was almost seven times higher than the rate in France. Rape statistics were similar: in 1938 France had 181 convictions for rape, or 2.3 rape convictions per million population; in 1936–1938 the United States averaged 1,815 rape convictions per year, or about 14 per million population—six times the conviction rate in France. Even allowing for the roughness of these comparisons, it is clear that levels of violence in the United States in the 1930s far exceeded those in France. When this level of criminality came to France with the US Army, the French were shocked and reacted negatively. Civilians who were used to a fairly quiet and secure existence were unhappy about the tumult and violence the Americans brought into their midst.[30]

In view of French complaints about the Americans' phlegmatic response to the crime wave unleashed by GIs, it is notable that the 729 investigations opened by the CID in Normandy in the fall of 1944 resulted in only 155 courts-martial. How many of these trials ended in conviction is another matter, but that 80 percent of the investigations went nowhere supports French contentions that the OPM was never serious about pursuing miscreant GIs.

Inferences about the low incidence of crime among the French are sup-

Table 8.1 Cases Investigated by CID of Normandy Base Section, August–December 1944

Crime	Aug.	Sept.	Oct.	Nov.	Dec.	Total
Major crime	10	21	18	12	12	73
Assault	18	54	24	13	12	121
Robbery/burglary	2	4	4	3	10	23
Minor crime	15	35	15	12	16	93
Rape	21	27	15	9	8	80
Murder	1	1	5	0	2	9
Attempted rape	12	23	16	16	3	70
Aggravated assault	13	9	19	10	9	60
Aggravated theft	8	27	70	63	32	200
Courts-martial	—	22	43	49	41	155

Source: Report on Normandy Base Section, NARA, RG 498, HQ ETO, Provost Marshal, box 4340.

Note: These numbers were taken from a bar chart and are approximate.

ported by crime statistics collected by French police in the Meurthe-et-Moselle. Most crimes committed in the department while the war still raged in March 1945—although the fighting was moving further into Germany and away from France—involved theft and black-market sales. A Polish man and some accomplices were arrested for illegally transporting three tons of potatoes; twelve people were arrested for stealing cloth from a train station, two for stealing gasoline, and thirty-seven for unspecified misdemeanor thefts. Forty-nine people were given citations (but not arrested) for illegal solicitation of prostitutes on public roads. In March 1945, 110 people—presumably women—were detained but not arrested in the campaign to suppress illegal prostitution; fifty women were forcibly hospitalized for showing symptoms of VD. Things quieted down after the war, but black-market activity

Table 8.2 Felony Charges Filed against French in Meurthe-et-Moselle, 1945

Crime	Number
Murder	5
Premeditated murder	2
Voluntary homicide	4
Rape	6 (I was a foreigner)
Intelligence with the enemy	15
Arson	3
Burglary	3*
Counterfeiting	1
Complicity in theft	2*

Source: Resumé of arrests for all 1945, Archives départementales de la Meurthe-et-Moselle, WM 358.

*Thefts without violence were treated as misdemeanors in France; these crimes must have involved violence.

still ranked high among infractions. In January 1946 police in Meurthe-et-Moselle looked into 390 reported incidents, detained 147 people, and made 38 arrests, including one for murder. Three French soldiers and nine civilians were arrested for pillaging supplies from trains; two people were arrested for performing illegal abortions, two for selling goods at black-market prices, and six for illegal possession of rationed goods. Echoes of the war continued to reverberate: two were arrested for placing explosive charges—a common form of revenge against accused collaborators—and one for informing to the Germans. One was arrested for stealing an automobile, one for stealing a tire, and another for stealing a bike.[31]

In January 1946 police in Pont-à-Mousson made one arrest for criminal activity (unspecified) and detained five people at the request of the prosecutor's office. In February 1946 most arrests in the Meurthe-et-Moselle were for infractions of the rationing law and for dealing in black-market goods. One man was arrested for possessing 9,500 packs of foreign cigarettes. Police in Nancy broke up a ring of twenty-three people who sold 6,000 liters of wine illegally shipped in from the Var (in the south of France). Otherwise, two people were arrested for providing abortions, three for armed robbery, one for breaking and entering, and seven for breaking out of prison. This would have been a pretty quiet month in many American counties with a comparable population (529,000).[32]

Crime statistics for Troyes were similar, except that Troyes was even less exciting than the Meurthe-et-Moselle. French police made twenty-two civilian arrests in the last quarter of 1945, including ten arrests for burglary and three for black-market dealing in American goods; several women—one Polish—were arrested for theft. Police summaries for 1946 were even less eventful: in the first week of March, police made two arrests for drunkenness and two for fighting; two other people were picked up for trafficking in American goods. April was similar: six arrests, two for public drunkenness. Police who had been kept pretty busy while GIs were stationed in the Aube passed some very quiet weeks after they left. Many weeks passed in spring 1946 with nothing at all to report.[33]

In fact, most infractions by American soldiers were not violent offenses against French citizens but more prosaic wrongdoings, such as being AWOL, using government vehicles without authorization, or trading currencies on the black market. Most GI crimes handled by provost marshals were low-level offenses that resembled the types of crime routinely handled by French justice during peacetime. When GIs flooded into Paris after VE Day, JAG conducted dozens of summary trials for minor offenses every day, with around 2,000 trials held in July alone. There were so many AWOL offenses, and JAG was so short of personnel, that many offenders were simply sent back to their units for discipline. In June 1945 JAG's Seine section (Paris) tried six officers ranking from lieutenant to lieutenant colonel for dealing in currency on the black market. The first trial of a WAC was held in Paris; she was accused of being AWOL for two months. In October crowds of GIs showed up in Paris on three-day leaves from Germany with big wads of cash they wanted to send back to the United States via money orders. They all claimed it was gambling winnings, but JAG believed it was actually profits from selling cigarettes, looted watches, and other booty stolen from Germans. An air force captain was tried for attempting to sell diamonds and gold of suspicious origin on the Parisian black market. These were not the sort of offenses that overly troubled the French.[34]

After VE Day: Behavior Deteriorates

After Germany surrendered and France was again flooded with hundreds of thousands of GIs, their bad behavior increased. In June 1945 a brawl erupted between British soldiers and black GIs at a public dance hosted by the town of Port-de-Bouc. An argument between a Yugoslav and a GI turned into a fight; other Yugoslavs and some British soldiers joined to battle the Americans until MPs restored order. MPs blamed the violence on the Yugoslavs and took two of them away. In July a riot broke out at 10:00 p.m. in a bar in the old harbor district of Marseille packed with French civilians and black GIs. A drunken French sailor and one of the GIs got into a heated argument that quickly escalated; blows were exchanged, and pistols were drawn. Others joined the fracas, which eventually became a riotous tumult involving as many as 300 people. Shots were fired inside the bar and out on the street, but somehow, only two people were injured. Newspapers reported that it took MPs and French police an hour to restore order. As the Seine-et-Oise was overrun in the summer of 1945 by US troops transiting out of Europe, there were so many incidents that the prefect did not bother to enumerate them in his report to the interior minister; he simply noted that there were daily incidents and frequent brawls between French soldiers and GIs stationed at the air base in Etampes. French police closed all establishments that served alcohol in Suippes after a December 1945 melee between American soldiers and French civilians left one Frenchman dead and several badly injured. The prefect called on a unit of the CRS to help maintain peace in the small town. By the summer of 1945, the French were used to reading newspaper accounts of brawls involving GIs, so it is not surprising that they believed a story about a GI riot in Rouen that appeared in *Le Libre Soir* in August. The RG, however, called the Interior Ministry to correct the story: there had been no riot, only a street fight between a GI and a French civilian, who was not badly injured. This was the only report I found in which RG agents alerted Paris that things were really not so bad.[35]

After VE Day there was a noticeable uptick in GI attacks on French police. These incidents, which had been uncommon before May 1945, were particularly worrisome. It is possible that GIs' respect for French authority declined after the surrender of Germany because American soldiers in Germany were used to acting with impunity and deferred to no civil authority. French police reports before May 1945 revealed only scattered confrontations between GIs and French police. A municipal policeman in Laroche-Migennes was punched in the eye by an American soldier for no apparent reason in March. Also in March, a drunken and out-of-control GI in Neuves-Maisons, near Nancy, took on a group of French policemen trying to arrest him and had to be subdued by a gendarme's baton. GIs in Laon set upon and kicked a CRS officer on the street; the next day, GIs fought with CRS officers who prevented the Americans from entering a reception for returning

French POWs in Laon. The assistant commander of the police in Longwy punched a GI and threatened another with a pistol after the GIs attacked the policeman's son in the courtyard of police headquarters. MPs later arrested the policeman. The same day, MPs arrested another French police officer who had fought with a GI harassing civilians in a public square. This not only greatly alarmed French authorities but also changed the thinking of many French people, who had previously believed that only a few bad apples were responsible for the trouble. A police commissioner in Auxerre who had lost two teeth after being punched by a GI in November wrote in his report, "It should not stand that an American soldier punches a French police officer and I demand justice be done." If MPs prevented French police from protecting the civilian population from those bad apples, then the thugs and rogues had won. That prospect truly shocked the French populace and authorities alike. In early June police in Cannes reported that an American officer had been involved in a fight with French police. Several GIs got into fistfights with French police at a dance in Sauilly, near Verdun, in July. When other GIs joined in to support their comrades, a police commander pulled his pistol and was stabbed in the back. The policeman was taken away in an ambulance, and French authorities were irate; they wanted the GIs charged with attempted murder. French police and GIs exchanged gunfire in Maubeuge in November, slightly wounding two civilians. As bad as the robberies, beatings, intimidation, and harassment were, perhaps the greatest irritant to Franco-US military relations was not drunken, brawling GIs but MPs, who repeatedly intervened against French authorities to rescue GIs from justice.[36]

After Germany's surrender, reports also revealed more attacks on GIs by French civilians. This may have been connected to the increase in GI assaults on French police, as French civilians increasingly believed that if the French authorities could not protect themselves from marauding American soldiers, they surely could not protect civilians. Whatever the motive, French civilians more often resorted to arms to protect themselves. One resident of Troyes was attacked on the street by an American soldier without provocation and witnessed the same soldier punch a woman a few moments later; he reported the incidents to the French police, who told him there was nothing they could do. MPs, called to the police station, asked him to identify the soldier, which he was unable to do. The MPs also told him they could do nothing. Frustrated by this lack of response, the man wrote to the prefect, "In future I am going to go out armed and if attacked, shoot him like a dog. I am warning you, M. Prefect, that if the peaceful citizens of Troyes cannot be protected, we will protect ourselves." Only days later, Minister Tixier was informed that the citizens of Auxerre had mounted civil patrols to protect themselves. Groups of five men armed with *nerfs de boeuf* (hardened strips of cowhide used as weapons) and clubs took to patrolling the streets at night. After a string of attacks on Frenchmen and -women in Le Havre in June 1945, civilians organized patrols because they no longer believed the French police could or would protect them and their families. French authorities feared that clashes between Frenchmen and GIs could have grave repercussions. Indeed, on 2 August a crowd of French in Auxerre chased after GIs in a jeep who had attempted to drag a ten-year-old boy into the vehicle. The commissioner shuddered at the thought of what would have happened if the GIs had abducted the boy or if the crowd had caught up to the jeep. Days later, municipal police in Auxerre broke up a crowd that was threatening four GIs, yelling about all the recent aggression against French citizens. The police did not know whether these particular GIs had done anything to merit such attention, but the people of Auxerre were extremely upset about the recent abduction and rape of two young girls. French police discovered two GIs, battered by civilian parties unknown, in Auxerre the following week. When an American soldier savagely beat the madam of a bordello in Aix, only police intervention prevented a French mob from lynching him. MPs confiscated the pistol of a farmer in Crusnes-Village, Meurthe-et-Moselle, after he shot an inebriated GI who had invaded his house demanding cognac and women. French police intervened in another case, allowing a man in Beuvielle, who had shot at GIs attacking his neighbor's house, to keep his shotgun for self-defense. Police said he was probably going to need it. Even Provost Marshal Donald W. McGowan in Normandy had asserted in November 1944 that if SHAEF kept brothels off-limits to GIs, the ban on civilian weapons in Normandy should be dropped so that the French could protect themselves![37]

Serious incidents involving GIs seemed to occur in clusters, both geographically and chronologically. Divers elements caused outbreaks of bad behavior, and sometimes these elements combined to aggravate a volatile situation: a new unit moved into an area where MPs were not posted nearby, or a weak commander allowed bad elements to set the standard of comportment in his unit. Sometimes ethnic or racial tensions spilled out of the barracks and onto French streets. All these factors played a part in an incident in December 1945 involving American, Polish, and French attendees of a dance in Mailly. The gathering descended into a free-for-all after a drunken American lieutenant picked a fight—according to the gendarme who witnessed it—with some Polish soldiers. Four more GIs joined the fray before it was broken up by an American officer, who escorted the GIs out the door. More trouble ensued when a gendarme stopped a local prostitute from entering the dance hall; some of the Americans inside objected and attacked the gendarme. French civilians in attendance took offense at GIs assaulting a French policeman and joined the fracas to defend him. When the dance broke up shortly thereafter, the four GIs evicted earlier returned, armed with pistols, and followed the gendarmes in a small truck until the police left the road. Reports trickled in the next day that the GIs were plotting an attack on the gendarmes. When the commander of the gendarmes heard that armed US soldiers were looking for his men, he ordered them to return to their barracks and remain armed and vigilant, but not to confront the soldiers. MPs stationed thirty miles away in Châlons-sur-Marne were summoned, but until they arrived, the GIs cruised around Mailly in cars, shooting at random, threatening people, and breaking windows. They shot out the tires of the town's bus and cut electrical and telephone lines.[38]

Policing in this region of the Aube was left entirely to French police and Polish MPs; American MPs had been withdrawn from the region, which French police blamed for the recent deterioration of GI civility. The chief of the gendarme section in Mailly emphasized that relations between the American soldiers and the population of Mailly had been excellent until that time. Colonel H. McE. Pendleton, head of Civil Affairs in the region until May 1945, also told the prefect in Troyes that excellent relations had existed between US forces and the locals, who were "entirely friendly and hospitable to the extreme." The gendarme chief asserted that relations had degraded as US troops left and were replaced by new units unfamiliar with the area and its population. However, he guessed that the arrest of two very bad American troublemakers, who had exerted a malevolent influence on other soldiers, would help restore calm. No more trouble was reported at dances; however, the gendarme chief had recommended that all dances be canceled, so that might explain the calm. This episode in Mailly featured drink, the pursuit of Frenchwomen, bad actors, ethnic rivalries, and a lack of American MPs to enforce the law. Poor leadership and lax discipline can probably be added to the mix. One must wonder where the American officers were while GIs were marauding around Mailly in US Army vehicles. Such a combination, no doubt, was seen often enough around France in 1945 without causing serious incidents, but this case illustrates that a small number of "bad characters" could lead others into trouble.[39]

Sometimes a "bad apple" really was the main problem: A police inspector in Paris reported that one of his men shot and wounded an American "soldier well known to the people of the quarter as a violent troublemaker" who led a band of deserters and was always armed with a pistol. The French policeman shot him while attempting to arrest him, but he got away. Removing him from the scene would have solved a big headache for the French police.[40]

The inspector general's report on lawlessness in Normandy concluded:

> The facts speak for themselves as to the lawlessness of American soldiers in Normandy. It is a disgrace to the American Army. This record of crime stands without justification, and no excuses can be made, nevertheless, there are certain factors that have definitely contributed to their high incidence: Intoxicants; weapons in the hands of troops, not required for defense against the enemy; the loss of command control inherent in operations over greatly lengthened supply lines; male sex desires spurred by alcohol and undeterred by a sense of moral restraint. There can be no overemphasis on the importance of stiffening command control, moving swiftly to apprehend the criminal and taking punitive action against the guilty . . . that lawless acts committed by American soldiers against civilians in the Normandy area justify the fear [of] the French people and the concern of their civil and military officials, and reflect discredit to the United States Army.[41]

Although the inspector general's report was issued in November 1944, its conclusions apply to the entire period of the US military presence in France: June 1944 to January 1946. Leadership at the top made a difference in the behavior of the troops: when misbehavior was tolerated, it occurred; when discipline was imposed, bad behavior mostly disappeared. A few out-of-control soldiers could and did affect the comportment of others. Removing problem GIs went a long way toward imposing discipline on the rest. MPs also made a difference, but if MP patrols were purely decorative, they had little impact on GI criminality. Increasing the number of MP patrols and conducting joint patrols with French police went a long way toward reducing civilian complaints. Serious policing, oversight by senior commanders, and removing bad actors from the ranks quickly encouraged better behavior by the remaining troops and kept relations with civilians cordial. It was always preferable for American commanders to take steps to reduce incidents of bad behavior rather than forcing the French to take matters into their own hands. By the time the French had to close cafés, declare them off-limits to GIs, or set up armed civilian patrols, the situation had already degraded too far to maintain good relations.

The prefect in Laon reported in October 1945, "Relations with the civilian population are much better now thanks to good working relations between MPs and gendarmes. Before in Laon there were daily fights, break-ins, and breaking of fences. Now, calm has been restored." And the commissioner from Rouen reported, "On the whole, relations between the civilian population and American troops have improved, except in the region of Rouen, where incidents continue to occur. Abuses by Americans at d'Alizay continue. A joint post by MPs and French police has been posted at the most dangerous intersection in Alisay [*sic*]. Thefts from farmers in Igoville and Alizay have diminished. Intervention by American and French authorities has improved relations between troops and civilians."[42]

There is little doubt that the number of incidents involving French police increased after Germany surrendered. Germany's defeat removed a lot of incentive for the French people to put up with the various inconveniences imposed on them by the large American military presence. The French had endured much to win the war. Once it was won, there was little reason for them to tolerate all the burdens of what felt like an American military occupation. Uncontrolled drunkenness and criminality wore out the welcome that many French had extended to their liberators.

The problem of out-of-control GIs existed everywhere GIs were found in France. The response by the American officers responsible for their behavior varied from unit to unit. In many cases, it is hard not to conclude that these officers shirked their duty and failed to intervene when they should have. I have found no case in which the official French reaction was unjustified. Everyone, including the French people, expected some misbehavior by GIs, but many were unprepared for the amount of objectionable conduct and the failure to curb it. Drunkenness was one thing, but assault, vandalism, theft, rape, and murder shocked the French and provoked outrage. Large-scale R&R sites, such as Nice and Paris, were heavily policed by both American and French authorities because GIs who came directly from battle zones were expected to "unwind," perhaps to excess. Yet the lack of police reports and the lack of outrage among prefects suggest that the pervasive police presence in these areas kept the GIs' behavior within permissible bounds. When MPs became scarce, especially in late 1945, and American policing almost disappeared, the results were disastrous: French complaints about GIs abounded. GIs could be controlled by competent policing and leadership, but when both were lacking, problems flourished.

9

The 101st Airborne Division in France

The Failure of US Army Justice

American troops stationed in France often brought Stateside levels of violence with them, to the chagrin of the French forced to endure it, but the airborne divisions that helped liberate France in 1944 raised the tumult to shocking levels that eroded much of the goodwill born of the liberation. More important, the failure of the 101st Airborne Division (ABD) to render justice to aggrieved French produced outrage beyond that caused by the misdeeds of the few. As US Army units were repositioned in France for eventual transfer overseas, General Maxwell Taylor's 101st ABD began to arrive in the Yonne on 3 August. French police reported that drunken GIs attacked gendarmes in Seignelay and broke shop windows; others attacked a young woman in Sens and stole her purse; soused paratroopers in the train station in Sens engaged in fistfights with one another, broke windows, and damaged doors; GIs raped two young girls in Poinchy. Over the next three days, as more units of the 101st poured into their accommodations in Auxerre, they beat up a number of French civilians and robbed them of money, jewelry, and wristwatches; tried to make off with a young boy in a jeep; broke into a house, attacked its residents, and stole some items; tried to break into several other houses, causing damages in the process; threatened a young woman with a pistol; attempted to steal several automobiles; beat a French soldier, attacked a French policeman, and engaged in fistfights with one another in a barracks; provoked a general brawl between Frenchmen and paratroopers; and raped the widow of a *résistant* who had been murdered by the Gestapo and stole 500 francs from her fiancé. All this occurred in Auxerre alone; there were other incidents in Sens, Migennes, and Tonnerre.[1]

Prefect Paul Gibaud was out of the department during this initial mayhem, and General Taylor had not yet arrived. Moreover, French police had not yet established contact with MPs for the 101st, so there was a dearth of leadership and authority during this crucial transition period. Newspaper reaction to the havoc wrought by the 101st was strongly negative, boosting a wave of latent anti-Americanism that needed little encouragement. If the chaos unleashed by the men of the 101st was not bad enough, the reaction of its leadership, including the Office of the Provost Marshal, made the situation worse. The American leaders refused to take responsibility and provide the leadership necessary to rein in the out-of-control paratroopers.

Police in the Yonne had anticipated trouble because men from the departing 13th ABD had warned the French that the 101st was made up of daredevils and parolees from prison. Thus, the population awaited their arrival with dread, and once the paratroopers got there, they lived up to their reputation. An initial Renseignements Généraux report noted, "They have behaved badly, often drunk, they accost women in the streets, and steal their silver and jewelry, and have raped women and even children." Police called to a cinema in Sens on 4 August to quiet a horde of GIs and to enforce the theater's no-smoking rule could neither gain the GIs' cooperation nor impose order. The theater owner threatened to bar all GIs in the future. Relations with French police got off to a bad start in Auxerre on the night of 6 August when four officers came across three sisters "well known to the police" drinking in a bar with a large number of paratroopers. The police attempted to escort the women out of the bar, but about ten GIs objected. One American threw a glass at an officer, and a police inspector was knocked to the floor and surrounded by threatening GIs. The Didier sisters then intervened and convinced the soldiers to back off and allow the police to leave, which they did after extracting a promise from the sisters to present themselves at police headquarters the next day. When Commissioner Jean Mairey drove from Dijon to meet with General Taylor and his staff as a courtesy, his vehicle nearly collided with an army truck upon entering Auxerre, and he was pretty upset about it when he met with Taylor. Mairey was not alone. The prefect's chief of cabinet left work to meet his fiancée and found her being accosted on the street by some GIs who were trying to pick her up, so the 101st got off to a bad start with French officialdom as well. When Prefect Gibaud returned to Auxerre, police presented him with a list of twenty-seven incidents provoked by the Americans since their arrival in August. They had had a busy few days.[2]

Local newspapers reported all the mayhem occurring in the Yonne and commented unfavorably. *L'Yonne Républicaine* ran an article titled "Certain Regrettable Incidents" that enumerated some of the outrages. It applauded one young woman—identified in a police report as an eighteen-year-old who had been riding her bicycle along the river—who had fought back against her attackers. They threw her into the river and stole her bike. In other incidents, pistol-wielding GIs had invaded people's apartments or forced people out of their cars, which they then stole. General Taylor wrote a letter in response to the article, assuring readers that these incidents had been perpetrated by a small number of bad actors, and everything possible was being done to cooperate with French police to apprehend the offenders and bring them to justice. Taylor, who spoke French, then called on all officials in the town to mend relations. He ordered a report from his divisional inspector general (IG) and provost marshal (PM) and demanded that steps be taken to correct the situation in the Yonne. Reports were written and delivered, steps were taken, and orders given, and General Taylor and his staff believed that would be the end of the trouble. They were wrong. The article in *L'Yonne Républicaine* had attracted the attention of people in Paris, and the conduct of the 101st became the subject of discussion in both SHAEF and the French ministries. However, of greatest interest to both the Americans and the French was not the misbehavior of the paratroopers but the phlegmatic response by their commanders.[3]

The IG of the 101st, Major Robert L. Bogard, investigated the events and concluded that the paratroopers' behavior had been exaggerated by French police and the press; it was really just a case of soldiers blowing off a little steam. Initially, no one in the 101st took responsibility for these incidents, and they all denied the seriousness of the situation. The PM, the IG, and General Taylor all tried to brush off criticism of the division and its soldiers. The IG of XVI Corps received Bogard's report and initiated his own investigation; he too concluded that the claims of misdeeds were "exaggerated," but he admitted that armed robbery was not "just blowing off steam." The rape of twelve- and sixteen-year-old girls was completely inexcusable, and he demanded that the 101st's PM follow through on the investigation. When questioned by the corps IG, General Taylor had said the seven or eight incidents reported in the 101st's first few days in Auxerre "did not seem excessive and did not cause any particular concern." Then he had read "the inflammable [*sic*] article in the French press" that provoked his published response, which in turn inspired another paper, *La Vie de l'Yonne,* to run a highly critical article under the headline "In Berlin Fraternization—In Auxerre Occupation?" Taylor thought most of the commotion in town was just "rowdyism," and he agreed with his PM and the French police that all the robberies had been committed by same "really bad characters of the criminal type." He failed to mention the rapes. He added that parachute volunteers differed from other soldiers; they were "a pretty vigorous type of soldier . . . definitely more of a handful than an older and more mature man when in a rest area." He concluded that crimes had been committed by a few bad characters, but by 6 August, the situation was under control.[4]

XVI Corps' IG sympathized with Taylor's point of view, reporting to his commander, Brigadier General George S. Eyster, that the problems were the result of "the entry of a new unit into the area and some natural 'airborne boisterousness' the first two or three nights after pay day (August 2–4)." A few criminals took advantage of the situation, and an "inflammatory article [appeared] in the local paper," portraying the situation as worse than it really was. Most of the incidents had not been reported to the OPM by the French police, and the complaint to Paris had been made by a subprefect while Prefect Gibaud was away; relations between General Taylor and the prefect were very good. In any event, there had been no incidents in the last two days, and some cafés had closed voluntarily. Eyster reported to Eisenhower's chief of staff, Major General Leslie Rooks, that complaints of misbehavior by the 101st were "probably exaggerated," the 101st had taken swift action, and everything was under control.[5]

The IG's report landed on the desk of assistant military attaché David Rockefeller in Paris. He thought everything was far from "under control" and asked the IG for the European theater of operations (ETO) to pick up the investigation, which turned into an inquiry into the behavior of not only the men of the 101st but also its PM and IG. The IG for ETO headquarters in Paris was not pleased with what he found. He characterized the behavior as egregious and very bad for Franco-American relations, and he believed the officers of the 101st should accept the blame for permitting such outrageous and undisciplined behavior. The report agreed with earlier assessments that there had been a temporary loss of control for the first three to four days after the 101st moved from Austria to the Yonne, after which the number of incidents decreased due to increased patrols, reimposed discipline, and greater control over GIs' liberties. However, the gravity of the incidents had not diminished; not enough had been done to find the culprits, and when they were found, too little punishment was imposed. The IG in Paris echoed the views of many French: the division's MPs were concerned with protecting GIs, not civilians. Enforcement had been slack, and discipline in the unit was lax. The 101st's PM had cited too little cooperation from French police, yet when General Taylor complained about French merchants illegally selling alcohol to GIs out the back door, the prefect asked for a list of such merchants, which the PM failed to provide. Despite increased MP patrols, incidents deemed "trivial" in Taylor's 10 August report continued: the ETO IG counted ten incidents on 5 August and ten more on 6 August. Between the signing of the corps IG's report on 10 August and the submission of the ETO IG's report on 20 August, French police recorded another twenty-eight serious incidents, including the 15 August death of a sixty-year-old Frenchman shot by an inebriated GI who had started waving a pistol around after being ejected from a dance; four GIs running amok in the village of Chemilly, resulting in the exchange of gunfire between French and American soldiers; and a French soldier whose nose was broken and his left eye seriously injured when he was attacked by three GIs in Joigny. One night in Auxerre, two French policemen were beset by five drunken GIs, and when they took the matter up with MPs, the French police got into a fight with the MPs, who had also been drinking and were then arrested! Two GIs assaulted a French couple, pushing them off the bicycles they were riding, beating the man, and stealing the bikes. On the afternoon of 20 August, a fifteen-year-old French boy was killed by an American car while riding his bike, and another fight broke out between French soldiers and GIs in Auxerre. Misbehavior by soldiers of the 101st continued to produce echoes in Paris for months afterward. The French government sent another complaint to the US Mission in Paris that resulted in a meeting with French officials on 15 September. The American ambassador apologized to French foreign minister Georges Bidault for the actions of the 101st, and the US Mission fired off a memo to the 101st, asking whether any trials had resulted from the actions of the division's PM.[6]

One of the reasons Paris took such an interest in the affairs of the 101st ABD in Auxerre was the horrific nature of one of the crimes: the rapes of two young girls from Poinchy, aged twelve and sixteen, in Milly, in the countryside east of Auxerre. The IG in Paris followed events, and the US Mission in Paris inquired in November about the results of the investigation. The initial report was taken by local police in Chablis and forwarded to the police commissioner in Auxerre. The PM of the 101st interviewed the girls through a translator and concluded that they "seemed confused" and were unable to pick out their attacker from a lineup of soldiers "named George" (because one girl said her attacker wore a wrist bracelet etched with "George"). However, the PM was careless about the facts of the case—including the girls' ages and their hometown—which is rarely a good sign. As of the date of the IG's report, 12 August—nine days after the attack on the two girls—no assailant had been identified, and the IG of XVI Corps was unimpressed with the progress of the investigation or the steps taken to date by the 101st's PM, Major John W. Urban. The commander of the French military district, Colonel J. Lanquetot, met with General Taylor about the rapes and other disturbances caused by his paratroopers, and he came away unconvinced that Taylor took the situation seriously. Lanquetot said he was going to set a 10:00

p.m. curfew for his soldiers and suggested that General Taylor do the same for his. Taylor replied that this seemed too drastic and suggested an 11:00 p.m. curfew six nights a week and midnight on Saturday. The rapes had occurred between 10:45 and 11:00 p.m. Otherwise, MP patrols were increased, and liaison with French police was strengthened by joint patrols and the assignment of two French police commissioners to work with MPs. Colonel Lanquetot "told General Taylor that [the curfew] would be alright providing he stopped the incidents."[7]

The incidents did not stop, and the two girls in Milly were not the 101st's only rape victims that summer. On 5 August a small gathering of friends at a house in central Auxerre was interrupted by two pistol-wielding paratroopers who ordered Mme. M.—a widow whose husband had been murdered by the Gestapo in the town jail in 1943—into a separate room, where she was raped by one of the intruders. The other stole 500 francs from her fiancé, who wrote to the OPM that he could forgive the offenses by the US Army—and the attack on his fiancée was by far the worst—if justice were rendered. On 12 September a drunken paratrooper accosted twenty-six-year-old Mme. T., who was married to a police official in nearby Joigny. He tried to kiss her, and when she resisted he hit her in the head with a rock, grabbed her by the throat, and pushed her into an alley, where he raped her. Afterward, the stunned woman, bleeding profusely from the head, was found by another GI who took her to the MPs, and they took her to the US military hospital. Stung by the 101st's phlegmatic response in past cases, army headquarters in Paris dispatched two seasoned American detectives to take over the serious cases attributed to the 101st. One night, MPs actually witnessed a GI attack a woman in Auxerre; the soldier fled and, incredibly, was never identified. At least the OPM kept rape cases open, although we cannot know what kind of resources were devoted to them. A shocking number of cases involving attacks, thefts, robberies, and vandalism were closed after a few days with the notation, "Case closed. No identification."[8]

Ultimately, the IG's investigation of misconduct by soldiers of the 101st ABD concluded that an untrained and inexperienced PM, supported by inadequate and incompetent assistants, was unable to control the soldiers under his authority and take effective corrective action. The IG found that although the number of incidents declined after corrective measures were taken, their seriousness did not. Serious incidents, such as the fatal shooting of a Frenchman or four soldiers "running amuck," kept occurring, indicating that the situation was not under control. The IG laid most of the responsibility for the sad situation in the Yonne on the OPM, but he also concluded that there was a serious leadership problem in the division. Without ever naming General

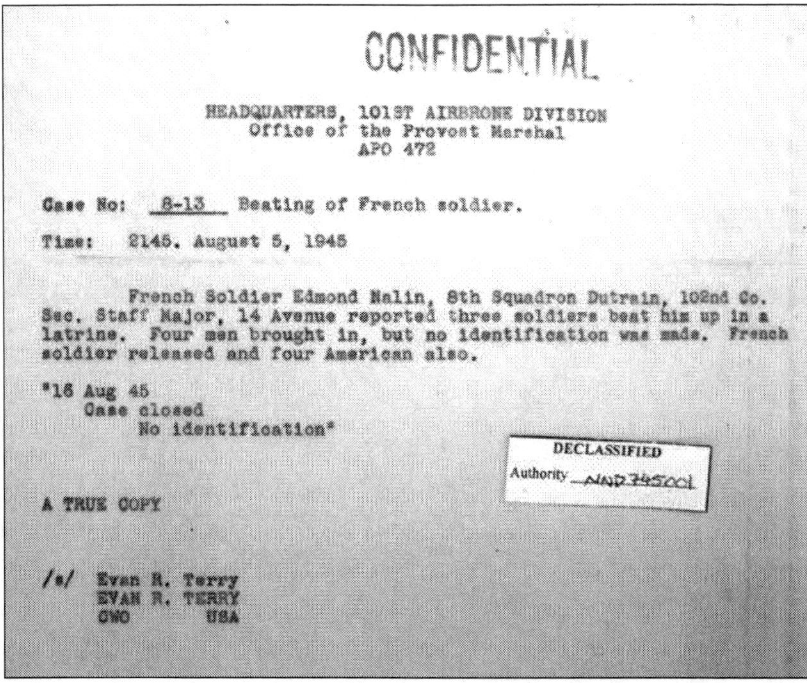

CONFIDENTIAL

HEADQUARTERS, 101ST AIRBRONE DIVISION
Office of the Provost Marshal
APO 472

Case No: 8-13 Beating of French soldier.

Time: 2145. August 5, 1945

French Soldier Edmond Malin, 8th Squadron Dutrain, 102nd Co. Sec. Staff Major, 14 Avenue reported three soldiers beat him up in a latrine. Four men brought in, but no identification was made. French soldier released and four American also.

"16 Aug 45
Case closed
No identification"

DECLASSIFIED
Authority NND 745001

A TRUE COPY

/s/ Evan R. Terry
EVAN R. TERRY
CWO USA

Inspector general's report, 101st Airborne Division. (Courtesy of the National Archives and Records Administration)

Taylor, the IG pointed out that "lack of discipline and control" could not simply be dismissed as "airborne boisterousness," a direct challenge to Taylor's earlier report on the matter. He also criticized "the commander's" failure to follow through and see that culprits were discovered, caught, and charged. Although the IG's investigation and report addressed a general degradation in the behavior of American paratroopers, rape was considered the most serious crime, and the report concentrated on it. The rape of the two young girls was one of the few in which the perpetrators were unknown yet the case remained open. From this, we can conclude that at least the US military considered rape a grave offense. Four rapes were attributed to the 101st during the division's sojourn in the Yonne. Another GI, a service soldier who was not with the 101st, was accused of rape in the department during this period.[9]

Incidents involving GIs declined, but they continued to occur. Most police reports involved offenses against property rather than violence by GIs against French citizens, which, though still objectionable, was an improvement. After two incidents involving MPs and French police—a French police officer accidentally shot an MP, and MPs shot and wounded a French soldier in a jeep—stricter rules for arrests and for the discharge of firearms were drawn up and agreed to by both forces. Rules regarding MPs arresting French citizens or entering French property were tightened to favor the French. French police in Sens declared that mixed patrols by MPs and French police had been tremendously successful in reducing incidents and lessening tension between the two services. Still, French officials and some police believed that MPs were not really interested in apprehending or punishing miscreants. The French police complained that when they arrested GIs and turned them over to MPs, which was standard procedure, the MPs escorted the suspects back to base and let them go, and that was the end of the case. MPs did not enforce the curfew or pick up obviously drunken GIs, even when they had illicit bottles of alcohol on them. Hence, as late as November 1945, French police still had complaints about publicly inebriated GIs and MPs who failed to do their job. As the man whose fiancée had been raped wrote to General Taylor, he could forgive the crime if the army found and punished the guilty party, but that is exactly what the 101st ABD failed to do. The greatest irritant to the French people, both officials and the public, was the Americans' failure to render justice. The OPM frequently disposed of cases, "case closed—no identification," with no investigation at all. GIs got away with mayhem, murder, and rape, and the responsible officers of the 101st made no effort to deliver justice.[10]

American airborne divisions set records among US Army units for disrupting French civilian life. In part, this may have been due to the type of individual attracted to paratroop units—as claimed by General Taylor. Both the 82nd ABD and the 13th ABD (stationed in France but never deployed in combat in Europe) racked up many complaints from French police, prefects, and commissioners. Yet the commander of the 13th ABD, General Eldridge Chapman, took many steps to ingratiate the division with the French population of the Yonne, and he took additional steps to induce discipline among his paratroopers and MPs. The prefect of the Yonne reported that most civilians eventually warmed up to the GIs. Violent clashes between paratroopers of the 82nd ABD and French police in Longwy in July and August 1945 convinced the division's PM to flood the town with MPs, restrict liberty hours, and institute mixed patrols of MPs and municipal police. This worked to lessen, but not eliminate, the outrages committed by GIs. The leaders of both the 13th and 82nd ABDs admitted there were problems and took steps to correct them. The leaders of the 101st either did not recognize the problems or did little to fix them. The PM and IG of the 101st failed to deliver justice to the aggrieved French, which soured their opinion of American GIs.[11]

10

The American "Occupation"

"N'oubliez pas que vous êtes en pays occupé et que nous sommes les occupants" (Don't forget that you are an occupied country and we are the occupiers). These words, spoken in heat by an American MP during a sharp exchange with French workers in Cherbourg in February 1945, carried little truth. However, the claim was probably taken seriously by both the American GI who made it and the French workers he was yelling at. Many French seemed to believe that the Americans were the new occupying power, and many GIs behaved as if it were true. In fact, it was not. The Americans responsible for directing Allied affairs in France, down to the town majors scattered across much of the country, neither believed it nor wanted it to be true. They had enough to worry about, and the expanding strength of the provisional government established by General de Gaulle was a blessing, not a curse. Both administrations employed hardworking, capable, smart, and determined staff who understood the importance of close cooperation with each other. Even de Gaulle, unrelentingly hostile to the United States to the end, understood the importance of close coordination and acted accordingly. Yet the behavior of some GIs belied the benign intentions of the United States and helped convince many French that they were saddled with a new occupation. Other French came to resent the American presence for reasons that had little to do with GIs and more to do with French politics, which was beyond the control of the Americans.[1]

Remarks by the commissioner in Orléans fairly represented the views of many French officials in the fall of 1944. The Americans he dealt with were courteous and competent, but the policies they implemented and defended were obnoxious to the French: seizing all purported German property as war booty, (generously) treating POWs according to the Geneva Convention rather than handing them over to the French as laborers, to do with as the French thought fit, and requisitioning too much wood. These grievances would remain until the end of the war and would never be settled to the satisfaction of the French while American forces remained in France. These American actions were also visible to the public and caused much ill will. Commissioner Marcel Grégoire had nothing but complaints about the US Army, which had largely taken over Reims and Châlons-sur-Marne as SHAEF's base of operations against Germany in the fall of 1944. His protest that the US Army had requisitioned Troyes's entire output of undergarments to clothe Russian and Polish DPs elicited no reply from General Charles O. Thrasher, in charge of the Oise base section. Passing the matter to Paris for handling produced a compromise: two-thirds of the underclothes would be left for the French. "Otherwise I have been able to achieve no satisfaction from American authorities here on any question of requisitions or the seizure of booty," Grégoire complained. "They requisition whatever they want without regard to French needs or wishes." To some extent, the officials that General de Gaulle appointed to positions of authority mirrored his stiff and righteous manner, at least toward the Americans. Thus, Grégoire's complaints ought to be considered in that light. Nevertheless, his attitude reflected the thinking of many French officials about the Americans' conduct during their stay in France.[2]

On 5 November 1944, only a week after the United States recognized the provisional government, Commissioner for Inter-Allied Relations François Coulet fired off a letter to SHAEF full of recriminations about mostly petty grievances. Coulet assured SHAEF that overall relations with "the Allies" (his letter was really about the Americans) were excellent, but he lamented that officers in the lower echelons did not always implement the agreements between SHAEF and the provisional government. He cited disagreements over war booty and requisitions as the biggest irritants for the French. Coulet argued that repeated transgressions created a bad impression on the French, and although the French press had been discreet, "reports from Prefects and Republican Commissioners are very clear that opinion is turning against the allies" (meaning the Americans). He repeated complaints about Patton and protested that civil affairs officers asked nosy questions about bank holdings. He urged SHAEF to understand that such transgressions against French sovereignty created a bad impression among the populace. He protested the American attitude toward "certain populations in Lorraine as if they were the enemy" and argued that the public could easily see the lenient treatment meted out to German POWs, while homeless and refugee French suffered. This was not just Commissioner Coulet using public opinion as leverage to convince SHAEF to take action—although he was certainly doing that. French opinion was indeed drifting in a hostile direction.[3]

French complaints about interference in matters of French politics and justice were rare because the Americans scrupulously stayed out of such affairs. General Koenig had requested that French tribunals be attached to American armies advancing through France to hear cases of French citizens accused of collaboration. Although his concern was understandable, especially in view of the "justice" meted out by the FFI's ad hoc courts, and although Civil Affairs recommended approval of the suggestion, the idea was rejected by SHAEF because it involved the US Army in questions that should be handled solely by the French. Coulet made repeated references to American interference in French politics, but his protests lacked specifics, conviction, and perhaps sincerity. The only case he could point to was the supposed election of a municipal council in Hagondange (Moselle) in September 1944. There was little evidence that such an event ever occurred, and the scanty proof presented had every sign of being phony. A letter about the "election" purportedly written by two civil affairs officers, "Daviz" and "Fitzhugg," was apparently concocted by someone, although it was probably not a Communist ploy, as the Americans had confirmed Rubeck, a PCF member, as mayor. Although there was no "election" in Hagondange and the French were free to install whatever candidate they pleased as mayor, the issue of the "election" lived on and became a bone of contention for the Gaullists. This issue was surely a product of paranoia and was kept alive by Gaullist appointees to serve a larger purpose.[4]

Many French had exaggerated expectations about the fruits of liberation. Nicole (Braux) Taflinger remembered: "We had wings on our feet. Dreams, ambitions, everything could now come true. In one morning we could see a whole new life unfolding—full of laughter, fathers returning home, the sun shining, jazz music, and no sound of boots in the night—and maybe even some food! . . . The streets had a holiday air and we whiffed the smell of cooking as women prepared some of their preciously hoarded food." Having suffered through shortages of everything during the German occupation, they unrealistically believed that abundance would arrive in the van of the Americans. Some French who had secretly hoarded delicacies such as chocolate, coffee, or canned peaches decided that it was time to break them out and consume them, because soon there would be plenty more. In Villers-lès-Nancy, teenager Nicole Braux celebrated the arrival of Americans in jeeps and tanks by giving a precious can of sardines to her cat. Popular discontent mounted when food became even less plentiful in the wake of liberation. There was much grumbling about the lack of food that started when the Americans arrived, even though Allied soldiers seemed to have more than adequate stores of food available to them. Many French blamed their own government rather than the Americans. People called for Paul Giacobbi to be replaced as supply minister. In fact, after Giacobbi (Radical) was replaced by Paul Ramadier (SFIO) on 16 November 1944, there was no apparent improvement in food supply; Ramadier was booed when he visited Troyes in May 1945. Many French rightfully blamed de Gaulle's campaign to stomp out the black market for the disastrous consequences on the food supply. Thus, legitimate public gripes about the lack of food were not aimed entirely at the Americans, but the US image suffered along with that of the GPRF in the sour atmosphere.[5]

The US Information Service attributed most of the negativity toward the United States to unrealistic expectations of an immediate economic revival, lax American treatment of German POWs, and explosions of "time bombs" left behind by the Germans. By February 1945, 30 percent of French gave the Americans a "satisfactory" rating and 56 percent "unsatisfactory"; by June 1945, opinions had not changed much—25 percent "satisfactory" and 48 percent "unsatisfactory." The Americans responsible for interpreting these polls believed that the negative attitudes in the fall and winter were inspired by the lack of military progress against the Germans and the scarcity of food in France.[6]

French unrest over food supplies was linked to resentment over the "benign" treatment of Axis POWs. These two issues came up repeatedly in surveys conducted by French pollsters for the US Army: the consensus was that the Americans provided too little material support for the French and treated German POWs too leniently. Although many recognized that the Americans were not primarily responsible for the food shortage, they became angry when food that could have fed French civilians was diverted to POWs. In the winter of 1944–1945 the cry from French civilians and officials was practically universal: give us the food you are now feeding to POWs! To make matters worse, Americans were taking housing that could have been used for homeless French to shelter POWs. The people in the Ardennes resented having to surrender more land and buildings in the winter of 1944–1945 to hold German POWs when Allied requisitions in the department were already burdensome. One reaction was to knock down English-language road signs put up by the Allies. The poor condition of many of the French POWs who returned from Germany and the horrific newsreels of the concentrations camps ("slaughter houses") liberated by Allied troops heightened French anger toward Germany. A torrent of news stories about German atrocities negated any sympathy the French might have shown toward German civilians who were themselves experiencing the horrors of liberation by the Red Army.[7]

The French hunger to avenge the humiliation of defeat and occupation was heightened by the barbarity of the German withdrawal from France in

1944. Many American soldiers respected German soldiers and held them in high regard, although this tended to decrease after the discoveries of the concentration camps in Germany in April and May 1945. Nevertheless, French animus against the Germans generally exceeded that of GIs. Exceptions were the riflemen who had experienced all the horrors of meeting German soldiers on the front lines; they often grew to hate their opponents and wish them only ill. Pierre Maillaud, who served with Leclerc's Second Armored Division in France, met a GI outside Argentan during the Battle of the Falaise Pocket. The two men surveyed the devastated town after it had been liberated, retaken by the Germans, and then lost again. The American corporal said to Maillaud, "It's not war. It makes me sick to see the town in this poor state. . . . I know they'll blame us, but it's those filthy Germans. They use everything for shelter, your homes, your civilians, your children. That's their sort of war. . . . They've left booby traps and time bombs all over town. Yesterday they took twenty-seven prisoners, including several Red Cross men. We found their bodies. They'd been shot in the back. I don't know how long I'll be in this but I know I'll take no more prisoners." Most American front-line soldiers felt the same way after witnessing too much carnage. But most GIs were not front-line infantry; they served in logistical units or in supporting functions within fighting units. These soldiers generally harbored less vindictive feelings toward their foes.[8]

French attitudes toward the Americans waxed and waned with the fortunes of war. When Allied armies advanced, the French generally held them in high esteem; when they stalled, the French grew wary and irritable. It is also possible that as the Allies advanced, French police and other civil authorities were reestablished, offering a means to convey complaints about GIs that may have been festering for a while. Renseignements Généraux and the commissioners of the Republic funneled regular reports to Paris in September and beyond, and those reports often conveyed grievances against the Americans, so perhaps long-standing grievances were finally heard. Regardless, it is probable that the initial enthusiasm for their liberators dimmed after the excitement of liberation died down and bored supply troops settled in for some serious drinking. The shock of the initial success of the German Ardennes offensive surprised the French public, and their high opinion of the US Army never quite recovered its former luster. People in the Aube, who had little reason to gripe about the Americans—other than some distasteful encounters with drunken GIs—carped about the US Army after Christmas 1944. They grumbled that the United States wanted all the glory for defeating Germany, so the Americans had done the minimum to set the French army back on its feet. Opinion was turning sour in Marseille as well. The prefect asked General Ratay to temporarily increase the milk ration so children could have warm milk at Christmas, and he refused. Quaker Relief immediately offered 150 cases of milk for children of Marseille. In the wake of this incident, Commissioner Haag noted that the public continued to favor the "correct" British over the Americans, who caused too many accidents with their reckless driving and showed too much sympathy for German POWs.[9]

Many French took a serious interest in important questions, such as American recognition of de Gaulle's provisional government and France's role in peacemaking. Impatience over official recognition was not limited to small circles in Paris and government offices in the administrative districts. Stalin and Churchill had both urged American recognition of de Gaulle's GPRF as the legitimate government of France during the summer of 1944; even the taking of Paris and the reestablishment of de Gaulle's ministries there did not convince Roosevelt that de Gaulle was the real leader of France. Roosevelt did not send an ambassador to Paris until 23 October 1944, which rankled many French, particularly de Gaulle, who assumed bad faith on the part of Washington in its dealings with the French. When de Gaulle visited Roosevelt in Washington in July 1944, rumors continued to swirl in Algiers that the US government was still secretly negotiating with Marshal Pétain to establish a government in France headed by Camille Chautemps. Journalist A. J. Liebling heard the same rumor in Paris, even after its liberation in August 1944. Chautemps, dispatched by Vichy to the United States in 1940 with a vague mission to improve relations, tried to convince émigrés and Americans that de Gaulle was a fascist. When Chautemps proved ineffective, Vichy recalled him to France, but he chose not to return. Instead, he offered his services to the Free French in the United States and was refused; he offered to help out an independent anti-Vichy group based in Philadelphia called France Forever, but it declined; later, he tried to join with General Giraud and then the US Army, but no one wanted his services because he was tainted by his association with the death of the Third Republic in 1940. And still the Gaullists believed that the United States wanted to install Chautemps as the leader of liberated France. General de Gaulle and many in his entourage assumed that Eisenhower dragged his feet over liberating Paris because he had been ordered not to enter the French capital until Washington had reached an accord with Pierre Laval to transfer the Vichy government to Paris and keep Pétain in power. Indeed, as late as 19 October 1944, Roosevelt cabled Churchill that the time had not yet arrived to recognize de Gaulle's GPRF, and Secretary of State Hull informed the American representative to Paris that Roosevelt had decided to extend only de facto recognition of the GPRF. Eisenhower implored Roosevelt to formally recognize the GPRF as soon as possible. On 22 October he did.

Late in 1944 some French still believed that the US government wanted to set up a military government and thus occupy France. De Gaulle never dropped his suspicions about Roosevelt in particular and about American intentions and motives more generally. Even though he got along well with Eisenhower, de Gaulle always assumed that the SHAEF commander had to toe some secret line dictated by Washington.[10]

Many French believed that France was deliberately kept in an inferior position by the Allies and not treated as an equal partner. In fact, France was not an equal partner with the United States or Britain because, even at the end of the war, it could not supply its own military with weapons. De Gaulle gave a speech in March 1945 urging the Allies, especially the Americans, to divert some of their enormous war materials away from Germany to help the French "on the Atlantic front" retake French towns from the Germans. Complaints that the FFI were not receiving adequate supplies and armaments to defeat the Germans on the western coast of France could *only* be directed at the United States because only it could provide the supplies necessary to do the job. France's armaments industry was not yet back on its feet and thus could not supply its own armed forces; the French army remained dependent on the United States and Britain for years after the war. Thus, FFI frustrations with the US Army seemed unavoidable, even if there was little the United States could do about it. Eisenhower was unwilling to deprive the main offensive against Germany of supplies in order to reinforce a sideshow like the Atlantic enclaves. Despite these frustrations, the commissioner in Rennes noted in December 1944 that the FFI got along well with American soldiers in the region. When the Americans launched massive B-24s raids against the German Atlantic stronghold of Royan in April 1945, the French were very pleased, and French newspapers had only praise for American help in retaking the Gironde estuary.[11]

The French generally reacted badly whenever France was treated like a secondary power of little importance. French historian Henri Amouroux claimed that de Gaulle offered the French "greatness" in early 1945 because he could not offer them bread. Most French were angry that de Gaulle had been excluded from the "Big Three" talks in Yalta in February 1945; neither de Gaulle nor the French people accepted that France's defeat in 1940 relegated it to a secondary role in the world. De Gaulle's refusal to meet with Roosevelt in Algeria after the Yalta Conference produced mixed reactions among the French. Some, including the PCF and much of the French press, thought it was a mistake; they believed he missed an opportunity to improve relations between the two nations. Yet, according to the Sûreté Nationale, the majority of French approved of de Gaulle's snub of Roosevelt. Negative reactions to Allied slights of de Gaulle should not be interpreted as love for de Gaulle, however; they were received as insults to France. In November 1944 some people in Troyes were upset that Rue Thiers had been renamed Rue de Générale de Gaulle, especially because President Adolphe Thiers had been so important to the creation of the Third Republic in 1871, with parallels to 1944 France. The French did not necessarily love de Gaulle, but they believed he deserved respectful treatment by Washington because France deserved respect. In their view, America owed more to France for its centuries-long *mission civilisatrice* (spreading civilization to the world) than France owed to the United States for its fleeting role in the world wars. French history demonstrated the greatness of France and its empire of 100 million, which military defeat and four years of Nazi occupation could not erase. This was (and is) a view held by many French, who saw relations between France and the United States as much bigger and more important than de Gaulle's dealings with Roosevelt.[12]

Opinions about the United States tended to be harsher in Paris than in the rest of the country. Perhaps this was because Parisians were more influenced by international events, such as de Gaulle's exclusion from the Yalta and Potsdam Conferences, which rebounded more against the United States and Britain than against the Soviet Union. Opinions about the United States were particularly negative in Paris before May 1945 and warmed after VE Day—at least until de Gaulle was excluded from the Potsdam Conference in July and August. French attitudes toward the USSR, which were generally favorable in the earliest surveys and grew warmer over time, were largely positive. The warmth of opinion toward the Soviet Union after the German surrender failed to reflect Stalin's contemptuous attitude toward the French contribution to victory and the American push to take France seriously as one of the victors. In fact, the French zone of occupation in Germany was carved out of the American zone because the Soviets refused to realign the zones to take the French into consideration. De Gaulle was excluded from Potsdam at Stalin's insistence and against the wishes of Churchill. A bitter dispute between Generals Eisenhower and de Lattre about transferring French-conquered Stuttgart to American control rose to the presidential level less than two weeks after Truman took office. Eisenhower's protest that he could not count on French cooperation in the final days of the war and de Gaulle's testy defense of "French national interest" gave the new president in Washington little incentive to argue for de Gaulle's inclusion in the upcoming talks in Potsdam.[13]

As French regard for the Western (Anglo-Saxon) Allies dimmed, opinions about the Soviet Union brightened. Stalin received de Gaulle in Moscow in December 1944, adding to the Soviet Union's prestige, which had risen by leaps since the Red Army's victory at the Battle of Stalingrad two years earlier. Just as French bulletins were full of stories of shortages in France and inadequate supplies for French troops fighting in the Vosges Mountains, de Gaulle was greeted in Moscow with great fanfare, while the US Army was bogged down in eastern France. In the spring of 1945, 40 percent of French thought good relations with the Soviet Union were more important than good relations with either the United States (15 percent) or the United Kingdom (28 percent). After VE Day, those numbers changed only slightly: USSR, 37 percent; United States, 24 percent; United Kingdom, 36 percent. Historians Andrew Knapp and Claudia Baldoli convincingly assert that the destructive bombing raids by the Western Allies and their seeming stalemate against the Germans compared badly with the USSR, which did not bomb France and had an unbroken string of victories in the east. Opinion favored the distant, victorious Soviet Union over the too-close, bumbling Western Allies. As the collapse of Germany seemed imminent in April, the French were distracted by worries over the high cost of living and the exciting prospect of a German defeat. According to reports by the French police, most French credited primarily the USSR for the defeat of Germany; Stalin was held in greater esteem than either Churchill or Roosevelt. This helps explain why 10,000 people turned out at a PCF rally in Troyes to hear Communist hero André Marty give a speech, while local Radicals (who had been preponderant in the Aube before the war) held their meeting in a café. The unflinching focus of France's Communist press on the heroic exploits of the Red Army and its silence about the victorious push of the Anglo-Saxon armies against Nazi Germany helped promote positive thinking about Stalin and the Soviet Union in the spring of 1945 and discounted the Western Allies' contribution to Germany's defeat.[14]

In the last prewar elections of 1936, PCF candidates won 15 percent of the vote; in the first postwar elections in October 1945, the PCF won 26 percent of the vote, making it the largest political party in France. Certainly, the PCF grew in prestige during the war, yet many (perhaps most) French did not trust it. In many ways, French attitudes toward the Communist Party mirrored attitudes about the United States: backers of the PCF overwhelmingly held skeptical or hostile views of the United States. According to the commissioner at Bordeaux, reactions to a liberty ship captain who failed to salute during the playing of the Soviet anthem were divided by class: workers sympathetic to the Soviet Union thought it was an insult, whereas the local "property-owning class" took it as a reassuring sign that the United States was not wholeheartedly aligned with the USSR. Some French thought the US Army lingered in France in 1945 to stomp out a Communist revolution should one erupt. Many anti-Communist French hoped this were true. In fact, de Gaulle saw the Anglo-Saxon Allies' armies in France as his best defense against a Communist coup, just as the Allies saw de Gaulle as the best French bulwark against a Communist takeover. Both camps suspected the motives and intentions of the PCF and viewed mutual cooperation as their best guarantee against Communist machinations. De Gaulle was anxious to have either the Americans or the French army accept the Germans' surrender in the Atlantic pockets because he did not want the prestige (and the captured armaments) to go to the FFI, which de Gaulle perceived as being thoroughly dominated by the PCF. There was actually little prospect for a PCF putsch: the PCF followed orders from Moscow, and while the war raged, Stalin wanted no trouble behind the western front that would interfere with a speedy victory over Hitler. After Germany surrendered, that was a different matter, but by May 1945, the French state was sufficiently resurrected under de Gaulle's GPRF and the FTP had largely been neutralized, rendering the likelihood of a successful Communist coup remote.[15]

The French directed their war-weariness against the Americans in part because the US military presence was pervasive and preponderant in France, even more conspicuous than the French military. Although there were Canadian and British troops in France throughout the war, they failed to arouse the same levels of antagonism provoked by the Americans. The US Information Service, attached to the Psychological Warfare Division, surveyed French public opinion in partnership with the French Institute of Public Opinion in mid-November 1944 and found that the French viewed the British more favorably than the Americans: 53 percent of the French respondents said the American attitude toward France was "not satisfactory"; 22 percent said the same of the British attitude. Regardless of the sincere efforts of American civil affairs officers, the British dealt more successfully with French officials at all levels. The British set up regular meetings with local and regional French officials to discuss mutual concerns and try to resolve them then and there, if possible. The British took pains to involve French officials in almost all their interactions with the French, such as inspecting French armaments factories, whereas American officers appeared alone and unannounced to poke around, arousing French suspicions. The British were acutely aware of French sensitivities on the issue of sovereignty and tried to accommodate them whenever possible. American officers in Paris dealt with their French counterparts with sensitivity, but they spent a lot of time apologizing for American officers lower down the chain who did not. Civil affairs officers often promised that agreements would be upheld, but they were in no position to keep those promises.[16]

American soldiers also compared badly to British troops, in the opinion of the French. Reports from Normandy frequently contrasted the objectionable behavior of American soldiers to the good behavior of British soldiers and noted the French public's affection for the latter. As tens of thousands of GIs crowded into the "cigarette" camps in the Seine Inférieure, waiting to be shipped to the front, crime rates mounted, and the French thought back fondly to the days when British troops were quartered in the region. In December 1944 the commissioner in Rouen reported to Paris that the Americans "have created terror in the regions of their camps . . . [and] affection rebounds on the English." When people around Dieppe heard the news that British troops would soon depart for Antwerp and be replaced by Americans, they shuddered in horror, given the stories they had heard about rape, murder, and armed robbery committed by GIs elsewhere in Normandy. Commissioner Raymond Aubrac in Marseille noted that French in the south preferred the British—deemed "correct" by the French—over the Americans. This sentiment was echoed by a French couple Janet Teissier du Cros met in Valence, who told her, "'We prefer the English' because, only the English understood what things had been like in France, only the English had tact and consideration in their dealings with the French." Marie Osmont in Normandy was initially sadly disappointed by the lax discipline, thievery, and laziness of the British soldiers quartered at her house, who had displaced the "correct" Germans. But ultimately she decided that the British, with their easy ways and love of pranks, more resembled the French than the Germans had. Belgians were also surprised that the behavior of Allied troops contrasted badly with that of the German occupiers. Belgians were rudely surprised by the lax discipline among British and Canadian soldiers compared with the Germans, but they were shocked by the Americans, whose behavior was the worst. People in Antwerp remarked that women had never been afraid to go out at night during the German occupation, but once the Allies took over, women stayed inside after dark.[17]

Some Americans also perceived social differences between themselves and the French that produced friction. Major Robert L. Bogard of the 101st ABD claimed that soldiers of the 13th ABD, previously stationed around Auxerre, had poisoned the atmosphere by frightening the locals with stories about the savagery of the men of the 101st. He added that the paratroopers of the 101st were "not well impressed with French soldiers they contacted in Miesbach . . . [and] the boys had heard that they were not wanted in France." There were rumors that women who went with American GIs had their heads shaved, and this prejudiced the Americans against the French. Bogard noticed that French girls were rarely seen in public with GIs and thought this might be because the girls wanted to avoid getting bad reputations. He speculated that maybe "the French do not place as much emphasis on the casual greeting as does the average American, which . . . he may interpret as coolness." All this mutual mistrust and misunderstanding, Bogard mused, had fueled the violence unleashed by some GIs upon their arrival in France. General Taylor told an IG investigator that tensions between the French and his paratroopers grew because the French were "aloof" and had "snubbed" the GIs, who resented that the French would not attend dances put on by the 101st.[18]

The crime waves that accompanied the new American troops genuinely alarmed and frightened French civilians and the officials who had to respond to them. People who had welcomed the Americans as liberators were shocked at the thuggish and criminal behavior of some GIs. In late July 1944 two-thirds of the Normans surveyed in the Cotentin Peninsula had no complaints about the "Allied soldiers"—who were nearly all American. However, more than one-fifth believed they "drank too much" and were "undisciplined." Only 9 percent of these respondents said that drinking to excess was the only problem; the rest linked drinking to other objectionable behavior, such as treating women poorly. Four percent said GIs were thieves, and 4 percent said they were rapists. Officers in the Psychological Warfare Division, which was responsible for the survey, concluded that widespread rumors and "tales" about rape had had an enormously negative impact on the public's view of American soldiers. Even if only a small fraction of GIs were thugs who preyed on French civilians, these few had a disproportionate influence on French thinking about American soldiers.[19]

In a report brimming with complaints about the Americans, the commissioner in Châlons-sur-Marne wrote in March 1945, "The American mentality is so opposed to that of the French that only our debt to them for liberation prevents a complete rupture which is beginning in public opinion." The corrupting influence of the Americans was so profound, he warned, that "I fear for future attitudes of the French." Commissioner Grégoire's view was shared by others: the problem was not what the Americans *did;* it was who they *were.* Americans were fundamentally incompatible with the French, and the two civilizations had little affinity. Many French believed that the enormous influence of German Americans in the United States explained the natural affinity between Germans and Americans and the sympathy GIs expressed for German POWs. They believed the same probably held true for the large Italian American population, which conditioned the GIs to look favorably on Italian POWs as well. Moreover, Americans did not know what it was like to live under the boot of the Germans and Italians.[20]

French Catholics sometimes evinced hostility toward Americans for their own reasons. On the feast day of Saint Vincent de Paul, the canon of the Nancy cathedral harshly criticized American soldiers for their "dissolute morals" that allowed them to rape and attack innocent civilians. He went on to preach that Russians and Americans were partners in denying Christ and rejecting his morality, and he warned that the French were in danger of following the same immoral path; France would never regain its former greatness unless it "restored Christ to his proper place." This sort of anti-American propaganda had been preached by the Vichy regime since November 1942, with Vichy claiming that the capitalist societies of the Anglo-Saxons cared nothing for Christian values and morality; they cared only about their ledgers. The Americans reported numerous sermons in Nancy churches that were hostile to the United States. Such Catholic-grounded views of Americans as materialistic, cold, calculating, and lacking in charity surfaced in other objections that were not couched in specifically Catholic terms. The French populace was aghast at the US Army's waste of food, clothing, wood, and all kinds of articles since it arrived in France. Astonishment at Americans' wantonness and their dearth of charity only increased as the army disposed of supplies on its way out of France. Mayor Marius Choltus of the Nancy suburb of Saint Max expressed "incomprehension" in a letter to a local newspaper protesting that the Americans had had the POWs burn beds, tables, chairs, mattresses, and other equipment before leaving Camp Fruhinsholz in Nancy. The mayor was "astounded" that the Americans would deny such useful materials to the French, many of whom had lost everything in the aerial bombardment and the fight for liberation. Mayor Choltus then wrote that the US Army's culture of waste reflected something more profoundly wrong with America than the simple waste of good supplies: "The Americans are like that. In 1933, while millions starved to death, they destroyed crops. They have no compassion, no spirit . . . beautiful speeches, beautiful principles, and beautiful charters . . . good intentions mask an empty heart, cold egoism, a lack of ideals. . . . What could one expect from such people?" The people of Digosville—next to Cherbourg—were appalled when the Americans dumped five tons of potatoes into a trash heap. Locals dug through the garbage and salvaged "many perfectly good" potatoes. Days later, the Americans dumped a huge quantity of soap, doused it with gasoline, and set it on fire. The angry residents, who in September 1945 still suffered from a shortage of soap, could not understand the actions of the US Army. The subprefect in Mondidier protested that as the Americans prepared to leave air bases in the Somme, they burned vast quantities of supplies rather than declaring them surplus: huge quantities of linen, several tons of sugar and conserves, 500 pairs of shoes, and even gliders and an airplane. French workers who had witnessed the pyres with their own eyes spread stories of the destruction to neighboring town and villages. They said the Americans had burned usable garments in front of people who had given their own precious clothes to downed American airmen, been deported for helping them, and now had nothing. Such depravity could only be a manifestation of a commercial mentality that weighed all things by their placement on ledgers. This view of Americans had a long history in France and was not invented by Vichy; however, it was repeatedly broadcast by Vichy propagandists to a receptive audience, evidently with some success. It remains alive and well in France today.[21]

At a meeting of Femmes de France in Villefranche, in the Maritime Alps, a returned French POW gave a talk on 15 March and finished by saying, "I'm happy to be back, but it's rather annoying to be liberated by your 'allies' with a submachine gun in your stomach." He did not elaborate on what he meant, but it was certainly not warm praise for the Allies. The audience immediately erupted in an uproar, and blows were exchanged between those who agreed with the speaker and those who supported the Americans. The next day in a Cannes cinema, when a newsreel showed a French boxer beating an American in a match, French soldiers in the audience erupted with "à bas les américains!" (down with the Americans) and "les américains au poteau!" (Americans to the execution post). Afterward, French soldiers brandished guns and fired them at random, calling for the expulsion of the Americans by force. Interestingly, there had been no recent serious violent incidents involving GIs in the region. This may not have represented the majority opinion among French troops or civilians, but it certainly revealed a deep animosity toward Americans among some of them. Renseignements Généraux in Sens pointed out in March that when American troops appeared on movie screens, they were often met by whistles and catcalls, and GIs did not salute the French flag during the playing of the "Marseillaise." The wife of the deported mayor of Sens, Lazare Bertrand, was much criticized in town for trying to promote Franco-American collaboration, and many people found her "intimacy" with the Americans far greater than what they deserved. Efforts in Auxerre to organize a "welcoming committee" for the 13th ABD went nowhere, and when the 13th's band staged a concert, the French audience of around 2,000 received each piece with only lukewarm applause. Rumors circulated in Nancy in mid-July 1945 that there was a plan afoot on Bastille Day to shave the heads of local women who consorted with Americans. The US Counter Intelligence Corps (CIC) also got wind of the rumor and wanted to ensure that it did not happen. Whereas the US military had largely stood by during the head shavings that occurred in f 1944, this time, it feared clashes between GIs and French civilians. MPs had no authority to act against French civilians, except under extraordinary circumstances, but the army planned to post extra MPs around Nancy during the July celebrations, and the CIC sought the aid of French authorities to prevent any incidents.[22]

The exasperation of many French civilians influenced the attitudes of the officials responsible for their welfare. Commissioner Bourdeau de Fontenay in Rouen noted at the end of October that although French officials continued to enjoy good relations with their American counterparts, the people were fed up with the boorish behavior of GIs waiting to leave Europe in the summer and fall of 1945. Accidents, too many of them fatal, caused by careless GIs alienated many French citizens who were already exasperated by drunken GIs behaving like thugs. They protested that French police were powerless to intervene, and MPs did not respond to appeals for help, leaving civilians without any protection at all. Many felt that they could no longer patronize their own cafés. Subprefect Daussin in Montdidier, described by his superior as "a resistance hero with great affection for our Allies," complained that American soldiers exhibited a brutal and coarse attitude toward the French, and scenes of drunkenness and orgy were common. "It is currently heard said that German soldiers conducted themselves better in an 'enemy country' than American soldiers in a 'friendly country.'" Americans were seen as hard hearted, profit driven, and without charity. By July 1945, Commissioner Pierre Pène in Laon was fed up with the Americans. He reported that relations between GIs and the local population had become particularly tense, and after a stream of depressing reports from his prefects and subprefects depicting the Americans as out-of-control gangsters, the commissioner was ready to give up trying to work with them. "As dozens of thousands of French who were tortured by the Gestapo for hiding and helping downed aviators, I can see why the population is discouraged. All approaches to address these problems have been without result."[23]

Despite such tensions, events on the world stage brought France and the United States closer together. The inclusion of a French delegation at the San Francisco Conference that founded the United Nations helped boost French morale and convinced many that France was returning to a place of importance in the world. American and British insistence that France be a member of the United Nations Security Council—over Soviet objections—was recognized and appreciated by the French public. Diplomatic problems related to Poland were raised at the San Francisco Conference in May and inspired genuine concern among many French, who harbored great sympathy for the Poles. The fate of democracy in Poland fueled real skepticism among many French about the USSR and Stalin's intentions. Such mutual concerns helped bring the French and the Americans closer and led to greater empathy between the two. Such empathy was possible only when American and French interests aligned, as they had in their mutual fight to defeat Nazi Germany.[24]

After overcoming numerous difficulties to unite the Free French, rid France of Nazi and Vichyist foes, and wrest recognition from his allies, de Gaulle left the provisional government and French politics before the US Army finally sailed away. Once a Constituent Assembly was elected in October 1945, maneuvering by the various political parties began right away. The Communists gained the most votes and formed the largest political bloc, which, with the revived Socialist Party (SFIO), held an absolute majority in the Assembly. This was de Gaulle's (and the Americans') worst nightmare: he detested political parties and generally held politicians in low regard, but he could never cooperate with a government dominated by Marxists. When the new legislature started to strip away the powers of the president, de Gaulle resigned in a huff, expecting to be called back by popular acclaim after a period of chaos. Fifteen years would pass before he returned. When de Gaulle left in January 1946, American soldiers still raced along rural French roads in jeeps, sipped French beer in cafés, and lolled on French beaches in the Basque country. But soon they too would be gone.

Some of the frustrations experienced by French officials and the public were most likely unavoidable, given the difficult circumstances. Some of the frustration, such as the unhappiness over the trivial resources devoted to capturing the German-held Atlantic enclaves, reflected a refusal to see the American point of view. Some of it was the product of paranoia, such as fears about having Pierre Laval or Camille Chautemps foisted on the French as their ruler. However, that paranoia was no doubt fed by Roosevelt's refusal to recognize de Gaulle as the legitimate leader of France and thus could have been avoided. Much of the rancor was a reaction against GI indiscipline. Perhaps those who claimed that French and Americans were two different peoples with conflicting mentalities were right. German levels of discipline never would have been tolerated by conscripted GIs, leading a small number of American soldiers to behave very badly indeed. Such miscreants could usually be brought into line, but while they were out of step with the rules, their commanders, and their own comrades, they caused much damage to the reputation of the US Army. However, they did not do as much damage as President Roosevelt would have inflicted if he had gotten his way and imposed a military government—AMGOT—on France. In the unlikely event that the

British could have been persuaded to go along, it is difficult to imagine how the Allies could have forced the French to accept an AMGOT, especially with hundreds of thousands of armed FFI behind the front lines. Despite what some Americans and French might have believed, and notwithstanding what President Roosevelt wanted, there was no American occupation of France.

Epilogue

Yankees Go Home

VE Day was greeted with incredible joy by the French, who proudly displayed all their British, French, American, and Soviet flags. Janet Flanner wrote, "VE-Day here was like an occupation of Paris by Parisians. They streamed out into the city's avenues and boulevards and took possession of them, filling them from curb to curb. They paved the Champs-Elysées with their moving, serried bodies." WAC Frances DeBra found it impossible to get to work on VE Day because the crowds of French were so deep along the Champs-Elysées. Franco-American concord had seemingly reached a high point with victory. That a brawl erupted shortly thereafter among French civilians in Villefranche over criticism of their American ally indicates that while some French detested the Americans, others were literally willing to fight for them. Paris quickly filled up with American soldiers on leave, all of them looking for souvenirs to take home. DeBra noted in June that the city was overrun with GIs, who picked the stores clean. Everyone continued to complain about the high prices caused by the "unfair" exchange rate. American tempers flared during "de Gaulle Day" parades in Paris on 18 June, as GIs became frustrated by the snarled traffic and delays. Fistfights fights broke out on the Champs-Elysées between American soldiers and French police, soldiers, and bystanders. French onlookers reacted badly to American indifference or exasperation, and numerous shouting matches and shoving incidents occurred. When one WAC tried to cross the street through the parade, she was knocked to the ground by a French soldier. French police also noted an increase in fights between police and GIs at night. WAC Betty Magnuson noted, "People were no longer so happily allied, and several unpleasant incidents occurred among the parade bystanders." For Betty and other Americans, Bastille Day was just another excuse for the French to stage yet another military parade. These displays were becoming tiresome, and most Americans had no interest in watching yet more soldiers marching down the Champs-Elysées. To the WACs and GIs stationed in Paris, the parade simply meant that they were unable to get to work. Frances DeBra avoided the Bastille Day parade, too; however, she and other WACs gathered atop the Hotel Windsor to enjoy the fireworks and the monuments lit up with floodlights that night.[1]

Fights became more common between GIs and French soldiers on Rue Pigalle, although, because many French soldiers and returning DPs wore US uniforms, it was frequently difficult to distinguish them from actual American soldiers. Regardless, the Office of the Provost Marshal recorded an increase in scuffles and brawls between American and French soldiers around Paris. Many Americans, Betty among them, were tired of France, and now that the war was over, they just wanted to go home. Even Captain Robert Gerdy, a dedicated Francophile who loved Paris and Parisians (or at least *parisiennes*), was growing less fond of Paris by late May. He observed, "I am coming to be more critical of [the French]." In late June, as Gerdy walked on the streets of Paris with a Russian woman, some French sailors insulted him. "Everywhere you turn there's stupidity—and we're not the smartest people in the world either," he noted. "The French are getting kind of desperate about food and they have every reason to, and a lot of people go around saying the French don't think the Americans are gentlemen because so many soldiers are rolling around the gutters and accosting dames all the time. That was true in England, too, and the British used to get browned off at us all the time." Gerdy was right: many French had indeed gotten "browned off" at misbehaving GIs.[2]

With the war over and the Americans expecting to move 2.5 million soldiers through France on their way home or to the Pacific theater, SHAEF anticipated new requisitions of facilities in northern France. In some cases, it needed to requisition buildings that had only recently been returned to French possession. Paris commanded that no decisions concerning new requisitions by the Allies were to be made by prefects or mayors; all such determinations would be made by commissioners of the Republic, acting in the name of the GPRF. The expansion of the "cigarette camps" in the Seine-Inférieure exacerbated an already bad situation. The camps filled up with so many soldiers waiting to cross the Atlantic that some GIs complained they spent all their time standing in chow lines: the lines were so long that as soon as soldiers finished one meal, they headed to the end of the line for their next meal. Frances DeBra, who was sent to Camp Philip Morris, complained that there was absolutely nothing to do; there was not even anything to read. Nor did soldiers waiting to ship out have any duties to distract them, as all the menial jobs were performed by German POWs.[3]

In October, Commissioner Bourdeau de Fontenay protested to the French liaison to the Allies in Le Havre:

> Until a few weeks ago problems with the American troops passing through was normal for an area with this many soldiers, but lately the incidents have multiplied, the civil population of Rouen and the region of Le Havre are very agitated. Orders have been issued to French police to use all means in their power to protect French citizens; MPs often intervened with insufficient energy and I want to avoid any incident between French police and MPs. If nothing is done to ameliorate this situation, a clash between French police and certain elements of the U.S. Army is to be feared. I don't know if this is just a small number of bad actors, but they are ruining the good reputation of the U.S. Army here.[4]

Police in Rouen received a steady stream of reports about criminal or at least objectionable behavior by GIs. The police commissioner in Rouen complained that incidents occurred every night, and women dared not go out alone. They were not safe even when accompanied by men; GIs accosted women even when they were with their husbands. Many young girls were seduced by the Americans; two girls, aged fourteen and sixteen, were kept for ten days at the US camp in Amfreville. "[GIs] intrude into people's homes and demand drink with menaces and accost the woman of the house. The population is outraged and people say aloud what they had previously only thought, *les Boches se tiennent mieux que les américains, ils ne se livraient pas comme eux au vandalisme; on ne dirait pas que les américains sont nos amis* [the Krauts behaved better than the Americans; they did not take to vandalism like (the Americans) do; one would not say that the Americans are our friends]." Actions taken by French officials had some impact. Gendarmes coordinated their patrols and improved their communications with MPs, which reduced the number of incidents in September, yet the prefect in Rouen reported that outrages continued to occur at Camp Lucky Strike and in nearby villages. For its part, the US Army limited the number of troops that could leave base at any one time to 15 percent, which reduced the number of scandals that, according to Bourdeau de Fontenay, "have set the French population against the Americans." At the same time, the Allies greatly increased their aid to damaged regions in Normandy, especially in the Calvados.[5]

With the war over, Allied military security was relaxed in Paris, and the number of stragglers increased. MPs and French police were kept busy chasing AWOL GIs around the city. Although the crime rates reported by French police remained about the same, MPs picked up more GIs for joyriding in army vehicles; they impounded 163 vehicles during just three days in July.

MPs were especially interested in GIs involved in crime—both petty and serious. Several American deserters were accused of murder; others were deeply involved in the black markets around Paris, and MPs joined French police in conducting raids on buildings known or suspected to be black-market centers. GIs were accused of audacious robberies and attacks. Three GIs chased two Frenchwomen down a street in Saint-Denis and shot at them with pistols on 3 January 1946, hitting one woman. Two days later, GIs were reportedly staging stickups on Paris streets in broad daylight. Inter-Allied relations at the top were hardly better than those at the base. By August, grave incidents involving GIs in Paris had not diminished, provoking Interior Minister Tixier to request a meeting with General John Lee to discuss the situation. Lee did not respond for two weeks, and then he (or someone in his office) replied to Assistant Minister Haas-Picard and not to Minister Tixier.[6]

Prefects and commissioners in departments all over France where US troops were quartered sent letters and reports in the summer of 1945 with similar complaints about out-of-control GIs. They often included long lists of incidents recorded by the police and passed on to higher authorities. The secretary-general of police in Marseille sent a six-page list "of the most notable incidents" in his jurisdiction to Commissioner Haag, summarizing the incidents involving GIs from June to October 1945. The following incidents occurred during a single week in July:

> June 30/July 1, midnight, soldier Dablanc, stationed at the Audoud Barracks in Marseille was wounded by a revolver bullet in the neck as he returned to his quarters, by an American soldier of color.
>
> July 3, 11:30 p.m. At a place called "Traverse de l'Hermitage" in a suburb of Aygalades, near Marseille, MMs Kouyoumdjian and Torossian, both of Armenian origin, were killed by shots from a revolver fired by four American soldiers of color. M. Argelas, taken away by ambulance, was also a victim gravely wounded by the same men.
>
> July 4, 10 p.m. Some American soldiers assaulted the Bar Honoré at 21 rue Coutellerie, in the course of a fusillade fired into the doorway of the bar, the owner Eyssautier and a Spanish resident, Yglesias-Gomez, were killed. Several other bar customers were wounded as well as three American soldiers.
>
> July 5, 12:10 a.m. Jean Cecchini, harbor pilot, . . . was attacked in front of his home and wounded in the head by six American soldiers.
>
> July 5, two American soldiers who found themselves on the No. 26

> tramway made advances on the wife of a corporal in the French army, provoking a violent fight. Both [Americans] were detained.
>
> July 7, 12:15 a.m. , . . . two American soldiers who set upon a French soldier were apprehended and remanded to the MPs. The wounded [French soldier] was taken to hospital.

This went on and on for six pages, listing the incidents in which someone was injured or killed through October.[7]

The Americans' departure from France did not go smoothly. However, despite the notes of chaos and bedlam introduced by GIs, their exit in 1945 and 1946 was more peaceful than their entrance in 1944. And, everything considered, the winding down of the US military presence in France proceeded in a fairly orderly fashion, aided by French and American officers and officials who, by the summer and fall of 1945, had gained much experience working together. All over northern France, French officials tallied up what the Americans owed for services rendered and received claims from French citizens against the US Army for rent, damages, sales, and such. The AFA in Beauvais submitted an invoice to the Americans for 170 million francs for roadwork, wages for French workers, lumber, fuel, water, and the like, and it had no concerns about getting paid. The AFA had been submitting monthly invoices for routine goods and services since late 1944, and they had always been settled without a problem. But Lend-Lease lasted only as long as a state of war existed, so both France and the United States had to decide how to pay all the bills that had accumulated after it lapsed in September 1945. As the Americans closed air bases and left buildings in the Haute-Marne in October, the Bureau des Ponts et Chaussées (PC) in Chaumont passed along ninety-five invoices to the prefect's office, expecting payment. Because the Americans were still there, the prefect had no worries about getting the 4.6 million francs owed for services and goods rendered to the US Army in October. In December 1945 the prefect in Beauvais sat on a pile of 893 dossiers for requisitions by the US Army, but his staff had little time to settle them before the Americans were scheduled to leave. Resolving claims for road accidents involving US Army vehicles was a never-ending headache for the French. As the Americans cleared out of Troyes, Chaumont, and Châlons-sur-Marne, Commissioner Marcel Grégoire was pleased to take back the newly available hotels, schools, and factories. He also reported that his office had a huge backlog of affairs to settle, but the Americans were proving cooperative, and the stack was diminishing.[8]

The vanishing army bureaucracy made satisfying claims more urgent for the French. Civil Affairs was eliminated on 14 July 1945. That same day, SHAEF was dissolved, and the US Forces, European Theater Mission, took over. The Americans were leaving faster than claims could be processed. American liaison officers who knew the ropes and were familiar faces to their French counterparts were disappearing at a worrisome pace and being replaced—if at all—by new officers who did not know the ropes and were unfamiliar with the cases under discussion. Or worse, US offices closed, and French officials had no idea how they or their citizens were supposed to get paid. Nonroutine claims, such as for damages and irregular requisitions, took up huge amounts of time, and the French feared they would never see any compensation from the Americans, who were eager to get out and go home. M. Menant, the manager of a sports club in Avallon, complained that a long-gone American colonel had altered the facilities and promised to reverse the changes before the Americans departed. Now the soldiers were leaving, and no one had made the promised restorations; nor had anyone fixed his damaged fields, which the manager claimed would cost 50,000 francs. The Americans replied that they had neither the personnel nor the equipment to make the repairs—and the amount requested for the fields, $1,000, seemed excessive. This sort of thing was common as the Americans left France, and Menant would have to submit a claim to the AFA, like everybody else. To ease the process, Prefect Gibaud had newspapers print instructions on how to submit claims and where to find the AFA office in Auxerre. The American office in Fontainebleau that had received claims from the French public in the Seine-et-Marne closed suddenly and without warning in November, leaving the French with a huge stack of unsettled claims. There were unpaid bills for routine goods and services rendered in October worth 10.5 million francs ($210,000); this was down from 25.7 million francs for June 1945, revealing how drastically the American presence had already been reduced. The largest amount owed (7 million francs) was for French workers' wages (down from 10 million francs in June); this amount was due to the AFA office, which paid the French workers directly. As elsewhere, the Americans still owed a lot of compensation for roadwork and auto accidents that were subject to negotiation, and now the AFA office in Melun wanted to know who was going to negotiate these charges. The AFA in Paris was deluged with similar questions emanating from many departments in northern France.[9]

The Americans' departure from many bases around France produced anxiety among both officials and civilians, who worried what came next. What about all the promises American officers had made to French communities? Were the towns going to receive surplus goods? As the Americans began to pull out of big air bases in the Aisne, French officials worried about the fate of the facilities. They did not want the Americans to burn the temporary barracks, which would make excellent housing for DPs, refugees, and French displaced by the war. The prefect in Laon wanted to move in homeless French as soon as possible because he feared if the buildings were left unattended for even a short time, they would be subject to looting. He wanted to move in Republican Guards (a unit of the gendarmerie) to live there and protect the premises from looters as soon as possible. Officials in the Seine-Inférieure fretted over what was to become of the huge cigarette camps once the GIs shipped out. The commissioner in Rouen expressed frustration over the fate of the surplus from the camps; the population had expected to get a stream of usable supplies but so far had received only trickles. In late November the commissioner was equally nervous about the disposal of surplus in the Eure; by the end of December, he had still heard nothing. The prefect in Laon oversaw a territory full of warehouses rented by the US Army; these warehouses had constantly leaked supplies onto the black market, and now he expressed great anxiety about the fate of the contents as the Americans pulled out. He wanted the material to be inventoried by the French as soon as possible so that a vast new supply of goods did not disappear into underground markets. Officials became alarmed when they heard that the Americans were destroying supplies rather than handing them over to the French. The commissioner in Laon complained to Paris that the departing US Army had burned twenty tons of tires in July; most of them still had tread and could have been enormously helpful to the French. When the mayor of one small town in Normandy heard that departing Americans were going to burn used clothing, he asked the camp commander to turn the clothes over to him instead. The commander complied. At the same time, the mayor of Orival, near Rouen, reported that his town had received five truckloads of clothes and boots from another American commander.[10]

The US Mission set up procedures for French who were interested in buying surplus army property, and many French were interested. The US Liaison Office in Paris distributed lists of equipment for sale and arranged for prospective buyers to inspect the items. The port director in Marseille had to get approval from Paris in February 1946 to buy surplus US Army clothes for port workers: 200 pairs of snow boots (170 francs, or $3.40 a pair), 200 raincoats (350 francs, or $7 each), 200 pairs of pants, 200 coats, 3,000 handkerchiefs (10 francs, or 20 cents each), 2,000 towels, and so forth. The "emergency order" indicated that all these items had been manufactured in France for the Americans. The PC submitted a similar request to buy clothing for its workers. The price list attached to the PC request—50 cents for a pair of socks, $4 for overalls, $4 for a wool shirt—reveals that these were not fire-sale bargains, but given the difficulty of acquiring clothes at any price in France, the prices were probably reasonable.[11]

By the beginning of 1946, one group of American soldiers remained in France: the Graves Commission, which was responsible for locating and moving the bodies of American soldiers scattered around France. Before the American dead could be consolidated into large cemeteries, they had to be located, which required help from the French. Prefects all around France sent circulars to mayors, asking whether they knew of any war dead buried in their communes. This included Axis dead, which the Americans assumed responsibility for as well. American officers were dispatched to sites of plane crashes to look for Allied remains in the area. The prefect in Troyes identified nineteen communes with downed Allied planes, but there was no way to tell whether they were American or British. The American major in charge of the Graves Commission in the Meurthe-et-Moselle remained in Nancy until May 1946, after gathering the American dead into four cemeteries in the department. Ceremonies were held at the four cemeteries on Memorial Day, 30 May 1946; they were attended by large numbers of French civilians as well as French military honor guards. The French were not pleased that land in the village of Andilly, acquired by the Americans for a cemetery, was then used to bury dead Germans. Fifty GIs stayed in Auxerre searching for the remains of Americans and Germans in May 1946; an appeal for more information on uncollected war dead by the prefect's office in September 1947 elicited only a "non" from mayors in the Yonne. The American military maintained a small presence in France for many years after the war; the United States kept small bases in the north and east of France and a presence in Marseille, mostly to support logistics for US occupation troops in Germany. These soldiers required support troops and staff, such as transportation troops to move them and MPs to police them. By spring 1946, the hordes of GIs who had dominated Nancy and Metz for much of 1945 were gone; the US Army maintained small forces in Lorraine throughout the rest of the 1940s. Otherwise, only Graves Commission troops remained, along with the 43,739 American soldiers they had laid in their graves. The rest of the Yankees had gone home.[12]

Stationing an enormous military establishment in a foreign country during wartime offers limitless opportunities for clashes, mishaps, and even tragedy. Both the French and the Americans struggled to minimize occasions and areas for friction, and to a large degree, they succeeded. It would have been nothing short of miraculous if the two allies had managed to avoid all conflict, and such a miracle failed to appear. The American military remained in France for only about a year and a half, from June 1944 to January 1946.

It was fortunate that de Gaulle's committee in Algiers took the initiative and proposed an agreement covering the payment for services before the Allied invasion of France. Even though both the Allies and France proved effective in solving problems as they surfaced, having some basic ground rules in place before the event proved wise. Unlike the Germans, the Allies undeniably did not set out to fleece France of its wealth—far from it. They did what little they could to restore France to health. Nevertheless, Allied largess did not come free, and the French were expected to pay for services rendered that did not directly serve the Allied cause.

Some problems were best left to decision makers at higher levels—SHAEF and French authorities in Paris. Trying to settle problems at the local level sometimes failed because civil affairs officers had little real authority over US troops. The provisional government of General de Gaulle was determined to stamp its authority on France and sought to centralize decision making to the extent possible. In contrast, SHAEF set policies and granted wide discretion to the lower-level officers who were expected to implement those policies. It is possible to conclude that French and Allied authorities who dealt with problems locally often solved them more quickly and successfully than when Paris or SHAEF were in charge; however, both sides could and did appeal to higher authorities when problems could not be worked out satisfactorily at the local level. Centralized decisions handed down from Paris served the French by challenging American decisions that were contested by local officials. Given the vast differences in power between a provincial French mayor and an American colonel in charge of a US garrison that was disturbing the local peace, appealing to Paris was often the only avenue available to the French. Policies established locally by American officers were sometimes unwise, such as barring Frenchmen from dances hosted by the Americans, straining relations with Frenchwomen, young Frenchmen, and French parents alike, for different reasons. Despite French protests, this practice continued. Problems generated by slack discipline or impulsive and inconsistent polices, as occurred with the 101st Airborne Division in the Yonne or General Patton's often capricious regulations in Lorraine, could be resolved only when Paris or SHAEF interceded. In some cases, the GPRF in Paris left the management of affairs mostly in local hands, which worked remarkably well when authority was bestowed on the right person, such as chief engineer Le Bel in Marseille.

SHAEF often proved inflexible when minor accommodations would have soothed raw French nerves. War booty inspired the most acrimonious disputes between the two allies. SHAEF's intransigence on the disposition of captured goods ensured that this remained a sore spot for as long as the

US military remained in France. The practice of claiming all German war matériel as war booty only heightened tensions. Strictly enforcing regulations covering the transfer of US Army property to civilians produced more ill feeling. Confiscating US Army property from French civilians after the war was over served no good purpose. Keeping US Army goods out of French black markets was a common goal of both the French and the Americans, and they cooperated to do that. But chasing down cans of food and cloth caps given as gifts by well-meaning GIs only harmed French opinion of the US Army while it remained a guest in France.

If US Army intransigence on some questions was puzzling, the GPRF's obstinacy on seemingly unimportant questions was less mysterious. De Gaulle's government remained nervous about proving its sovereignty until his exit in January 1946. French officials—usually in Paris or among the commissioners appointed personally by de Gaulle—frequently refused to budge on small questions, such as who got to hand out socks to men in need, when making minor concessions would have smoothed over problems. This situation should have receded as French sovereignty became more securely established. Certainly, by the spring of 1945, the French were in control of their own affairs, and Gaullist truculence should have abated. There is little evidence that it did. The personnel appointed by de Gaulle often mirrored his own rigid personality, such as Adrien Tixier and François Coulet. This maintained the momentum of Gaullist prickliness as long as they held office.

In some cases, there was no clash over policies or interests; there were simply problems that bedeviled both partners and defied resolution, such as finding housing for DPs in France. The Americans were happy to dump the problem of caring for DPs in the lap of the French provisional government, but no one could find housing for them. The French army was just as likely as the American army to be occupying living space that could have been used for DPs. All involved wanted to find a solution, but wartime conditions (not American obstinacy) made that very difficult. Only the exit of the US Army freed enough housing to shelter DPs. Similarly, only the Americans' departure ended the high demand for wood from French forests and the competition with French civilians for fuelwood and wood for construction. Once the French took charge of the Axis POWs, they faced their own challenges about finding enough wood to meet their needs.

Oddly enough, money and bills due occasioned few real difficulties between the two allies. Neither side devoted much time or energy to complaining about payments because, by and large, they had a system for resolving questions when they arose—and they did. US and French financial officials got along well and had procedures in place for making payments or recording credits. Questions that could not be answered locally were kicked up to Paris and SHAEF; problems that baffled officials at these higher levels were deferred to the Treasury Department in Washington and the Finance Ministry in Paris. Rather than directing their ire at the Americans, French civilians overwhelmingly complained about the sluggishness of payments and the low rates of compensation set by their own government.

Problems that defied resolution, such as the treatment of POWs and the distribution of war booty, had to be managed rather than solved. Trouble provoked by undisciplined GIs is probably the best example of difficulties that were subject to management rather than solution. French officials protested to American officers, who listened to their complaints and then offered solutions—usually additional MPs working more closely with French police—that were implemented with varying degrees of success. GIs continued to behave badly as long as they remained in France, French officials continued to protest, and US officers continued to adjust procedures to address the grievances. It is difficult to call this process "success" or "resolution"; however, it did manage the problem of GI criminality, which was probably the best SHAEF could hope for. And perhaps the best the French government could hope for was to be taken seriously by the Americans. American officers, from civil affairs officers and town majors to army generals and staff officers at SHAEF, including General Eisenhower, listened to their French counterparts and dealt with them seriously to arrive at a working alliance. In the end, the alliance worked well enough to achieve its ends, even if many problems that separated the two allies ultimately proved irresolvable.

Acknowledgments

As always, the staffs at all the French departmental archives I visited to research this book were helpful, friendly, and eager to accommodate. The staffs at the departmental archives of Aube, Bouches-du-Rhône, Meurthe-et-Moselle, and Yonne all went out of their way to assist me, especially Véronique Raguseo in Marseille and Arnoud Fouanon in Auxerre. In particular, I want to thank Jérôme Leclerc of the Archives départmentale de la Meurthe-et-Moselle, as well as the late Professor Jean-Louis Etienne in Nancy, who took an interest in my work, was very helpful, and offered sage advice. Staff at the Archives nationales in Pierrefitte-sur-Seine were welcoming and made my research not only fruitful but also enjoyable. My visit to France was particularly pleasurable thanks to the good company and friendship of Dominique and Maryline Beuret. I thank Joëlle Prim for her hospitality in Saint-Denis, Christian Darmon in Auxerre, and Patrick Thierry in Troyes. Rich Noble and Eric Van Slander of the National Archives and Records Administration in College Park, Maryland, proved helpful and went out of their way to make my visit more enjoyable. Rutha Beamon and Sarah Lepianka of the NARA Still Pictures Branch helped find photos for the book cover. Dr. Richard Sommers and the staff of the US Army Heritage and Education Center of the War College in Carlisle, Pennsylvania, provided valuable assistance at the Military History Institute, as well as a General and Mrs. Mathew B. Ridgway grant to help defray the costs of undertaking research at the MHI. The staff of the Microforms Department of the Library of Congress were cordial and accommodating. Charles Robertson offered friendly and useful advice. I thank the staff of the University Press of Kentucky—Melissa Hammer, Sarah Olson, Natalie O'Neal, and Linda Lotz—for their fleetness and professionalism. The press's anonymous reviewers provided useful suggestions for improving this work. I thank Mia Partlow of Indiana University for preparing the map, using open-source software. I thank the many people in the United States who helped me in ways big and small: Phil Berger, Deborah Best and Vince Gianinni, Emily Best and Dennis Benjamin, Pam and

George Callan, the late Jane Clark, the late Kurt Eigner, Leslie Derr, Dave Eubanks, Tricia Fleck, Susan and Walter Haydel, Sarah and John Nash, Ken and Linda Norkin, Carl Peridier, and Tim Souweine and Lisa Reichenbach. My family provided lodging, food, and welcome distraction: Rick and Sue Fuller, my mother Marjorie Huntsberger Fuller, Michael Fuller, Jeff Fuller and Rebecca Baldwin, Chris and Yvonne Fuller, and Alyssa Wilson and her brood. My sister-in-law, Kathryn Ragsdale, offered valuable editorial suggestions on much of the work, which is better for her red pencil. Above all, I owe a debt of gratitude to my wife, Lynda Fuller Clendenning, who always provided counsel and support when I needed it. Thank you, Lynda.

Notes

Abbreviations

ADA	Archives départementales de l'Aube (Troyes)
ADBdR	Archives départementales du Bouches-du-Rhône (Marseille)
ADMM	Archives départementales de Meurthe-et-Moselle (Nancy)
ADY	Archives départementales de l'Yonne (Auxerre)
ANF	Archives nationales de France (Pierrefitte-sur-Seine)
CA	Civil Affairs (Allied army department charged with liaising with French civilian administrators)
Chef Ing.	Chef Ingénieure (head engineer)
Comm. Police	Commissaire de Police (police commissioner)
Comm. Rép.	Commissaire de la République (commissioner of the Republic)
CS	chief of staff
CWO	chief warrant officer
Dir.	director
ETO	European theater of operations
For. Min.	foreign minister
FRUS	*Foreign Relations of the United States* (documents published by the US State Department)
HQ	headquarters
IGO	inspector general's office
MHI	Military History Institute (US Army War College, Carlisle, PA)
Min. Int.	Ministre de l'Intérieure (minister of the interior)
MTO	Mediterranean theater of operations
NARA	National Archives and Records Administration (College Park, MD)
NATOUSA	North African Theater of Operations United States Army
n.d.	no date
n.p.	no place of publication
PFC	private first class
Préf.	Préfet (prefect)
Pres.	president
PWB	Psychological Warfare Branch (propaganda branch, sometimes called PWD)

PWD	Psychological Warfare Division
QMC	Quartermaster Corps
Ravit. Gén.	Ravitaillement Général (General Supply)
Ren. Gén.	Renseignements Généraux (government domestic intelligence agency)
RG	Record Group
Sec. Gén.	Police Secrétaire général de la Police (top police official)
Sous-Préf.	subprefect
Svc.	service
TSFET	Theater Service Forces, European Theater (specialist army offices to support SHAEF)

Introduction

1. Comm. Rép., Marseille, to Min. Int., 15 February 1945, ANF, F1a 3304; G. Le Bel, "Proposition d'Attribution de Distinction Honorifique au Major Marcus de l'Armée Américaine," 25 April 1945, ADBdR 6 S 10/10.

2. On AMGOT, see Charles L. Robertson, *When Roosevelt Planned to Govern France* (Amherst: University of Massachusetts Press, 2011).

3. On German-occupied France, see Thomas Johnston Laub, *After the Fall: German Policy in Occupied France, 1940–1944* (New York: Oxford University Press, 2010); Allan Mitchell, *Nazi Paris: The History of an Occupation, 1940–1944* (New York: Berghahn Books, 2008); Philippe Burrin, *France under the Germans: Collaboration and Compromise,* trans. Janet Lloyd (New York: New Press, 1993).

1. France and the United States, Allies in War

1. There are many valuable books on this period. I relied most heavily on Raoul Aglion, *Roosevelt and de Gaulle: Allies in Conflict; a Personal Memoir* (New York: Free Press, 1988); Winston S. Churchill, *The Second World War,* 6 vols. (Boston: Houghton Mifflin, 1949–1950), vol. 2; Charles de Gaulle, *The Complete War Memoirs of Charles de Gaulle,* trans. Jonathan Griffin and Richard Howard (New York: Da Capo Press, [1984]); Richard Griffiths, *Pétain: A Biography of Marshal Philippe Pétain of Vichy* (Garden City, NY: Doubleday, 1972); Cordell Hull, *The Memoirs of Cordell Hull,* 2 vols. (New York: Macmillan, 1948), vol. 2; Julian G. Hurstfield, *America and the French Nation, 1939–1945* (Chapel Hill: University of North Carolina Press, 1986); Jean Lacouture, *De Gaulle,* 2 vols., trans. Patrick O'Brian (New York: W. W. Norton, 1990), vol. 1; William L. Langer, *Our Vichy Gamble* (New York: W. W. Norton, 1966); William D. Leahy, *I Was There: The Personal Story of the Chief of Staff to Presidents Roosevelt and Truman* (New York: Whittlesey House, [1950]); G. E. Maguire, *Anglo-American Policy towards the Free French* (New York: St. Martin's Press, 1995); Henri Michel, *Histoire de la France Libre* (Paris: Presses Universitaires de France, 1972); Milton Viorst, *Hostile Allies: FDR and Charles de Gaulle* (New York: Macmillan, 1965).

2. On North Africa, see Harry C. Butcher, *My Three Years with Eisenhower* (New York: Simon and Schuster, 1946); Mark W. Clark, *Calculated Risk* (New York: Harper and Row, 1950); Dwight D. Eisenhower, *Crusade in Europe* (New York: Doubleday, 1948); Arthur L. Funk, *Charles de Gaulle: The Crucial Years, 1943–1944* (Norman: University of Oklahoma Press, 1959); Henri Giraud, *Un Seul But, la Victoire, Alger 1942–1944* (Paris: R. Julliard [1949]); Harold Macmillan, *The Blast of War, 1939–1945* (London: Macmillan, 1967); Général Charles Mast, *Histoire d'une Rébellion, Alger, 8 novembre 1942* (Paris: Plon, 1969); Robert Murphy, *Diplomat among Warriors* (New York: Doubleday, 1964); Kenneth Whittemore Pendar, *Adventure in Diplomacy: Our French Dilemma* (New York: Da Capo Press, 1976); Richard W. Steele, *The First Offensive 1942: Roosevelt, Marshall and the Making of American Strategy* (Bloomington: Indiana University Press, 1973).

3. Hervé Coutau-Bégarie and Claude Huan, *Darlan* (Paris: Fayard, 1989); Bernard Pujo, *Juin, maréchal de France* (Paris: Albin Michel, 1988); Alphonse Juin, *Mémoires,* 2 vols. (Paris: A. Fayard [1959]), vol. 1; de Gaulle, *Complete War Memoirs,* 357.

4. Macmillan, *Blast of War,* 232, 253–54, 294–95; Eisenhower, *Crusade in Europe,* 129; Murphy, *Diplomat among Warriors,* 145–46, 174–76; Butcher, *My Three Years,* 225, 230, 232–36; Robert E. Sherwood, *Roosevelt and Hopkins: An Intimate History* (New York: Harper Brothers, 1948), 683–84.

5. Robertson, *When Roosevelt Planned,* 102–3; Harry L. Coles and Albert K. Weinberg, *Civil Affairs: Soldiers Become Governors* (Washington, DC: US Army Center of Military History, 2004), 11–12; Sir Frederick Morgan, *Overture to Overlord* (Garden City, NY: Doubleday, 1950), 227–30; Frank S. V. Donnison, *Civil Affairs and Military Government North-West Europe, 1944–1946* (London: Her Majesty's Stationery Office, 1961), 12–19; Forrest C. Pogue, *The Supreme Command* (Washington, DC: Office of the Chief of Military History, Department of the Army, 1954), 142–43; Edwin Wilson, Algiers, memo of conversation with de Gaulle, 10 November 1943, *FRUS,* 1943, 2:188–92; accord of 14 December 1943 between UK and CFLN, NARA, RG 331, SHAEF, G-5/652, box 12.

6. Pogue, *Supreme Command,* 144–46; Butcher, *My Three Years,* 512; Robertson, *When Roosevelt Planned,* 107; de Gaulle, *Complete War Memoirs,* 509; Chapin to Hull, 29 March 1944, *FRUS,* 1944, 3:660–65.

7. Butcher, *My Three Years,* 241, 513, 540; Lacouture, *De Gaulle,* 1:513, 517; Robertson, *When Roosevelt Planned,* 112–13; Franco-American accords signed in Algiers, March 1944, ANF, F1a 3304; François Coulet, *Vertu des temps difficiles* (Paris: Plon, 1967), 219–20.

8. Franco-American accords, March 1944; Ordonnance du CFLN, Algiers, 4 April 1944 (on the AFA), ADBdR, 6 S 10/10; "Draft No. 5, Arrangements for Civil Administration and Jurisdiction in French Territory Liberated by an Allied Expeditionary Force," n.d. (attached cover letter suggests May 1944), NARA, RG 331, SHAEF, G-5/2, box 12; Coles and Weinberg, *Civil Affairs,* 667–70.

9. Hull to Chapin, 2 June 1944, *FRUS,* 1944, 3:696.

10. Donnison, *Civil Affairs,* 80–81.

11. Coulet, *Vertu,* 215, 220; de Gaulle, *Complete War Memoirs,* 554; Pogue, *Supreme*

Command, 400–403, 458–59; Coles and Weinberg, *Civil Affairs,* 667–68; George McJimsey, ed., *Documentary History of the Franklin D. Roosevelt Presidency,* vol. 47, *Establishing Civil Government in Occupied Europe* ([Bethesda, MD]: University Publications of America, 2001), 114–16; Eisenhower to Marshall, 21 March 1944, in *The Papers of Dwight D. Eisenhower. The War Years: III,* ed. Alfred D. Chandler (Baltimore: Johns Hopkins University Press, 1970), 1781–82. On AMGOT, see Robertson, *When Roosevelt Planned.*

12. Lacouture, *De Gaulle,* 1:528–30; Coulet, *Vertu,* 228–32; Robertson, *When Roosevelt Planned,* 151; Lt. Col. D. R. Ellias, report on British zone, 9–12 June 1944, NARA, RG 331, SHAEF, G-5, box 64.

13. Coulet to Koenig, 3 July 1944, ANF, F1a 4005; weekly report of labor inspector to Coulet, 29 July 1944, ANF, F1a 4006; minutes of weekly G-5 Staff Conference, 11 July 1944, NARA, RG 331, SHAEF, G-5, box 64.

14. Coulet to Koenig, 24 June 1944, ANF, F1a 4004; minutes of weekly G-5 Staff Conference, 4 July 1944, NARA, RG 331, SHAEF, G-5, box 64; Operations Report, A1A1 Detachment, 7 July 1944, NARA, RG 498, First Army HQ, G-5, box 2950.

15. Coulet to Koenig, report on visits to Granville and Avranches, 4 August 1944, ANF, F1a 4006; Coulet to Koenig, report on visit to la Manche, 31 July 1944, ANF, F1a 4005.

16. Robert Gildea, *Fighters in the Shadows: A New History of the French Resistance* (Cambridge, MA: Belknap Press, 2015), 327.

17. P. Laroque to Koenig, report on Rennes, 13 August 1944, ANF, F1a 4006; Coulet to Koenig, 17 August 1944, ibid.

18. De Gaulle, *Complete War Memoirs,* 592–93; Butcher, *My Three Years,* 526; Eisenhower, *Crusade in Europe,* 247–48; Eisenhower to F. d'Astier, 17 March 1944, in Chandler, *Papers of Eisenhower,* 1771–72.

19. Robert Aron, *Histoire de la Libération de la France, Juin 1944–Mai 1945* (Paris: Libraire Arthème Fayard, 1959), 180; S. J. Lewis, *Jedburgh Team Operations in Support of the 12th Army Group, August 1944* (Fort Leavenworth, KS: Combat Studies Institute, 1991), x; Marcel Vigneras, *Rearming the French* (Washington, DC: Office of the Chief of Military History, Department of the Army, 1957), 304–5; Claude Delasselle, Joel Drogland, Frédéric Gand, Thierry Robin, and Jean Rolley, *Un département dans la guerre 1939–1945: Occupation, collaboration et résistance dans l'Yonne* (Paris: Editions Tirésias, 2006), 463–66, 468, 470, 484. Nelson Douglas Lankford, ed., *OSS against the Reich: The World War II Diaries of Colonel David K. Bruce* (Kent, OH: Kent State University Press, 1991), and William Dreux, *No Bridges Blown* (South Bend, IN: University of Notre Dame Press, 1971), offer lively accounts of American officers working with FFI behind German lines.

20. Dir. of Ravit. Gén., Yonne, to Commandant of FFI, Auxerre, 1 September 1944, ADY, 1 W 324. ADY, 1 W 319, is full of complaints about FFI misbehavior, much of it quite serious.

21. Maginnis log, 11–15 June 1944, MHI, Maginnis Papers, box 1; John J. Maginnis and Robert A. Hart, eds., *Military Government Journal: Normandy to Berlin* (n.p.: University of Massachusetts Press, 1971), 5–6, 15.

22. Maginnis log, 16–22, 23, 25, 26 June, 8, 17, 19, 28 July, 5 August 1944; Maginnis and Hart, *Military Government Journal,* 14–19, 21.

2. Requisitions

1. Sabatier to mayor of Pradet, 13 December 1943, 14 October 1944; mayor of Pradet to Sabatier, 15 January 1944; receipt for 17,680 francs, 19 June 1944, all in ADBdR, 9 W 38.

2. Franco-American accords, March 1944, ANF, F1a 3304; Ordonnance du CFLN, Algiers, 4 April 1944 (on the AFA), ADBdR, 6 S 10/10; "Draft No. 5," NARA, RG 331, SHAEF, G-5/2, box 12; minutes of weekly G-5 Staff Conference, 11 July 1944, ibid., G-5, box 64; "Arrangements for Civil Administration and Jurisdiction in French Territory Liberated by an Allied Expeditionary Force," n.d. (attached cover letter suggests May 1944), ibid., G-5/2, box 12; Arrêté sur la requisition des voitures, 13 July 1944, ANF, F1a 4005.

3. Col. Wayne Allen, General Purchasing Agent, US Army, to Col. Laroque, office of Comm. Rép., Bayeux, 16 August 1944, ANF, F1a 4006.

4. Réunion des déléguées régionaux d'AFA, Paris, 6–8 January 1945, ANF, F1a 3304; Min. of Supply Giacobbi to Comms. Rép., Regional and Dept. Dirs. of Supply, 26 October 1944, ADY, 1 W 579; circular from Comm. Rép. to Préf., Auxerre, with arrêté of 29 February 1944, 6 November 1944, ibid.; Gen. Supply, Yonne, note to the press, n.d. [fall 1944], ADY, 1 W 324; Dir. Gen. Supply, Yonne, to Préf., 20 January 1945, ibid.; Ren. Gén., Nancy, report, 19 December 1944, ADMM, WM 1521; Capt. Leonard McCormick, AFA liaison officer, memo, 18 July 1945, NARA, RG 498, HQ ETO, box 1488; Brig. McKeswick, report, 17 November 1944, NARA, RG 331, SHAEF, G-5/2/10, Financial Reports, box 5.

5. Réunion des déléguées régionaux d'AFA, Paris, 6–8 January 1945, ANF, F1a 3304; Préf., Châlons-sur-Marne, report, 9 January 1945, ibid.; Vehicles, vol. 2, June 1945, NARA, RG 498, HQ ETO, box 1492, file 451.2.

6. Préf. Haut-Rhin, Colmar, to Min. Int., 18 April 1945, ANF, F1a 3303; Comm. Rép., Bordeaux, to Min. Int., 15 May 1945, ibid.; dossier on sequestrations, ADBdR, 9 W 38; Dir. of Ravit. Gén., Yonne, to Commandant FFI, Auxerre, 1 September 1944, ADY, 1 W 324; Parquet, Joigny, complaint by M. Druge, farmer, Arces, 18 November 1944, ibid.; Head of Ravit. Gén., Bléneau, to Dir. Ravit. Gén., Yonne, 25 November 1944, ibid.

7. Min. Air, Paris, to Regional Air Commandants, 13 December 1944, ADA, 1576 W 117; ADA, 1576 W 287, contains a thick dossier on the Grandes-Chapelles requisitions; Coulet to Koenig, 26 July 1944, ANF, F1a 4005; Réunion des déléguées régionaux de l'Aide aux forces Alliées (AFA), 6–8 January 1945, ANF, F1a 3304.

8. ADBdR, 47 W 3, contains the registers; Arrêtés Nos. 573 and 574, 19 October 1944, ADBdR, 6 S 10/10; Le Bel to Lt. Col. Philippon, chef de requisitions, Marseille, 13 September 1944, ibid.

9. Ren. Gén., Marseille, to Comm. Rép., 17 January, 14 March 1945, ADBdR, 149 W 182; Sec. Gén. Police, Marseille, memo, 13 January 1945, ADBdR, 5 W 394; Préf.,

Alpes-Maritime, to Min. de Guerre, 15 October 1945, ANF, F1a 3305; Pres. Syndicat de Tourisme de Alpes-Maritimes to Préf., 8 October 1945, ibid.; Purchasing Agent McCormick, memo, 16 July 1945, NARA, RG 498, HQ ETO, box 1488; Le Bel to Dir., Compagne de Docks, 10 March 1945, ADBdR, 6 S 10/10; Soc. de Travaux et Ind. Maritime, Marseille, to Le Bel, 26 September 1944, ibid.; Le Bel to STIM, Marseille, 29 September 1944, ibid.

10. *Exposé des circonstances dans lesquelles il a été procédé à la réquisition de la Tour Blanche par autorités Américaine,* 5 September 1944; note to Préf., Marseille, 20 September 1944; Dir. Dr. Marrot to Préf., 17 November 1945; Conseil Gen. to Dir. Adm. of Public Assistance, 18 December 1945; Dir. of Tech. Services to Préf., 26 March 1948; Préf. to Head of Military 2nd Bureau, 3 March 1949; Military Intendant, 3rd Div., to Préf., 2 September 1952, all in ADBdR, X 2 Bis 6655.

11. Mitchell, *Nazi Paris,* 78; Min. of Ed. to Min. of War, 31 January 1945, ADA, SC 24642 B; Min. of Ed. to Prefs., 2 February 1945, ibid.; Comm. Rép., Dijon, report, 15 November 1944, ANF, F1a 3304,; Comm. Rép., Loan–St. Quentin, 20 January 1945, ibid.; Réunion des déléguées régionaux de l'Aide aux Forces Alliées (AFA), 6–8 January 1945, ibid.; Maj. Gen. John T. Lewis to Coulet, 22 January 1945, ANF, F1a 3305.

12. Lt. Col. Charles Wolff, memo, 25 June 1945, NARA, RG 498, HQ ETO, box 1488; Col. Lévy, memo, 26 June 1945, ibid.; Purchasing Agent McCormick, memo, 16 July 1945, ibid.; Préf., Châlons-sur-Marne, report, 9 January 1945, ANF F1a 3304.

13. Haas-Picard to Min. Int., 26 October 1944, ANF, F1a 3304; Comm. Rép., Orléans, report, 18 November 1944, ibid.; no author to Haas-Picard, 1 December 1944, ibid.; Réunion des déléguées régionaux d'AFA, 6–8 January 1945, ibid.; Préf., Châlons-sur-Marne, report, 9 January 1945, ibid.; Sous-Préf., Toul, to Préf., Nancy, 6 November 1944, ADMM, WM 1521; Préf. to Maj. Harold McGugin, USAAF CA, 16 January 1945, ADA, SC 24642 B; requisition orders for 4,500 square meters of wood, 20 January 1945, ADA, ED 220/14; Roland G. Ruppenthal, *Logistical Support of the Armies,* 2 vols. (Washington, DC: US Army Center of Military History, 1953), 2:498.

14. Minutes of meeting of delegates, Capt. Cachera, Min. of Ind. Prod., 1 February 1945, ANF, F1a 3304; Sous-Préf., Lunéville, to Préf., Nancy, 2 and 11 October 1944, ADMM, WM 1521.

15. Ruppenthal, *Logistical Support* 2:497–98; Comm. Gen. for Tourism to Min. Int., 2 August 1945, ANF, F1a 3305; Mission Milt. Fr. Liaison, Biarritz, to Juin, Paris, 12 December 1945, ibid.; Comm. Rép., Bordeaux, report, 15 September 1945, ANF, F1a 3304; Comm. Rép., Dijon, report, 3 August 1945, ibid.; Préf., Nice, to Coulet, 13 September 1945, ANF, F1a 3306.

16. Comm. Rép., Châlons-sur-Marne, report, 1 March 1945, ANF, F1a 3304; Comm. Rép., Nancy, n.d. [July 1945], ibid.; Comm. Rép., Loan–Saint Quentin, report, 31 March 1945, ibid.; Comm. Rép., Châlons-sur-Marne, report, 15 June 1945, ANF, F1a 3305; Louis Stone to Col. Wayne Allen, 11 September 1945, NARA, RG 498, HQ ETO, box 1489; Vigneras, *Rearming the French,* 402.

17. Comm. Rép., Nancy, to Haas-Picard, 1 December 1944, 16 January and 1 March 1945, ANF, F1a 3304; Préf., Metz, report, 15 December 1944, ibid.

18. Comm. Rép., Nancy, to Haas-Picard, 1 December 1944, 16 January and 1 March 1945, ANF, F1a 3304.

19. Comm. Rép., Nancy, report, 16 January 1945, ANF, F1a 3304; Charles Codman, *Drive* (Boston: Little, Brown [1957]), 227.

20. De Gaulle to Tixier, 2 February 1945, ANF, F1a 3305; Tixier to Préfs. and Comm. Réps., 5 February 1945, ANF, F1a 3304.

21. Theater Service Forces, European Theater (TSFET), Seine Section, Historical Reports, French Liaison, July and September 1945, NARA, RG 498, HQ ETO, box 4342; Insp. Académique, Nancy, to Préf., 3 August 1945, ADMM, WM 1521; Préf. to Insp., 13 September 1945, ibid.; Préf. to Mayor of Homécourt, 30 October 1945, ibid.; Préf., Nancy, to Lt. Col. Harky, G-5, 17 September 1945, ibid.; Dir. Ecole Sup. de Chimie to Préf., Nancy, 13 September 1945, ibid.; HQ Oise sec., US Army, to Préf., 21 September 1945, ibid.; Comm. Rép., Châlons-sur-Marne, report, 15 June 1945, ANF, F1a 3305.

22. Préf., Alpes-Maritime, to Min. de Guerre, 19 October 1945, ADBdR, 149 W 182; no author [Préf., Nice] to Dir. Gen. Sureté Nat., 25 January 1945 [*sic,* 1946], ANF, F1a 3305; Comm. Rép., Marseille, 7 December 1945, ibid.; Gen. Ratay to Préf. Haag, 9 January 1946, ibid.; Haag to Gouin, 16 January 1946, ibid. .

23. Comm. Rép., Rouen, reports, 28 November, 26 December 1945, ANF, F1a 3304; Préf., Aube, report, November 1945, ibid.; Min. de Travaux Pub. et des Transports to Ing. en chef, P. et C., 6 July 1946, ADA, 1576 W 117; ledger, Département de l'Aube, Affaires Terminées Troupes Américaines et Françaises, Immeubles et Mobiliers, n.d., ADA, 220/15. ADBdR, 47 W 9, contains a thick dossier devoted to Mme. Beuchat's case. I thank Jérôme Leclerc for information about the French attributing all damages to the Americans.

24. Juin to Cabinet, 4 July 1945, ANF, F1a 3306;, Comm. Rép., Nancy, report, n.d. [July 1945], ANF, F1a 3304; Svc. Central for Alsace-Lorraine to Min. Int., 11 April 1945, ANF, F1a 3303 (this file is full of letters protesting requisitions by the French army following the US Army); AFA regional delegate to Préf., Nancy, 1 October 1945, ADMM, WM 1521; Préf. to Dir. Dept. for POWs, Deportees, and Refugees, 30 October 1945, ibid. (this file contains abundant correspondence about the fate of hospitals in Nancy starting in spring and into the fall 1945); Félix Gouin, Pres. Constituent Assembly, Paris, to Comm. Rép. 7 December 1945, ADBdR, 149 W 182; Gen. Ratay to Haag, 9 January 1946, ibid.; US Mission Report, 17 October 1945, NARA, RG 498, HQ ETO, box 1489.

25. Pres. Soc. pour la defense du Commerce et de l'Ind., Marseille, to Comm. Rép., 16 November 1945, ADBdR, 149 W 182; Préf., Marseille, to Gen. Commandant, XVe Milt. Region, 3 August 1945, ibid.; Préf., Auxerre, to Comm. Gen., US Army in Auxerre, 23 February 1945, ADY, 1 W 328; Ren. Gén., Auxerre, tele. message, 29 October 1945, ANF, F1a 3305.

26. E. Mathieu, Salon Massilia, J. Magalon & Cie., to Haag, 31 October 1945, ADBdR, 149 W 182; Préf., Rhône, report, 15 July 1945, ANF, F1a 3304.

27. Préf., Haut-Rhin, to Min. Int., 18 April, 5 May 1945, ANF, F1a 3303; Svc. Centrale de Alsace-Lorraine to Min. Int., 3 September 1945, ibid.; Préf., Moselle, to Min.

Int., 16 May 1945, ibid.; Préf., Strasbourg, to Min. Int., 18 May, 8 June 1945, ibid.; Préf., Metz, to Min. Int., 1 June 1945, ibid.; Comm. Rép., Strasbourg, to Min. Int., 18 May, 7 June 1945, ibid.; Min. Int. Tixier to Pres. de Gaulle, 24 May, 5 July 1945, ibid.; Conseilleur d'Etat de Préf., Strasbourg, to Min. Ind. Prod., 1 June 1945, ibid.; Purchasing Agent McCormick, memo, 16 July 1945, NARA, RG 498, HQ ETO, box 1488.

28. Svc. Tec. to Préf., Marseille, report, 10 July 1947, ADBdR, X 2 Bis 6655; Sister Marie, Religieuses Hospitalières de St. Augustines, to Préf., 7 August 1947, ibid.; Arrêté de Préf., 14 August 1947, ibid.

3. Transportation

1. SHAEF, memo no. 24, 18 July 1944, ADBdR, 6 S 10/10.

2. Comm. Police, Nancy, to Dir. Police, Nancy, 21 October 1944 ADMM, WM 1521; Maj. Harold McGugin, USAAF, to Préf., Troyes, 3 September 1944, ADA, SC 24642 B; poster, Avis à la Population, n.d., ADA, SC 39175; Lankford, *OSS against the Reich,* 188.

3. Ren. Gén., Nancy, 15 January 1945, ADMM, WM 1521; Office of Préf., Colmar, to Min. Int., 2 June 1945, ANF, F1a 3303; Comm. Rép., Nancy, report, 1 March 1945, ANF, F1a 3304; minutes of meeting of delegates from all ministries having relations with Allies, Paris, 30 October 1944, ibid.; Fiche, HQ Delbase, note, n.d. [probably December 1944], ADBdR, 149 W 182.

4. H. Heuzé, Chargé de Mission, Strasbourg, "Note sur l'interdiction de circuler dans la zone des opérations depuis le début de l'offensive américaine," 14 November 1944, ANF, F1a 3306. Heuzé's car joined that of the prefect of Moselle on the side of the road outside Verdun. His note is silent on whether Chenrion made it to Hayange.

5. Dir. Hosp., Troyes, to Préf., 2 August 1945; Préf. to Lt. Wilson, engineer, 8 August 1945; Dir. Hosp. to Préf., 24 September 1945, all in ADA, SC 24642 B.

6. PC to Préf., Troyes, 2 October 1944, ADA, SC 24642 B; External Relations Svc., Marseille, meeting notes, 30 December 1944, ADBdR, 149 W 182; Réunion des déléguées régionaux d'AFA, Paris, 6–8 January 1945, ANF, F1a 3304; Circular no. 30, 24 November 1944, NARA, RG 498, ETO HQ, box 1489; no author, report, 9 May 1945, NARA, RG 331, SHAEF, G-5, box 4; Xavier de Guerpel, *1939–1945, Une Certaine Vie de Château au Bocage Normand* (Conde-sur-Noireau, France: Editions Ch. Corlet, 1973), 231–32.

7. Joseph Bykofsky and Harold Larson, *The Transportation Corps: Operations Overseas* (Washington, DC: US Army Center of Military History, 1957), 331–35; William F. Ross and Charles F. Romanus, *The Quartermaster Corps: Operations in the War against Germany* (Washington, DC: US Army Center of Military History, 2004), 399; Haas-Picard to Min. Int., 29 November 1944, ANF, F1a 3305.

8. Préf., Seine-et-Oise, to Min. Int., 24 November 1944, ANF, F1a 3305; Min. Int. to Comms. Rép., 4 November 1944, ibid.; HQ Comm. Z, liaison to Commandant Henry Camerlynck, 29 October 1944, ibid.; Arlo Benzmann, CA, to Préf., Troyes, 17 October 1944, ADA, SC 24642 B; press release, Office of Préf., Troyes, 26 October 1944,

ibid.; Bykofsky and Larson, *Transportation Corps,* 335; Janet Teissier du Cros, *Divided Loyalties* (New York: Alfred Knopf, 1964), 337–40, 346.

9. M. Guyot to Préf., Auxerre, 14 March 1945, ADY, 1 W 328; Gen. Chapman to Préf. Gibaud, 2 April 1945, ibid.; gendarme message, Auxerre, 3 March 1945, ADY, 1 W 319; Préf., Troyes, to CA, 19 October, 7 November 1944, ADA, SC 24642 B; gendarme report to Préf., 15 August 1945, ibid.; Comm. Rép., Lille, to Min. Int., notes sur les incidents . . . du Nord, 28 November 1945, ANF, F1a 3305.

10. Investigation of injuries to Renée Touboul, French infant, aged nine years, 17 July 1944, NARA, RG 492, MTO Special Staff Investigations, box 2016.

11. Préf., Marne, to Min. Int., 18 January 1946, ANF, F1a 3305; Préf., Manche, report, 30 March 1945, ibid.; HQ Delta Base Section Office of Transportation, 8 January 1946, NARA, RG 498, HQ ETO, box 4339.

12. Statements of Ferdinand Froitères, forest ranger, and Oscar Hella, Sens, 5 February 1945, NARA, RG 498, HQ ETO, box 2947; US Mission, report, 15 September 1945, ibid., SHAEF, box 1489; Capt. Gall, note, 22 January 1945, ADBdR, 6 S 10/10; Comm. Rép., Rouen, report, October 1945, ANF, F1a 3304; Comm. Rép., Marseille, report, 2 January 1945, ibid.; Préf., Rouen, report, July 1945, ibid.; Comm. Rép., Rouen, report, 31 October 1945, ibid.; Préf., Oise, reports, November and December 1945, ibid.; Comm. Rép., Châlons-sur-Marne, report, 15 November 1945, ibid.; Préf., Marne, reports, 31 August and 31 July 1945, ibid.; Préf., Troyes, report, November 1945, ibid.; Comm. Rép., Lille, to Min. Int., notes sur les incidents . . . du Nord, 28 November 1945, ANF, F1a 3305; Préf., Troyes, to CA, 15 November 1944, ADA, SC 24642 B; Lt. Arlo Benzmann, CA, to Préf., 27 November 1944, ibid.; Préf. to Dir. SLEE [electric company], 8 December 1944, ibid.

13. David L. Cohn, *This Is the Story* (Boston: Houghton Mifflin, 1947), 106; Ross and Romanus, *Quartermaster Corps,* 664–66; Maginnis and Hart, *Military Government Journal,* 123; Préf., Aude, report with attached appeals, 27 November 1944, ANF, F1a 3304; Préf., Aude., report attachment, lists of gas cans collected, n.d. [19 January 1945], ANF, F1a 3305.

14. Svc. Inter-alliées to Col. P. J. T. Pickhall, G-5, SHAEF, 2 November 1944 and annex letter; Dir. Gen. Etudes et Recherches, Paris, to Coulet, 8 November 1944; Adj. relations interalliées, Min. Etrange, to Min. Int., 21 November 1944; Haas-Picard to Min. Int. and Min. Int. to Coulet, 23 November 1944, all in ANF, F1a 3304.

15. On Wybot, see André Dewavrin, *Souvenirs [par] Colonel Passy,* 2 vols. (Monte Carlo: Raoul Solar, 1947), 2:17–24; Roger Wybot, Direction de la Surveillance du territoire (DST), Sûreté Nationale, Paris, to Min. Int., 18 October 1945, ANF, F1a 3305; CID report on incident involving Sgt. Chester Krol, MP, 15 November 1944, ibid.; Brig. Gen. T. F. Bresnahan to R. Wybot, DST, 23 November 1944, ibid.; Wybot to Bresnahan, 5 December 1944, ibid.; Wybot to Préf. and Min. Int., 22 January 1945, ibid.

16. Préf. Police, 17 Arron., Paris, report, 14 April 1945, ANF, F1a 3305.

17. Col. Bruce Easley, Adjutant Gen., SHAEF, to Haas-Picard, 30 December 1944, ANF, F1a 3304; Min. Int. to Coulet, 20 January, 7 February 1945, ibid.; Ross and Romanus, *Quartermaster Corps,* 667.

18. Civil Affairs, Sixth Army Group, to French Inter-City Civil Transport Service, 28 September 1944, ADBdR, 6 S 10/10; minutes of weekly G-5 Staff Conference, 1 August 1944, NARA, RG 331, SHAEF, G-5, box 64; memo, Col. Homer Jones to SHAEF, 9 September 1944, ibid.; Préf., Troyes, to Civil Affairs, 20 October 1944, ADA, SC 24642 B; Chef Ing., PC, note, 11 April 1945, ADMM, WM 1521; Bykofsky and Larson, *Transportation Corps,* 340–45.

19. Jean-Luc Leleu, Françoise Passera, and Jean Quellien, *La France pendant la Seconde Guerre Mondiale* (Paris: Fayard and le Ministère de la Défense, 2010), 269; Bykofsky and Larson, *Transportation Corps,* 342–43.

20. Préf., Bar-le-Duc, to Min. Int., 11 November 1944, ANF, F1a 3306.

21. Dine, SNCF, Marseille, to "cher monsieur" [Min. of Transportation?], 19 February 1945, ADBdR, 149 W 182.

22. Ren. Gén., Nancy, report, 30 March 1945, ADMM, WM 1521.

23. No author, report, 9 May 1945, NARA, RG 331, SHAEF, G-5, box 4; Juin to Cabinet, 4 July 1945, ANF, F1a 3306; "QG de TSFET" Lt. Col. C. E. Johnson, Paris, to Pres. Comm. Interalliée de Redéploiement, 2 September 1945, ibid., reports that the United States provided the French with 46,000 wagons, considerably more than the number counted by the Americans.

24. Johnson to Pres. Comm. Interalliée de Redéploiement, 2 September 1945, ANF, F1a 3306; HQ Delta Base Section Office of Transportation [Marseille], 8 January 1946, NARA, RG 498, HQ ETO, box 4339.

4. The Port of Marseille

1. Speech by Port Dir. Couteaud, 5 April 1946, ADBdR, 6 S 10/10.

2. Raoul Busquet, *Histoire de Marseille* (Paris: R. Laffont, 1998), 395; Laub, *After the Fall,* 265–66; Clark and Smith, *Riviera to the Rhine,* 140–42, 202; "Journal de la Direction du Port," 17–19, 21, 23 August 1944, ADBdR, 6 S 10/10.

3. "Journal de la Direction du Port," 24–29 August 1944.

4. "Journal de la Direction du Port," 17–29 August 1944; André Beaufre, *La revanche de 1945* (Paris: Plon, 1966), 274. Le Bel signed everything "G. Le Bel," so his first name remains a mystery.

5. "Journal de la Direction du Port," 25–29 August 1944; Le Bel to Port Comm., 5 September 1944, ADBdR, 6 S 10/10; Clark and Smith, *Riviera to the Rhine,* 204; Bykosfky and Larson, *Transportation Corps,* 295; Busquet, *Histoire de Marseille,* 396, reports 176 ships sunk by the Germans in the harbor.

6. Chef Ing., Le Bel, to Insp. Gen. of Ind. Prod., Marseille, 16 September 1944; Groupement d'Union des Negotiants Soutier to Dir. Svc. Transport, 23 September 1944; Le Bel to Dir. of Port, 25 September 1944; Soc. de Travaux et Ind. Maritime Marseille to Le Bel, 26 September 1944; Chef Svc., Transport Maritime, to Le Bel, 26 September 1944; Le Bel to Dir. des Docks Vinicoles, Marseille, 28 September 1944; M. Garrus, AFA, to Le Bel, 16 September 1944; Enterprise TTBT (Tous Travaux de Beton et Terrasement) to Le Bel, 23 October 1944; Transport Maritime to Le Bel, 8 December 1944;

Lt., Port, to Port Commandant, 15 January 1945; Le Bel to Lt. Col. Philippon, chief of requisitions, Marseille, 13 September 1944, all in ADBdR, 6 S 10/10.

7. Col. Boutaud de Lavilleon to Mayor of Saint-Tropez, 19 August 1944, ADBdR, 149 W 182; Note circulaire Marine nationale, Marseille, 14 September 1944, ADBdR, 6 S 10/10; Chef Ing. Le Bel to Military Commandant of the Port, 16 September 1944, ibid.; Port Dir. Peltier to Commandant of the Port, 16 September 1944, ibid.; order of Col. Clarkson, 22 October 1944, ibid. ADBdR, 6 S 10/10, contains a folder with details of the tug rental to French port authorities.

8. Bykosfky and Larson, *Transportation Corps,* 319–20; Ross and Romanus, *Quartermaster Corps,* 122, 124; Cohn, *This Is the Story,* 163; Clark and Smith, *Riviera to the Rhine,* 204, 207; note, "NSCO," Marseille, 12 September 1944, ADBdR, 6 S 10/10; Busquet, *Histoire de Marseille,* 414.

9. Le Bel to Chef Gendarmerie, 31 August 1944, ADBdR, 6 S 10/10; Le Bel to 4th Arron. Ing., 1 September 1944, ibid.; Le Bel to Enterprise Negri et Fils, 9 September 1944, ibid.; Le Bel file about recruiting workers, 14–21 September 1944, ibid.; Companie des Docks et Entrepots de Marseille to Le Bel, 3 October 1944, ibid.; "Displacement of Population in France," 10 March 1944, NARA, RG 331, SHAEF, G-5/2/10, Financial Reports, box 3; Cohn, *This Is the* Story, 166; Bykosfky and Larson, *Transportation Corps,* 319; Ross and Romanus, *Quartermaster Corps,* 121; Clark and Smith, *Riviera to the Rhine,* 202.

10. Note on conference with M. Vernant, 20 January 1945, ADBdR, 149 W 182; Comm. Rép., Marseille, to Min. Int., 2 January, 15 February 1945, ANF, F1a 3304; Pres. of Technical Comm. Port of Marseille to Comm. Rép., 22 March 1945, ADBdR, 6 S 10/10; Le Bel, "Proposition d'Attribution de Distinction Honorifique au Major Marcus de l'Armée Américaine, " 25 April 1945, ibid.

11. Comm. Rép., Marseille, to Min. Int., 15 February 1945, ANF, F1a 3304; Port Police, Joliette, to Comm. Rép., 15 January 1945, ADBdR, 149 W 182.

12. Svc. de Relations avec l'Exterieure, report, 16 January 1945, ADBdR, 149 W 182.

13. Soc. Marseillaise de Trafic Maritime to Peltier, 27 November 1944, ADBdR, 6 S 10/10; Port Commandant, report, 27 November 1944, ibid.; Foreman Landi [Lanci?] to Sec. Dockworkers Union, 13 October 1944, ibid.; Ren. Gén., Marseille, extracts of reports, 25 November 1944, ANF, F1a 3304.

14. Napoleon Lenci, chef du Batelage, Marseille, to Le Bel, 30 October 1944, ADBdR, 6 S 10/10; Enterprise Jean Negri et Fils to Le Bel, 20 November 1944, ibid.

15. Salaires des Ouvriers d'Entretien, 26 October 1944; Le Bel to Col. Hitt, 18 October 1944; Chef de Svc. Techniques, Chambre de Commerce, Marseille, to Port Dir. Peltier, 7 October 1944; Chef Ing. [Le Bel], Marseille, to AFA, 6 July 1945; Le Bel to M. Alexis, AFA, 30 January 1945, all in ADBdR, 6 S 10/10. The federal minimum wage in the United States in 1944 was 30 cents an hour.

16. Commandant, Port of Marseille, order, 1 October 1944, ADBdR, 6 S 10/10; Comm. Port, to Chef Ing., 26 January 1945, ibid.; orders for rations, 31 October, 2 November 1944, ibid.; handwritten note, n.d., ibid.; Capt. of the Port to Work Inspector, 15 May 1945, ibid.; Ross and Romanus, *Quartermaster Corps,* 210.

17. Le Bel to Comm. gendarmes, 6 September 1944, ADBdR, 6 S 10/10; Clark and Smith, *Riviera to the Rhine,* 219; Cohn, *This Is the Story,* 165; Busquet, *Histoire de Marseille,* 402–4. The Marseille black market is discussed further in chapter 7.

18. Order of Col. Clarkson, 22 October 1944, ADBdR, 6 S 10/10; Clarkson to Le Bel, 12 March 1945, ibid.; Le Bel to Companie de Docks, 10 March 1945, ibid.; Chef Ing. Civil Defense, Marseille, to Le Bel, 14 March 1945, ibid.; Chef Port Police to Div. Chef, Ren. Gén., 12 February 1945, ADBdR, 149 W 182.

19. Le Bel to Préf., 6 March 1945, ADBdR, 6 S 10/10; Port Police to Port Commander, 23 June 1945, ibid.; Chef Ing. J. Mathieu, PC, to Col. Clarkson, 25 October 1945, ibid.; Dir. des Ports Maritime, Paris, to Couteaud, Dir. Port, Marseille, 20 April 1946, ibid.; Dr. Serafino, Pres., Entr'aide Francaise, Marseille, to Gen. Ratay, 13 November 1945, ADBdR, 149 W 182; Lt. Col. B. H. Shipe to Port Chef Ing. Revel, 21 September 1945, ibid.; Revel to Ciaparra, 22 September 1945, ibid.; Ing., 3eme Arron., to Revel, 25 September 1945, ibid.; Revel to Dir. Tech. Svcs., Cham. Commerce, Marseille, 14 November 1945, ibid.; HQ Delta Base Section, Office of Transportation Officer [Marseille], report, 4 January 1946, NARA, RG 498, HQ ETO, box 4339.

20. Min. des Travaux publics et transport, Paris, to Le Bel, 16 June 1945, ADBdR, 6 S 10/10; Min. des Travaux, Rumpler, Paris, to Chef Ing. Port, attached circular about end of Lend-Lease, 12 February 1946, ibid.; Chef of Port Police to Chef Ing., 9 July 1945, ibid.; Min. Fin., Paris, to J. Lévy, AFA, 14 February 1946, ibid.; invitation to transfer of 6th Port [designation for all French Mediterranean ports], 5 April [1946], at Cap Janet, ibid.; allocution by M. Couteaud, Dir. Port, 5 April 1946, ibid.; Réunion des déléguées régionaux d'AFA, Paris, 6–8 January 1945, ANF, F1a 3304; arrêté de 30 Mai, *Journal Officiel,* 6 June 1945, ibid.; HQ Delta Base Section, Office of Transportation Officer [Marseille], report, 4 January 1946.

21. Chef Ing. Revel, PC, Marseille, to Dir. Tech Svcs., Marseille Chamber of Commerce, 13 August 1946, ADBdR, 6 S 10/10; Dir. Maritime Ports, Paris, to Port Dir. Couteaud, Marseille, 20 April 1946, ibid.; Min. Pub. Works, Paris, to Chef Ing. PC, Marseille, 9 September 1946, ibid.; Gen. Ratay to Comm. Rép. Haag, 9 Janusry 1946, ADBdR, 149 W 182; "QG de TSFET," Lt. Col. C. E. Johnson, Paris, to Pres. Comm. Interalliée de Redéploiement, 2 September 1945, ANF, F1a 3306; Report Mission to France, 17 October 1945, NARA, RG 498, HQ ETO, box 1489.

22. Speech by Gen. W. Allen to French delegates of AFA, 9 May 1945, NARA, RG 498, HQ ETO, box 1489; open letter of Col. Clarkson, 2 May 1945, ADBdR, 6 S 10/10; allocution by M. Couteaud, Dir. Port, 5 April 1946; www.theodore-roosevelt.com/trsorbonnespeech.

5. Displaced Persons

1. Michael R. Marrus, *The Unwanted: European Refugees in the Twentieth Century* (New York: Oxford University Press, 1985), 304–5.

2. "Plans for Displaced Persons," 4 June 1944, NARA, RG 331, SHAEF, G-5/2, Financial Reports, box 3; "The Displacement of Population in Alsace-Lorraine," 10

March 1944, ibid.; "Displacement of Population in France," 10 March 1944, ibid.; Leleu et al., *La France pendant la Seconde Guerre Mondiale,* 135.

3. Displaced Persons Branch, report, 7 September 1944, NARA, RG 331, SHAEF, G-5/2, box 47; cable from SHAEF to Bomber Command, Eighth Air Force, and Air Ministry (UK), 25 October 1944, ibid.; Ralph Bain, Dep. Dir. Civilian War Relief, report, 11 January 1945, ibid., box 54.

4. Min. for Inter-Allied Affairs Coulet to Min. of War Diethelm, 26 January 1945, ANF, F1a 3305; Maj. T. H. Brown, report, n.d. [April 1945], NARA, RG 331, SHAEF, G-5/4, box 48; "Notes for Conference," 17 May 1945, ibid., box 47.

5. DP forms, NARA, RG 331, SHAEF, G-5/2, box 30; "Notes for Conference," 17 May 1945; DP reports, Maj. M. J. Proudfoot, 17 and 28 April, 6, 9, 10, 19, 25, and 28 May, 4, 5, and 13 June, 6 July 1945, ibid., box 58; Col. A. H. Hoffit Jr., report, 24 June 1945, ibid.; Maj. F. W. Jones, Adj. Gen. Div., to SHAEF, 26 June 1945, ibid., box 47; Marguerite Duras, *The War: A Memoir,* trans. Barbara Bray (New York: Pantheon Books, 1986).

6. Agnès Humbert, *Résistance: A Woman's Journal of Struggle and Defiance in Occupied France,* trans. Barbara Mellor (New York: Bloomsbury, 2008), 224–45, 257–70.

7. Svc. Central Alsace-Lorraine to Min. of War, 22 May 1945, ANF, F1a 3303.

8. Memo from Col. P. Jacobsen, French liaison officer, to SHAEF, 21 April 1945, NARA, RG 331, SHAEF, G-5/4, box 48; memo from John T. Lewis, 17 April 1945, ibid.; Maj. T. H. Brown, report, n.d. [April 1945], ibid.; Duras, *The War,* 12–15, 30–34, 44–45; Donald Harrison, ed., *From the Letters of Robert S. Gerdy, 1942–1945: A Personal Record of World War II* (Philadelphia: Dorance, 1969), 313. Duras was obsessed with the returning DPs and POWs and bitterly critiqued anything that was not Communist. She even hated "American milk"—distributed in cans.

9. Préf., Loire, report, 16 December 1945, ANF, F1a 3304; Ralph Bain, Dep. Dir. Civilian War Relief, report, 11 January 1945, NARA, RG 331, SHAEF, G-5/2, box 54; W. H. G. Giblin, Dir. Civ. War Relief, report, 7 June 1945, ibid.; "Notes for Conference," 23 January 1945, ibid., box 58.

10. Ralph Bain, report, 11 January 1945, NARA, RG 331, SHAEF, G-5/2, box 54. See Crane Brinton, "Letters from Liberated France," *French Historical Studies* 2, no. 2 (1961): 151–54, on conditions in the southwest; for an alternative view, see Robert Gildea, *Fighters in the Shadows: A New History of the French Resistance* (Cambridge, MA: Belknap Press, 2015), 388, 411–12.

11. Inspecteur des Svc. d'Enfance to Préf., Auxerre, 22 January 1946, ADY, 1 W 328; ARC, Paris, to Pref., Auxerre, 7 February 1946, ibid.; Préf., Auxerre, to Croix Rouge, 13 February 1946, ibid.; Préf. to Mr. Dayton, Dir. Civilian War Relief, Paris, 13 February 1946, ibid.; Croix Rouge to Préf., 15 February, 17 June 1946, ibid.; Préf. to Entr'aide française, Dijon, 20 February 1946, ibid.; *Le Travailleur de l'Yonne,* 28 December 1945, ADY, 1222 W 11.

12. Préf. to Comm. Rép., 30 September 1944, ADMM, WM 1523; W. H. G. Giblin, report, 6 November 1944, NARA, RG 331, SHAEF, G-5/2, box 54; minutes of Weekly Staff Conference, 31 October 1944, ibid., G-5, box 64; US Mission to France, report, 17 October 1945, NARA, RG 498, ETO HQ, box 1489.

13. US Mission to France, report, 16 August 1945, NARA, RG 498, HQ ETO, box 1488; US Mission to France, report, 17 October 1945, ibid., box 1489; Comm. Police, Nancy, 15 March 1945, ADMM, WM 1523; report, 31 March 1945, ibid.; Préf., memo, 16 April 1945, ibid.; Préf., Marne, to Min. Int., 5 December 1945, ANF, F1a 3305; Maginnis and Hart, *Military Government Journal,* 127, 135.

14. Capt. Perry Waldner, report, 12 December 1944, NARA, RG 331, SHAEF G-5, box 47; US Mission, report, 15 September 1945, NARA, RG 498, HQ ETO, box 1488; Préf., Marne, to Min. Int., 5 December 1946 [1945], ANF, F1a 3305; Humbert, *Résistance,* 226, 268–69.

15. Report on Visit to Normandy Base Section, 25 February 1944 [1945], NARA, RG 498, HQ ETO, Insp. Gen. Sec., Reports 1944–45, box 4666; Gilbert Grandval and A. Jean Collin, *Libération de l'Est de la France* (Paris: Hachette, 1974), 225–26; Préf., Lyon, report, 15 August 1945, ANF, F1a 3304; "Fortnightly Report, 16–30 Nov. 44," 30 November 1944 [British army report], ANF, F1a 3306; Maginnis and Hart, *Military Government Journal,* 137–38, 142–43, 145.

16. Ren. Gén., Clermont-Ferrand, 6 December [January], 3, 5, 6, 7 January 1945, ANF, F1a 3305; Comm. Rép., Clermont-Ferrand, report, 3 January 1945, ANF, F1a 3304; Ren. Gén., Clermont-Ferrand, 11 January 1945, ANF, F1a 3306; Ren. Gén., Orléans, 14 January 1945, ibid.

17. Capt. Perry Waldner, report, 14 January 1945, NARA, RG 331, SHAEF, G-5/4, box 48; "Notes on Conference [with General Dragun]," 19 February 1945, ibid.; US Mission Report, 18 January 1945, ibid., box 58.

18. Gendarme report, Toul, 1 April 1945, ADMM, WM 1523; Comm. Rép., Bordeaux, report, 31 May 1945, ANF, F1a 3304; Préf., Seine-et-Marne, report, 15 September 1945, ibid.; US Mission report, 15 September 1945, NARA, RG 498, HQ ETO, box 1489.

19. Min. Int., note, 6 December 1944, ANF, F1a 3306; Tixier to Haas-Picard, 20 December 1944, ibid.; Comm. Rép., Alsace-Lorraine, to Haas-Picard, 23 December 1944, ibid.; Min. Int., note, 6 January 1945, ibid.; Commandante P. Sorbac, XX Corps, G-5, to Lt. Col. Clemencon, 12 AG, G-5, 24 November 1944, ibid.; W. H. G. Giblin, report, 6 November 1944, NARA, RG 331, SHAEF, G-5/2, box 54.

20. Comm. Rép., Strasbourg, to Haas-Picard, 9 December 1944, ANF, F1a 3306; Min. Int. to Haas-Picard, 4 January 1945, ibid.; Maj. Raymond Fisher, DP Branch, G-5, 23 May 1945, ADBdR, 142 W 21; Comm. Rép., Marseille, to Min. Int., 7 June 1945, ibid.; Cpt. Joseph Wall, CA, Vittel internment camp, to Préf., Vosges, 12 December 1944, ANF, F1a 3304.

6. Axis Prisoners of War

1. Sous-Préf. G. Hutin, Vendôme, to Préf., Loir-et-Cher, 7 October 1944, ANF, F1a 3304; "Some Recent Trends in French Attitudes toward the United States," 2 July 1945, NARA, RG 498, HQ ETO, box 1488; US Mission to France, report, 15 September 1945, ibid., box 1489.

2. Comm. Rép., Rennes, reports, 16 November, 1 December 1944, ANF, F1a 3304; Centre Entr'aide cantonal des Anciens Prisonniers du canton de Melle to Préf., Deux-Sèvres, 5 December 1944, ANF, F1a 3306; extract of report from Comm. Rép., Strasbourg, 31 May 1945, ANF, F1a 3303.

3. Memos from Col. R. H. Clarkson, Delta Base, copy to Dir. of the Port, 5 and 17 November 1944, ADBdR, 6 S 10/10; US Navy Port Office, Marseille, Regulations and Information, 3 April 1945, ibid.; Serv. for External Relations, notes on conference, 30 December 1944, ADBdR, 149 W 182; report on Cherbourg, 25 February 1944 [1945], NARA, RG 498, Inspector Gen. Reports, 1944–45, box 4666; Col. Cannon, Report of Investigation Concerning Alleged Lawlessness of American Troops in Normandy, extracts of gendarme reports for October, 7 November 1944, ibid., box 4673; "Some Recent Trends in French Attitudes toward the United States," 2 July 1945; Comm. Rép., Rouen, report, 15 January 1945, ANF, F1a 3304; Ren. Gén., Paris, to Haas-Picard, 3 January 1945, ANF, F1a 3305.

4. Centre Entr'aide cantonal des Anciens Prisonniers du canton de Melle to Préf., Deux-Sèvres, 5 December 1944, ANF, F1a 3306; Sarah Fishman, *We Will Wait: Wives of French Prisoners of War, 1940–1945* (New Haven, CT: Yale University Press, 1991), 59–60, 151–55; Nicole H. Taflinger, *Season of Suffering: Coming of Age in Occupied France, 1940–45* (Pullman: Washington State University Press, 2010), 152–56.

5. Comm. Rép., Loan–St. Quentin, report, 31 March 1945, ANF, F1a 3304; meeting of regional delegates of AFA, 6–8 January 1945, ibid.; minutes of meeting at prefecture in Marseille of French and Allied officers, 21 July 1945, ADBdR, 149 W 182; requisition order for Hôtel des Granges, Mézières, 20 January 1945, ADA, ED 220/14; requisition order for Château de Mézières, 22 May 1945, ibid.; requisition order for multiple plots of land, 28 May 1945, ibid.; multiple requisition orders for wood starting 5 February 1945, ibid.

6. Gendarme report, Nancy, 22 September 1944; note of telephone call from Préf., Nancy, to Sous-Préf., Lunéville, 1 December 1944; Gendarme report, Chambley, 2 December. 1944; Gendarme report, Lunéville, 10 December 1944; Gendarme report, Briey, 18 December 1944; Sous-Préf., Lunéville, to Col. Pinot, 18 December 1944; Sous-Préf., Lunéville, to Préf., Nancy, 17 and 23 April 1945; Ren. Gén., Nancy, reports, 23 February, 13 April 1945; Sous-Préf., Lunéville, to Dir. of Rural Management, Nancy, 12 April 1945; Pres. Dept. Comm. de Lib. to Préf., Nancy, 4 April 1945, all in ADMM, WM 1525.

7. Artillery officer Henri Gille to mayor, Nancy, 14 September 1945, ADMM, WM 1525.

8. Coulet to Koenig, 22 August 1944, ANF, F1a 4006; Gendarme report, Lunéville, 10 December 1944, ADMM, WM 1525; Gendarme report, Briey, 18 December 1944, ibid.; Sous-Préf., Lunéville, to Col. Pinot, 18 December 1944, ibid.; Sous-Préf., Lunéville, to Préf., Nancy, 17 and 23 April 1945, ibid.; Ren. Gén., Nancy, reports, 23 February, 13 April 1945, ibid.; Sous-Préf., Lunéville, to Dir. of Rural Management, Nancy, 12 April 1945, ibid.; Pres. Dept. Comm. de Lib. to Préf., Nancy, 4 April 1945, ibid.; Work Inspector to Préf., Nancy, 20 January 1945, ibid.; Centre Entr'aide cantonal des Anciens Pris-

onniers du canton de Melle to Préf., Deux-Sèvres, 5 December 1944, ANF, F1a 3306; Dir. Rural Management, Nancy, to Préf., Nancy, 7 December 1944, ibid. Rural laborers were excluded from the Law on Work Accidents of 1898, which was still in effect in 1944. The work inspector assured the prefect that demining workers would be covered by the law of 1898.

9. Chief Engineer Rural Management to Préf., Nancy, 26 April 1945; note to Préf., Nancy, 21 June 1945; under-Préf., Lunéville, to Préf., Nancy, 20 June, 26 September 1945, all in ADMM, WM 1525.

10. Min. Int. to Coulet, 11 December 1944, ANF, F1a 3306; Ren. Gén., Rouen, to Ren. Gén., Paris, 15 August 1945, ANF, F1a 3305; memo from Col. A. R. Brian, IGD, to COS NATOUSA, 24 June 1944, NARA, RG 492, MTO Special Staff Investigations, box 2021.

11. Comm. Rép., Dijon, report, 31 December 1944, ANF, F1a 3304; Comm. Rép., Marseille, to Min. Int., 15 February 1945, ibid.; minutes of meeting in Marseille of French and Allied officers, 21 July 1945, ADBdR, 149 W 182; memo, Comm. Rép., 11 July 1945, ADBdR, 6 S 10/10; Coles and Weinberg, *Civil Affairs,* 778–79; US Mission reports, 17 October, 16 November 1945, NARA, RG 498, HQ ETO, box 1489.

12. Comm. Rép., Loan–St. Quentin, report, 10 August 1945, ANF, F1a 3304; Préf., Oise, report, 29 September 1945, ibid.; US Mission reports, 15 August, 17 October 1945, NARA, RG 498, HQ ETO, box 1489; Ren. Gén., note, 16 October 1945, ADMM, WM 1521.

13. US Mission reports, 16 August, 17 October, 15 November, 15 December 1945, NARA, RG 498, HQ ETO, box 1489; Comm. Police, Auxerre, 27 October 1945, ADY, 1222 W 11; Revel to Dir. of Tech. Serv., Marseille, 14 November 1945, ADBdR, 6 S 10/10.

14. US Mission reports, 17 October, 15 November, 15 December 1945; Historical Report, n.d., NARA, RG 498, HQ ETO, ACOS G-2 & G-3, Seine Section TSFET, box 4339; Min. Int. to Préf., Aube, 16 April 1946, ADA, SC 4290; notes, 17 December 1945, ibid.; Charles Ferry, Assoc. Dept. Déportées et Internés Patriote, to Préf., 28 February 1946, ibid.; Préf., Marne, to Min. Int., 5 December 1946, ANF, F1a 3305.

15. Haas-Picard to Préf., Marne, n.d. [January 1946], ANF, F1a 3305; US Mission reports, 15 November, 15 December 1945; Min. of Justice, regional delegate, Troyes, to Préf., 12 February 1946, ADA, SC 4290; Comm. Rép., Nancy, report, 17 November 1945, ANF, F1a 3304.

16. Préf., Marne, to Min. Int., 5 December 1946, ANF, F1a 3305; Préf. report, Troyes, 24 March 1947, ADA, SC 24644; "Prisonniers de Guerre: 1948," list of monthly payments, 8 September 1948, ibid. By 1948, inflation had reduced the value of the franc to 263 francs to $1, so German POWs made slightly more than $1—less than they had in 1945.

17. French volunteers of the LVF—Legion des Volontaires Français contre le Bolchevisme—who fought on the eastern front, were eventually merged into the SS. Philippe Burrin estimates that 22,000 French, exclusive of Alsatians and Lorrainers, joined various German military units. It is difficult to separate volunteers from those drafted from

other formations such as the Milice or Todt Organization. See Burrin, *France under the Germans,* 433–36. US Mission reports, 15 September, 15 December 1945; Col. Alden Sibley, SHAEF, to Chief of Staff, Min. War, Paris, 14 October 1944, ANF, F1a 3303; de Gaulle to Min. Foreign Affairs, 21 October 1944, ibid.; note, "Situation des Alsaciens et des Lorrains faits Prisonniers par les Armées Alliées," n.d., ibid.; minutes of Defense Committee, Paris, 17 October 1944, ibid.; note [illegible] to Min. Int., 26 April 1945, ibid.; Tixier to Laffont and Marzolf, 28 April 1945, ibid.

18. Min. Int. to Haas-Picard, 4 January 1945, ANF, F1a 3306; Coulet to Haas-Picard, 18 February 1945, ibid.; Central Service for Alsace-Lorraine to Min. Int., 15 May 1945, ANF, F1a 3303; Gen. Juin to Chief of Staff for National Defense, 14 June 1945, ibid. ADBdR, 142 W 21, contains many undated lists of people held in US camps; these lists include only their names, providing no other information about them. One list identifies eighty-six as Alsace-Lorrainers.

19. Maj. Raymond Fisher, DP Branch, G-5, 25 March, 10 May 1945, ADBdR, 142 W 21; arrest report, Capt. Louisetti, Allied Military Govt., Merano, Italy, n.d., ibid.; Chef d'escadron Guignard to Préf., Var, 20 August 1944, ibid. This file contains lists of hundreds of people detained at Camp 404, about half of whom were determined to be French. For the fate of Milice stranded in Germany, see Paul Jankowski, *Communism and Collaboration: Simon Sabiani and Politics in Marseille, 1919–1944* (New Haven, CT: Yale University Press, 1989), 140. ADBdR, 5 W 272, contains thousands of index cards on individuals who were brought to Camp 404 by the Americans. The PPF, the largest and loudest of the collaborationist groups, was intensely anti-Communist. It was the principal promoter of the LVF.

20. Central Service for Alsace-Lorraine to Min. Int., 15 May 1945, ANF, F1a 3303; P. J. Moatti, Min. Int. cabinet, to Tixier, 19 June 1945, ibid.; For. Min. to Min. Int., 27 July, 17 August 1945, ibid.; Min. Int. to For. Min., 9 August 1945, ibid.; Préf., Haute-Marne, to Min. Int., 18 August 1945, ibid.; Svc. Central Alsace-Lorraine to Min. of Prisoners, Deportees, Refugees, 1 September 1945, ibid.; Allied Control Authority, Coordinating Committee, 3 October 1945, ibid.; Inspector Gen. of Camps to Haas-Picard, 26 October 1945, ibid.; US Mission report, 15 September 1945.

7. Black Markets and War Booty

1. Memo on black market, 17 July 1944, NARA, RG 331, SHAEF, PWD (Decimal File 381–884.5), box 26; Richard Vinen, *The Unfree French: Life under the Occupation* (New Haven, CT: Yale University Press, 2006), 225, 238; Eric Alary, Bénédicte Vergez-Chaignon, and Gilles Gauvin, *Les Français au quotidien, 1939–1949* (Paris: Perrin, 2006), 279; Françoise Passera and Jean Quellien, *Les Civils dans la Bataille de Normandie* (Bayeux, France: OREP Editions, 2014), 195.

2. Alary et al., *Les Français,* 282–84; de Guerpel, *1939–1945,* 138–44; memo on black market, 17 July 1944; Taflinger, *Season of Suffering,* 68–71.

3. Memo on black market, 17 July 1944. The detailed PWD report on the French black market included many tables with prices from different towns on different dates,

demonstrating the volatility of the market. Teissier du Cros, *Divided Loyalties,* reveals that even people living in the countryside had trouble obtaining enough food.

4. Memo on black market, 17 July 1944; Vinen, *Unfree French,* 220; Alary et al., *Les Français,* 287–88; Taflinger, *Season of Suffering,* 69–71; Mitchell, *Nazi Paris,* 111.

5. Brig. McKeswick, report, 17 November 1944, NARA, RG 331, SHAEF, G-5/2/10, Financial Reports, box 5.

6. Memo on black market, 17 July 1944; Burrin, *France under the Germans,* 278–80.

7. Memo on black market, 17 July 1944; Report on the Black Market in Italy, 20 July 1944, NARA, RG 331, SHAEF, PWD (Decimal File 381–884.5), box 26; memo from N. L. Halpern, 12 August 1944, ibid.; Lt. Col. J. H. Hynes, Dir. Food Branch, to SHAEF, 8 February 1944, NARA, RG 331, SHAEF, G-5, box 61; notes of meeting in War Office, London, 26 September 1944, NARA, RG 331, SHAEF, Gen. Staff Secretariat, Numeric Files, box 5.

8. Hilldring to McSherry, SHAEF, 1 March 1945, NARA, RG 331, SHAEF, Gen. Staff Secretariat, Numeric Files, box 5; memo from Brig. Gen. Robert A. McClure, chief PWD, 11 September 1944, ibid., box 28; memo, JAG, Seine Section, Railway Battalion Pilfering Cases, n.d., NARA, RG 498, IG Reports 1944–45, box 4681; Coles and Weinberg, *Civil Affairs,* 744; Frances DeBra Brown, *An Army in Skirts: The World War II Letters of Frances DeBra* (Indianapolis: Indiana Historical Society Press, 2008), 160.

9. IGO, memo, 28 October 1943; HQ NATOUSA, Note on Security of Property and Railway, 3 November 1943; Col. W. R. Watson, IGD, to Commanding Officer, 2 December 1943, all in NARA, RG 492, MTO Special Staff Investigations, box 2015.

10. Col. A. R. Brian, IGD, to Brig. Gen. H. S. Clarkson, 11 February 1944; Col. G. Pence to Commanding Gen., 21 January 1944; Brig. Gen. Clarkson to Provost Marshal, NATOUSA, 22 February 1944, all in ibid.

11. Gendarme reports, Troyes, 3, 15 November 1944, ADA, SC 24642 B; courts-martial of Pvts. Mack Richardson and William Ray, 4, 5 November 1944, NARA, RG 498, HQ ETO, Courts Martial, box 2907; court-martial of Pvt. Eugene Redmond, 14 December 1944, ibid.; court-martial of Staff Sgt. John D. Wright, ibid.; *Stars and Stripes,* Nancy ed., 25 January 1945. There was also a discrepancy in sentencing between judges, and the judge involved in the Versailles case was criticized by the Office of the Provost Marshal for the severity of his sentences. Investigation of black-market activities, 25 September 1944, NARA, RG 338, Third Army, IG Section, Reports and Investigations, July 1944–November 1944, box 2.

12. Investigation of shortage of cigarettes in ETO, 16 December 1944, NARA, RG 498, IG Reports, 1944–45, box 4674; John Savard, “My Life Until Now: The Story of a Boy Growing up in the Thirties,” MHI, Veterans’ Surveys, 2nd Infantry Division, box 1.

13. Investigation of shortage of cigarettes in ETO, 16 December 1944; memo, JAG, Seine Section, Railway Battalion Pilfering Cases, n.d.; statement of George E. Graham, 6 December 1944, NARA, RG 498, IG Reports 1944–45, box 4674; statement of Pvt. Cecil Charles Stokes, 5 December 1944, ibid.; court-martial of Captain William P. Olson, 13 November 1945, ibid.; JAG, Seine Section, Historical Report, NARA, RG

498, HQ ETO, Provost Marshal, box 4343; *Stars and Stripes,* Nancy ed., 25 January 1945; *Stars and Stripes,* Paris ed., 9 June 1945.

14. Ren. Gén, Marseille, to Comm. Rép., Marseille, 22 February, 14 March 1945, ADBdR, 149 W 182; Comm. Rép., Châlons-sur-Marne, report, 1 March 1945, ANF, F1a 3304; Janet Flanner, *Paris Journal, 1944–1965* (New York: Atheneum, 1965), 5–6; Delasselle et al., *Un département dans la guerre 1939–1945,* 514–15.

15. Gendarme, Marseille, report, 15 December 1945, ADBdR, 150 W 176; "Vol au prejudice des allies," 2 December 1944, ANF, F1a 3305; Préf., Rouen, report, July 1945, ANF, F1a 3304; Brown, *Army in Skirts,* 138, 176.

16. Préf., Troyes, to CA, 6 November 1944, ADA, SC 24642 B; Comm. Police, Auxerre, 12 November 1945, ADY, 1 W 328; note, Ren. Gén., Auxerre, 8 June 1945, ADY, 1222 W 11; Ren. Gén., Auxerre, telephone message, 29 October 1945, ANF, F1a 3304.

17. Investigation into burglary at *Stars and Stripes* office, Reims, 31 July 1945, NARA, RG 498, IG Reports 1944–45, box 4678; Sureté Nat. to Sec. Gén. pour la Police, 5 February 1945, ADA, 1265 W 188; US Navy Port Office, Marseille, Regulations and Information, 3 April 1945, ADBdR, 6 S 10/10; Min. Int. to Min. Guerre, 23 May 1946, ANF, F1a 3305; Comm. Police, Auxerre, 21 August 1945, ADY, 1222 W 11; Comm. Police, Joigny, 17 November 1945, ibid.; de Guerpel, *1939–1945,* 230.

18. Investigation into reports of misconduct by members of 101st ABD, HQ 101st ABD, OPM report, 11 August 1945, NARA, RG 498, IG Reports 1944–45, box 4678; Ren. Gén., Marseille, 8 January 1945, ADBdR, 149 W 182; Préf., Manche, report, 30 March 1945, ANF, F1a 3305; Haas-Picard to Min. Int., 10 April 1945, ibid.; Ren. Gén., note, 15 June 1945, ADY, 1222 W 11; Comm. Police, Sens, 25 October 1945, ibid.; Comm. Rép., Nancy, report, 17 November 1945, ANF, F1a 3304; Préf., Châlons-sur-Marne, 31 August 1945, ibid.; Comm. Rép., Dijon, report, 15 November 1944, ibid.; Préf., Laon, report, 1 December 1945, ibid.

19. Report on Pas-de-Calais, 17 November 1944, NARA, RG 331, SHAEF, G-5/2/10, Financial Reports, box 5; *Stars and Stripes,* Nice ed., 22, 23 March 1945; Comm. Rép., Strasbourg, extracts from report, 31 May 1945, ANF, F1a 3303.

20. *Stars and Stripes,* Nice ed., 26 March 1945; Amendes et Confiscations, Nancy, 1–15 February 1945, ADMM, W 1061 art.; Eisenhower to Hilldring, 6 December 1944, NARA, RG 331, SHAEF, G-5/14, Financial Reports, box 3; minutes of Weekly Staff Conference, G-5 Div., Col. W. F. Durbin to Brig. Field, 11 July 1944, NARA, RG 331, SHAEF, G-5, box 64.

21. *Stars and Stripes,* Nancy ed., 9, 10, 12 February 1945.

22. Sec. Gén. pour la Police, 27 October, 7 November 1944, ADA, 1265 W 188; gendarme, Romilly-sur-Seine, report, 30 September 1944, ADA, SC 24642 B; minutes of meeting at Prefecture between French and Allied officials, 21 July 1945, ADBdR, 149 W 182; Col. Mamier, Delta Base, to Gen., Commander of XV Milt. Region, 23 December 1944 and n.d. [30 December 1944], ibid.; Procureur de la Rép., Lyon, to Procureur Gén'l, Paris, 1 September 1945, ANF, F1a 3305; HQ, Lyon Depot, US Army, report, 30 July 1945, ibid.; Company B, 749 Tank Battalion, reports, 10, 26 July 1945, ibid.; Pierre

Tissier to Min. Int., 10 October 1945, ibid.; Maginnis and Hart, *Military Government Journal,* 98.

23. *Stars and Stripes,* Algiers ed., 3 February 1943; *Stars and Stripes,* Nice ed., 3 April 1945; notes of meeting in War Office, London, 26 September 1944, NARA, RG 331, SHAEF, Gen. Staff Secretariat, Numeric Files, box 5; Financial-France, report, 1 October 1945, NARA, RG 331, SHAEF HQ Files, box 1; message from Eisenhower to Hilldring, 6 December 1944, NARA, RG 331, SHAEF, G-5/14 Financial Reports, box 3. Lankford, *OSS against the Reich,* 189, gives black-market exchange rate.

24. Sous-Préf., Montdidier, Somme, to Préf., 10 July 1945, ANF, F1a 3305; Préf., Clermont-Ferrand, to Min. Int., 22 June 1946, ibid.; Special Service, Seine Section, Historical Report, n.d., NARA, RG 498, Adjutant General, box 4343; Violet A. Kochendoerfer, *One Woman's World War II* (Lexington: University Press of Kentucky, 1994), 119.

25. Coulet to Le Troquer, 26 August 1944, ANF, F1a 4006.

26. Ross and Romanus, *Quartermaster Corps,* 537–38, 728; Haas-Picard to Tixier, 26 October 1944, ANF, F1a 3304; Préf., Troyes, to CA, 27 September 1944, ADA, SC 24642 B; Sous-Préf., Vendome, to Préf., Loir-et-Cher, 7 October 1944, ibid.; Préf., Loir-et-Cher, to Min. Int., 12 October 1944, ibid.

27. Préf., Troyes, to CA, 27 September 1944, 21 February 1945; CA to Préf., Troyes, 19 October, 5 December 1944; Pujol to Préf., 17 January 1945; Pujol, memo, 27 April 1945, all in ADA, SC 24642 B.

28. Préf. to CA, 3, 4 October 1944, ADA, SC 24642 B; CA to Préf., 11, 23 September 1944, ibid.; [illegible] to Haas-Picard, 23 October 1944, ANF, F1a 3304; Haas-Picard to Tixier, 26 October 1944, ibid.; Comm. Rép., Orléans, to Min. Int., 18 November 1944, ibid.

29. Report, n.d., NARA, RG 331, SHAEF, G-5/2/10, Financial Reports, box 2.

30. Min. Int. Tixier to Comm. Réps. and Préfs., 3 January 1945, ADY, 1 W 579.

31. Préf. to CA, 7, 19 September 1944, ADA, SC 24642 B; CA to Préf., 11, 23 September 1944, ibid.; [illegible] to Haas-Picard, 23 October 1944, ibid.; Ross and Romanus, *Quartermaster Corps,* 729; Le Bel to Dir. des Docks Vinicoles, 28 September 1944, ADBdR, 6 S 10/10; Comm. du Port to Dir. of Societé Srevaux, 28 September 1944, ibid.; Chef de Serv. de Transport Maritime to Le Bel, 26 September 1944, ibid.; Groupement d'Union des Négociants Soutier to Dir. Serv. de Transport Maritime, 23 September 1944, ibid.

32. CA McGugin, memo, 24 September 1944, ADA, SC 24642 B; Préf., Troyes, to Chef de Bureau de recuperation des biens abandonnés, 26 September 1944, ibid.; CA to Préf., 28 September 1944, ibid.; Coulet to SHAEF, 5 November 1944, ANF, F1a 3304.

33. Min. des Aff. Etrangères, Déleg. AFA, to Haas-Picard, 16 December 1944, ANF, F1a 3304.

34. Haas-Picard to Min. Int., 12 October, 9 December 1944, ANF, F1a 3304; [illegible] to Haas-Picard, 23 October 1944, ibid.; Préf., Paris, note, 28 October 1944, ibid.; Min. Int. to Haas-Picard, 18 December 1944, ibid.; Police report, [place illegible], 23 January 1945, ANF, F1a 3305.

35. Comm. Rép., Chalons-sur-Marne, to Préf., Troyes, 26 December 1944; depart-

mental AFA to Chef Svc. de récupération des biens abandonnés, Troyes, 13 June 1945; attached inventories, 3 September 1944, 7 February 1945; Chef AFA, Aube, to Commandante Bocart, 18 September 1944; AFA lists of items turned over, 7, 23 February 1945, all in ADA, SC 24644.

36. ANF, F1a 3304, contains a folder "Récupération de matériel d'identité judiciaire dans la zone américaine d'occupation en Allemagne" dedicated to efforts to recover French property found in Germany in 1945.

37. Etat Major, 8eme Milt. Region, Dijon, to Comm. Rép., Dijon, 17 February 1945, ADY, 1 W 324; Comm. Rép, Strasbourg, extracts from report, 31 May 1945, ANF, F1a 3303.

38. Délég. Départ., AFA, Troyes, to regional Délég. AFA, Reims, 8 March 1945, ADA, SC 24644; "Chapitre XII," Préf., Aube, 1 March 1945, ANF, F1a 3304.

39. Ross and Romanus, *Quartermaster Corps,* 729–31.

8. Problem GIs and the GI Problem

1. Comm. Rép., Rouen, reports, 2, 16 November 1944, ANF, F1a 3304; Préf., Rouen, to Haas-Picard, 2 November. 1944, ibid.; Préf., Châlons-sur-Marne, to Provost Marshal, Reims, 20 August 1945, ANF, F1a 3305; Haas-Picard, memo, 5 September 1945, ADA, SC 24642 B.

2. Marie-Louise Osmont, *The Normandy Diary of Marie-Louise Osmont: 1940–1944,* trans. George L. Newman (New York: Random House, 1994), 13–17, 19–20, 22–23, 30. Osmont's guests were English and Scottish, so not only Americans compared badly to the Germans.

3. Investigation, interviews of Capt. Zuber, CA, 10 November 1944, and Alexander Weir, CID, 11 November 1944, NARA, RG 498, HQ ETO, Inspector General Reports, 1944–45, box 4678; investigation of reported misconduct by members of 101st Airborne troops in Auxerre, 12 August 1945, ibid. Etat major 8eme Reg. militaire: Avis, 12 November 1944, ADY, 1 W 579, lays out the agreement regarding cooperation between MPs and French police, assigning complementary tasks.

4. Lankford, *OSS against the Reich,* 144; HQ 3rd Army, Lt. Col. R. W. Hartman, to Préf., Nancy, 22 April 1945, ADMM, WM 1521; Comm. Police, Nancy, 7 November 1944, ibid.

5. Travaux publics de l'Etat engineer to Le Bel, 4 October 1944 ADBdR, 6 S 10/10; Ren. Gén., Auxerre, 25 October 1944, ADY, 1 W 319; SousPréf. delege. to AFA to Préf., Nancy, 15 June 1945, ADMM, WM 1521; gendarme, Nancy, report, 29 May 1945, ibid.; Comm. Rép., Lille, to Min. Int., Notes sur les incidents . . . du Nord, 28 November 1945, ANF, F1a 3305.

6. Betty Olson diary, 1 May 1945, Betty M. Olson Papers, MHI; Gabriel Mouchot, "Drinking and Its Control [in France]," in *Drinking and Intoxication,* ed. Raymond G. McCarthy (New Haven, CT: College and University Press, 1959), 152; courts-martial of Pvt. Lewis Fanning, Tech 4 Junior B. Freeman, Pvt. Hugo Magistrallie, Tech 5 James Jones, Sgt. Charles A. James, NARA, RG 498, HQ ETO, Courts Mar-

tial, box 2905; courts-martial of Sgt. Carl McLendon, Sgt. James Skillman, ibid., box 2906; Comm. Police, Sens, resumé of incidents during September, 2 November 1945, ADY, 1222 W 11.

7. McCarthy, *Drinking and Intoxication,* presents an excellent discussion of drinking habits in the United States after the war. The articles in his work agree that drinking in the United States increased during the war years and peaked in 1946, so most of the data from 1946 to 1950 should be viewed with that in mind. Nevertheless, the data and surveys presented make it clear that most Americans did not drink heavily. See Mouchot, "Drinking and Its Control," 151–52; H. Bastide, "Public Opinion [in France]," in McCarthy, *Drinking and Intoxication,* 158–59; John W. Riley Jr. and Charles F. Marden, "Who, What, and How Often?" ibid., 182–89; Milton A. Maxwell, "[Drinking] in One State," ibid., 199–200; Raymond G. McCarthy "[Drinking] in High School," ibid., 205.

8. Comm. Police, Joigny, 22 February 1945, ADY, 1222 W 11; gendarme report to Gendarme Commander, Laon, 22 June 1945, ANF, F1a 3305; Haas-Picard, memo, 5 September 1945, ADA, SC 24642 B; see, for example, Préf. to mayors of Aube, 26 July 1945, ibid.; [illegible] note to Port PC, Marseille, 18 September 1944, ADBdR, 6 S 10/10.

9. Corps de Sapeurs-Pompiers to Préf., 16 September 1944, ADA, SC 24642 B; Préf., Troyes, to CA, 19 October 1944, ibid.; Comm. Police, Laroche-Migennes, 16 March 1945, ADY, 1 W 319; Comm. Police, Auxerre, note, 16 August 1945, ADY, 1222 W 11; Ren. Gén., Marseille, to Comm. Rép., 30 June 1945, ADBdR, 149 W 182; court-martial of Pvt. Jesse Dickerson, 6 January 1945, NARA, RG 498, HQ ETO, Courts Martial, box 2905; Ren. Gén., Grenoble, 6 February 1945, ANF, F1a 3305.

10. IG report on Cherbourg, 25 February 1944 [1945], NARA, RG 498, IGO Reports, 1944–45, box 4666; arrêté of Comm. Rép. with "Avis à la presse," n.d., ADA, SC 24642 B; Préf. to mayors of Aube, 26 July 1945, ibid.; letter from Gen. Stuart Cutler, "A Nos Amis et Camarades Français," *Le Travailleur de l'Yonne,* 27 November 1945, ADY, 1222 W 11; Sous-Préf., Sens, to Préf., 7 August 1945, ADY, 1 W 328; Gen. Cutler to [Préf.?], 22 November 1945, ibid.

11. Taflinger, *Season of Suffering,* 125–26, 128; Brown, *Army in Skirts,* 119, 139; Insp. Limbourg to Comm. Police, Auxerre, 21 March 1945, ADY, 1222 W 11; Ren. Gén., Le Havre, note, 30 November 1944, ANF, F1a 3304; gendarme report to Gendarme Commander, Laon, 22 June 1945, ANF, F1a 3305.

12. Comm. Police, Joigny, 19 February 1945, ADY, 1222 W 11; court-martial of W.O. Selig Kaplan, 2 December 1944, NARA, RG 498, HQ ETO, Courts Martial, box 2905; court-martial of Pvt. Jesse Dickerson, 6 January 1945, ibid.; court-martial of Sgt. Charles A. James, 12 January 1945, ibid.; court-martial of Sgt. Carl McLendon, 12 January 1945, ibid., box 2906; court-martial of Cpl. Willis Trotter, 10 February 1945, ibid., box 2907.

13. Mme. Caiment, Pougy-sur-Aube, to Préf., 31 July 1945, ADA, SC 24642 B; Comm. Police, Berre-L'Etang, to Comm. Police, Marseille, 19 September 1945, ANF, F1a 3305; Ren. Gén., Châlons-sur-Marne, report, 10 September 1945, ibid.; Parquet, Châlons-sur-Marne, report, 12 September 1944 [1945], ibid.; Ren. Gén., Dijon, report,

13 August 1945, ibid.; Comm. Police, Auxerre, 24 September 1945, ADY, 1222 W 11; Kochendoerfer, *One Woman's World War II,* 120.

14. Comm. Police, Joigny, 10 March 1945, ADY, 1222 W 11; Ren. Gén., Auxerre, to Préf., 1 October 1945, ibid.; Comm. Police, Migennes, 30 March 1945, ADY, 1 W 328; Hilary Kaiser, *French War Brides in America: An Oral History* (Westport, CT: Praeger, 2008), 41, 87.

15. Gendarmerie, Fréjus, telegram to état maj. mil. region, Marseille, 5 December 1944, ADBdR, 149 W 179; Comm. Police, Fréjus, report, 5 December 1944, ibid.; Sec. Gén., Police, Marseille, to Comm. Rép., 30 June 1945, ibid.; Ren. Gén., Marseille, report, 9 December 1944, ADBdR, 149 W 182; Ren. Gén., Marseille, report, 15 February 1945, ANF, F1a 3305.

16. Comm. Police, Migennes, report, 30 March 1945, ADY, 1 W 328; gendarme, Frouard, report, 6 July 1945, ADMM, WM 1521; Comm. Police, Longwy, report, 27 August 1945, ibid.

17. Report of Investigation Concerning Alleged Lawlessness of American Troops in Normandy, 18 November 1944, interview of Col. Donald W. McGowan, Provost Marshal, 11 November 1944; interview of Lt.Col. Albert Du Bois, Provost Marshal, Le Havre and Rouen Base Section, 14 November 1944; conclusion of investigation, all in NARA, RG 498, HQ ETO, IGO Reports, 1944–45, box 4673.

18. Comm. Rép. Chailley-Bert, Nancy, report, 16 January 1945, ANF, F1a 3304; Préf., Nice, "secret" report, 17 May 1945, ibid.; Comm. Police to Sec. Gén. Police, Nancy, 27 January 1945, ADMM, WM 1521.

19. Court-martial of Maj. Willis T. Moran, 27 November 1944, NARA, RG 498, HQ ETO, Courts Martial, box 2906; Comm. Police, Joigny, 6 March 1945, ADY, 1222 W 11; Ren. Gén, Dijon, telephone message, 11 August 1945, ANF F1a 3305.

20. Court-martial of Pvt. Samuel Becker, 27 November 1944, NARA, RG 498, HQ ETO, Courts Martial, box 2905; Comm. Rép, Marseille, to Sec. Gén. Police, 6 July 1945, ADBdR, 149 W 179; Police Comm., Nancy, to Dir. Police, Nancy, 21 October 1944, ADMM, WM 1521.

21. H. Thibault, Insp. des Eaux et Forêts, Troyes, to Préf., Troyes, 9 June 1945; Charles Billiot to Préf., Troyes, 20 July 1945; Préf. to Mayor, Troyes, 23 July 1945, all in ADA SC 24642 B.

22. Curé, St. Victoret, to Comm. Rép., Haag, 18 June 1945, ADBdR, 149 W 182.

23. Comm. Rép., Haag, to Sec. Gén. Police, 6 July 1945, ADBdR, 149 W 179.

24. Report from Public Safety Section, 28 July 1944, NARA, RG 498, First Army HQ, G-5, box 2951; Report of Investigation Concerning Alleged Lawlessness in Normandy, 18 November 1944, interviews of Col. McGowan and Tech. Sgt. Alvin Small, CID, 11 November 1944; J. Robert Lilly, *Taken by Force: Rape and American GIs in Europe during World War II* (Basingstoke, UK: Palgrave, 2007), 83–84; Maginnis log, 21–22 June 1944, Maginnis Papers, MHI.

25. Report from Public Safety Section, 28 July 1944; Report of Investigation Concerning Alleged Lawlessness in Normandy, 18 November 1944, interviews of Capt. Bou-

loc, Sous-Préf., Cherbourg, M. A. Langevin, Leviandier, Col. McGowan, and Tech. Sgt. Alvin Small, CID, 11 November 1944; Police Comm., Nancy, 29 April, 24, 25, 26 July 1945, ADMM, WM 1521; Haas-Picard to Comm. Moutet, liaison with G-4, 8 January 1946, ANF, F1a 3305. Lilly, *Taken by Force,* 11–12, claims without substantiation that GIs committed about 3,600 rapes in France during World War II.

26. Interview of Capt. Dufossey, Gendarmerie, Cherbourg, 10 November 1944, NARA, RG 498, IGO Investigations, box 4673; Legentilhomme to War Minister, n.d., ibid.; General Slack investigation, n.d. [June 1945], NARA, RG 338, Third Army, IG Section, Reports and Investigations, July 1944–November 1944, box 4.

27. Ibid.

28. Interview with Capt. Robert Bouluc, Gendarmerie, Manche, NARA, RG 498, IGO Investigations, box 4673; interview of Yon Daniul, editor of *La Presse de Cherbourg,* 10 November 1944, ibid.; Legentilhomme to War Minister, n.d.; interview of Capt. Zuber, G-5, 10 November 1944; Ren. Gén., Marseille, to Comm. Rép, Marseille, 14 March 1945, ADBdR, 149 W 182; memo, n.d., Benjamin O. Davis Papers, box 20, MHI; NATO JAG report, 9 September 1944, ibid. Mary Louise Roberts, *What Soldiers Do: Sex and the American GI in World War II France* (Chicago: University of Chicago Press, 2013), 196–98, claims that reports of rapes by black GIs were, "at least in part, a hysterical response of French women to their fears concerning black men."

29. Interview of Capt. Dufossey, 10 November 1944; Ren. Gén., Versailles, extracts of report, 25 November 1944, ANF, F1a 3304; gendarme, Laon, report, 22 June 1945, ANF, F1a 3305; Préf., Seine-et-Marne, to Min. Int., 24 February 1945, ANF, F1a 3006; Ren. Gén., Versailles, telephone message, 25 February 1945, ibid.; Comm. Police, Nancy, report, 7 March 1945, ADMM, WM 1521; Sec. Gén. Police, Marseille, to Comm. Rép., 30 June 1945, ADBdR, 149 W 179.

30. *Statistical Abstract of the United States* (Washington, DC: Department of Commerce, 1934), 80; *Statistical Abstract of the United States* (Washington, DC: Department of Commerce, 1938), 85; *Statistical Abstract of the United States* (Washington, DC: Department of Commerce, 1940), 78, 86; *Annuaire Statistique de la France* (Paris: Ministère du commerce, 1939), 55, 58, 60, 66. On homicides in France, see *Annuaire Statistique de la France* (Paris: Ministère du commerce, 1946), 50. In the United States, there were 8,799 registered homicides in 1938; see *Statistical Abstract* (1940), 86. There was also a vast difference in conviction rates for murder: 60 percent in France (356 of 596 for 1934) versus 37 percent in the United States (3,700 of 10,000). If rape conviction rates were comparable, then the numbers of US rapes would presumably be higher.

31. Monthly reports of Sec. General pour la Police to Min. Int., March 1945 and January 1946, ADMM, WM 358.

32. Direction Général de la Police, Longwy, Pont-à-Mousson, reports, January 1946; summary report for Meurthe-et-Moselle, February 1946, all in ADMM, WM 358.

33. Sûreté Nat. quarterly report, Troyes, 26 December 1945; Comm. Police, Troyes, weekly reports for March and April 1946, all in ADA, SC 4259.

34. Historical report, Judge Advocate Section, Seine Section, n.d., NARA, RG 498, HQ ETO, TSFET, Provost Marshal, box 4343.

35. Ren. Gén., Marseille, telegram to Min. Int., 11 June 1945, ANF, Fla 3305; Préf., Marne, telephone report to Min. Int., 8 December 1945, ibid.; Ren. Gén., Rouen, telephone message to Min. Int., 18 August 1945, ibid.; Ren. Gén., Marseille, report, 5 July 1945, ADBdR, 149 W 179; Préf., Seine-et-Oise, report, 1 October 1945, ANF, Fla 3304.

36. Police, Laroche-Migennes, report to Préf., 14 March 1945, ADY, 1 W 319; Comm. Police, Auxerre, 12 November 1945, ADY, 1 W 328; gendarme report to Gendarme Commander, Laon, 22 June 1945, ANF, Fla 3305; Procureur Cour d'Appel, Amiens, to Garde de Sceaux, 26 July 1945, ibid.; Comm. Rép., Lille, to Min. Int., Notes sur les incidents . . . du Nord, 28 November 1945, ibid.; Comm. Police, Neuves-Maisons, to Préf., Nancy, 31 March 1945, ADMM, WM 1521; gendarme and Comm. Police reports, Longwy, 30 July 1945, ibid.; Sec. Gén. Police, Marseille, to Comm. Rép., 30 June 1945, ADBdR, 149 W 179.

37. André Tisserand to Préf., Troyes, 2 August 1945, ADA, SC 4290; Préf., Rouen, report to Min. Int., July 1945, ANF, Fla 3304; [Comm. Rép.?] "information," Dijon, 6 August 1945, ANF, Fla 3305; Ren. Gén., Dijon, telephone message, 8 August 1945, ibid.; Comm. Police, Auxerre, 21 August 1945, ADY, 1222 W 11; Sec. Gén. Police, Marseille, to Comm. Rép., 30 June 1945, ADBdR, 149 W 179; gendarme reports, Longwy, 10 August, 4 September 1945, ADMM, WM 1521; Report of Investigation Concerning Alleged Lawlessness in Normandy, 18 November 1944, interview of Col. Donald McGowan, Provost Marshal.

38. Gendarme reports, Mailly, 12, 21 December 1945, ADA, SC 4290; Col. H. McE. Pendleton, CA, to Préf., Troyes, 10 May 1945, ibid.; Ren. Gén., Troyes, report, 18 January 1946, ANF, Fla 3305.

39. Ibid.

40. Insp. R. Maestracci to Comm. Principale, 7eme section, Paris, 10 May 1945, ANF, Fla 3305.

41. Report of Investigation Concerning Alleged Lawlessness in Normandy, 18 November 1944.

42. Préf., Laon, report, 1 October 1945, ANF, Fla 3304; Comm. Rép., Rouen, report, October 1945, ibid.

9. The Final Descent and the Failure of US Army Justice

1. Ren. Gén., Auxerre, 10 August, 1 October 1945, ADY, 1222 W 11; "Liste des Incidents américains depuis février 1945," n.d., ibid.; Investigation of Reported Misconduct by Members of 101st Airborne Troops in Auxerre, 12 August 1945, NARA, RG 498, HQ ETO, Inspector General Reports, 1944–45, box 4678 (hereafter cited as IG 101st); M. Malet to Commanding Officer [Taylor], 7 August 1945, ibid.

2. Statement of Préf. Gibaud, IG 101st; "Informations," translation of subprefect's report to Préf., 7 August 1945, ibid.; Ren. Gén., Auxerre, 7 August 1945, ADY, 1222 W 11; M. Bogard, Sens, Pax Cinema owner, to M. le commandant américain [Harper], 4 August 1945, ADY, 1 W 328. The list of incidents handed to the prefect included only two rapes rather than three; several other incidents were also omitted.

3. "Regrettable Incidents," translation of article in *L'Yonne Républicain,* 8 August 1945, IG 101st; statement of Gen. Maxwell Taylor, ibid.; statement of Maj. John W. Urban, OPM, ibid.; Comm. Moutet, liaison, HQ, G-5, to Haas-Picard, 16 August 1945, ANF, F1a 3305.

4. Statement of Maj. Robert L. Bogard; statement of Gen. Maxwell Taylor; Gen. Maxwell Taylor to *L'Yonne Républicain,* 8 August 1945, all in IG 101st. "Inflammable" may have been a mistake by the clerk who transcribed Taylor's testimony; the general used "inflammatory" elsewhere.

5. Col. George Barker, CS XVI Corps, memo to Brig. Gen. George S. Eyster, 11 August 1945; Eyster, memo to Maj. Gen. Leslie Rooks, CS to Gen. Eisenhower, 12 August 1945, both in IG 101st.

6. IG, ETO HQ, report, 20 August 1945, IG 101st; Maxwell Taylor, report, 10 August 1945, ibid.; Comm. Police, Joigny, 13 August 1945, ADY, 1222 W 11; Comm. Police, Auxerre, 15, 16, 18, 20, 21 August 1945, ibid.; "Liste des Incidents"; US Mission to France, reports, 15 September, 15 November 1945, NARA, RG 498, HQ ETO, box 1489; US Ambassador to For. Min., n.d. [after 13 September 1945], ANF, F1a 3305.

7. Police Comm., Auxerre, 6 August 1945, ADY, 1222 W 11; [Préf.], note, 6 August 1945, ibid.; telephone message from Ren. Gén., Dijon, 5 August 1945, IG 101st; English translation of Police Comm. to Préf., Auxerre, 7 August 1945, ibid.; OPM to Gen. Taylor, 9 August 1945, ibid.; Taylor to editor, *L'Yonne Républicaine,* 8 August 1945, ibid.; Maj. Urban to Gen. Taylor, 9 August 1945, ibid.; interview with Col. J. Lanquetot, 17 August 1945, ibid.

8. Statement of M. Robert M____, 7 August 1945, IG 101st; Préf., note, 13 September 1945, ADY, 1222 W 11; Comm. Police, Auxerre, to Préf., 12, 13 September 1945, ibid.; Comm. Police, Joigny, 13 September 1945, ibid.

9. Comm. Police, Auxerre, 10 September 1945, ADY, 1222 W 11; "Liste des Incidents"; IG, ETO HQ, report, 20 August 1945, IG 101st.

10. Ren. Gén., Auxerre, 1 October 1945, ADY, 1222 W 11; Comm. Police, Sens, resumé of incidents during September, 2 October, 1945, and reports, 3, 25 October 1945, ibid.; "Note d'Information," Auxerre, 15 November 1945, ibid.; HQ, 101st ABD, OPM, French translation of agreement on policing, 14 October 1945, ADY, 1 W 328; Comm. Rép., Dijon, report, 17 September 1945, ANF, F1a 3304.

11. For many examples of problems caused by airborne divisions, see Investigation of Alleged Misbehavior and Vandalism by US Airborne Troops in Holland, 5 November 1944, NARA, RG 498, IG Reports 1944–45, box 4673; IG, report, February 1945, ibid., box 4666. On the 82nd ABD, see reports, June–September 1945, ADMM, WM 1521. On the 13th ABD, see reports, January–April 1945, ADY, 1222 W 11, 1 W 325, 1 W 328.

10. The American "Occupation"

1. Police Comm. Spec., Cherbourg, report, 13 February 1945, ANF, F1a 3305.

2. Comm. Rép., Orléans, 18 November 1944, ANF, F1a 3304; Comm. Rép., Châlons-sur-Marne, report, 9 January 1945, ibid.; Sûreté Nationale Bulletin Quotidien

d'Informations, 20 November 1944, ADA, SC 4260. On the commissioners, see Charles-Louis Foulon, *Le pouvoir en province à la libération: les commissaires de la République, 1943–1946* (Paris: Fondation nationale des sciences politiques, Armand Colin, 1975).

3. Comm. Rép. de Relations Interalliées to SHAEF, 5 November 1944, ANF, F1a 3304.

4. Minutes of Weekly Staff Conference, 4, 25 July 1944, NARA, RG 331, SHAEF, G-5/3006, box 64; Brig. Gen. G-5, SHAEF, to Bradley, 23 October 1944, NARA, RG 331, SHAEF, G-5/652, box 12; Bradley to SHAEF, n.d., ibid.; F. Conly [Coulet], Comm. Rép. to SHAEF, 14 October 1944, ibid.; Daviz and Fitzhugg [*sic*], CA, 13 September 1944, ibid.; Comm. Rép. de Relations Interalliées [F. Coulet] to SHAEF, 5 November 1944, ANF, F1a 3304; minutes of meeting of delegates from all ministries having relations with Allies, Paris, 30 October 1944, ibid.

5. Sûreté Nationale Bulletins Quotidiens d'Informations, 2 May 1945, ADA, SC 4259; Sûreté Nationale Bulletin Quotidien d'Informations, 15, 17 December 1944, ADA, SC 4260; Taflinger, *Season of Suffering,* 114–16; Comm. Rép., Bordeaux, report, 1 March 1945, ANF, F1a 3261.

6. Jerome Bruner, US Information Service, 5 January 1945, NARA, RG 331, SHAEF, PWD.

7. Note from Dieppe to Haas-Picard, 7 December 1944, ANF, F1a 3304; Comm. Rép., Loan–Saint Quentin, report, 31 March 1945, ibid.; Ren. Gén., Extraits du bulletin journalier de Pau to Haas-Picard, 8 December 1944, ANF, F1a 3305; Sûreté Nationale Bulletins Quotidiens d'Informations, 21, 23 April 1945, ADA, SC 4259.

8. William I. Hitchcock, *The Bitter Road to Freedom: A New History of the Liberation of Europe* (New York: Free Press, 2008), 79–80; Pierre Maillaud, *Over to France,* trans. Francis Cowper (London: Oxford University Press, 1946), 96–97.

9. Extracts Ren. Gén., Troyes, to Haas-Picard, 6 January 1945; Ren. Gén., report to Haas-Picard, 12 January 1945; Comm. Rép., Marseille, report, 2 January 1945, all in ANF F1a 3304.

10. Robertson, *When Roosevelt Planned,* 180; McJimsey, *Documentary History of the Franklin D. Roosevelt Presidency,* 47:182; Roosevelt to Churchill and Hull to Caffrey, 19 October 1944, *FRUS,* 1944, 3:741–43; Caffrey to Hull 20 October 1944, ibid.; Abbott Joseph Liebling, *Normandy Revisited* (New York: Simon and Schuster, 1958), 234–35; Hurstfield, *America and the French Nation,* 84–87; Aglion, *Roosevelt and de Gaulle,* 124; de Gaulle, *Complete War Memoirs,* 635–37 (just one example of the suspicion of Washington he exudes throughout); Sûreté Nationale Bulletin Quotidien d'Informations, 17 December 1944, ADA, SC 4260.

11. De Gaulle to Int. Min. Tixier, 2 February 1945, ANF, F1a 3305; Comm. Rép., Rennes, 1 December 1944, ANF, F1a 3304; Sûreté Nationale Bulletin Quotidien d'Informations, 22 March, 16 April 1945, ADA, SC 4260. Stephen Alan Bourque points out in *Beyond the Beach: The Allied War against France* (Annapolis, MD: Naval Institute Press, 2018), 92–94, that the multiple air raids on Royan were fiascoes that cost many hundreds of French lives (probably more than a thousand) and razed the town.

12. Sûreté Nationale Bulletin Quotidien d'Informations, 12 October, 17 and 25

November, 17 December 1944, 5 March 1945, ADA, SC 4260; Police Comm. Spec., Cherbourg, report, 13 February 1945, ANF, F1a 3305; Henri Amouroux, *Les Règlements de comptes* (Paris: Robert Laffont, 1991), 392–95.

13. G-2 and G-3, Seine Section, Historical Report, n.d., NARA, RG 498, HQ ETO, TSFET, box 4339; Eisenhower, *Crusade in Europe,* 412–13; See *FRUS,* 1945, 4:680–85, for the series of testy messages inspired by the Stuttgart affair.

14. Jerome Bruner, US Information Service, 5 January 1945, NARA, RG 331, SHAEF, PWD; "Some Recent Trends in French Attitudes toward the United States, 2 July 1945," NARA, RG 498, ETO HQ, box 1488; Sûreté Nationale Bulletins Quotidiens d'Informations, 3, 6, 9, 10 April 1945, ADA, SC 4259; Sûreté Nationale Bulletins Quotidiens d'Informations, 13 November 1944, ADA, SC 4260; Olivier Wieviorka, *Divided Memory: French Recollections of World War II from the Liberation to the Present,* trans. George Holoch (Stanford, CA: Stanford University Press, 2012), 24; Claudia Baldoli and Andrew Knapp, *Forgotten Blitzes: France and Italy under Allied Air Attack, 1940–1945* (London: Continuum, 2012), 234.

15. Comm. Rép., Bordeaux, 15 September 1945, ANF, F1a 3304; Sûreté Nationale Bulletin Quotidien d'Informations, 12 October 1944, ADA, SC 4260. Leclerc's aide-de-camp, Jean Chatel, reported de Gaulle's insistence that the Atlantic pockets not fall to the FFI; see Henry Maule, *Out of the Sand: The Epic Story of General Leclerc and the Fighting Free French* (London: Odhams, 1966), 274–75. On Moscow's advice to the PCF, see Henri-Christian Giraud, *De Gaulle et les communistes,* 2 vols. (Paris: Albin Michel, 1988–1989), 1:305.

16. Jerome Bruner, US Information Service, 5 January 1945, NARA, RG 331, SHAEF, PWD; minutes of meeting of delegates from all ministries having relations with Allies, 30 October, 13 November 1944, ANF, F1a 3304; report on meeting of regional delegates of AFA, Paris, J. Levy presiding, 6–8 January 1945, ibid.; Min. Int. Tixier, memo to Préfs. and Comm. Réps., 5 February 1945, ibid.; Préf., Nord, report [on British cooperation], 28 February 1945, ibid.; Comm. Rép., Orléans, report [on Americans snooping in French banks], 18 November 1944, ibid.

17. Minutes of meeting of delegates from all ministries having relations with Allies, 30 October, 13 November 1944, ANF, F1a 3304; extraits de rapports de Comm. Rép., Rouen, December 1944, ibid.; Teissier du Cros, *Divided Loyalties,* 340; Osmont, *Normandy Diary,* 50–100; Peter Schrijvers, *Liberators: The Allies and Belgian Society, 1944–1945* (Cambridge: Cambridge University Press, 2009), 224–27.

18. Investigation of 101st Airborne troops in Auxerre, 12 August 1945, statements of Maj. Robert L. Bogard and Gen. Maxwell Taylor, NARA, RG 498, HQ ETO, Inspector General Reports, 1944–45, box 4678.

19. "A Survey of Attitudes of Normans to Allied Landings," 21 August 1944, NARA, RG 331, 93A, SHAEF, PWD; Préf., Rouen, to Haas-Picard, 2 November 1944, ANF F1a 3304.

20. Comm. Rép., Châlons-sur-Marne, report, 1 March 1945, ANF, F1a 3304; Sûreté Nationale Bulletin Quotidien d'Informations, 13 March 1945, ADA, SC 4260.

21. Ren. Gén., Nancy, report, 27 July 1945, ADMM, WM 1521; "Incompréhension

Américaine [in Lorraine]," 16 November 1945, ibid.; Préf., Manche, report, 1 October 1945, ANF, F1a 3304; Sous-Préf., Montdidier, Somme, to Préf., 10 July 1945, ANF, F1a 3305; Baldoli and Knapp, *Forgotten Blitzes,* 122, 127–28 (Vichy propaganda).

22. Comm. Rép., Marseille, report, 22 May 1945, ANF, F1a 3304; Comm. Police, Migennes, 3 March 1945, ADY, 1222 W 11; Ren. Gén., Auxerre, 5 March 1945, ibid.; Ren. Gén., Sens, 10 March 1944 [1945], ibid.; Ren. Gén., Nancy, note, 13 July 1945, ADMM, WM 1521.

23. Comm. Rép., Loan–St. Quentin, report, 31 July 1945, ANF, F1a 3304; Comm. Rép., Rouen, report, 31 October 1945, ibid.; Sous-Préf., Montdidier, Somme, to Préf., 10 July 1945, ANF, F1a 3305.

24. Sûreté Nationale Bulletin Quotidien d'Informations, 19 April, 7 May 1945, ADA, SC 4259.

Epilogue

1. Flanner, *Paris Journal,* 26; Brown, *Army in Skirts,* 180, 192; Betty Olson, letter, 27 June 1945, Betty M. Olson Papers, MHI; Sûreté Nationale Bulletins Quotidiens d'Informations, 8 May 1945, ADA, SC 4259; Comm. Rép., Marseille, 22 May 1945, ANF, F1a 3304.

2. Brown, *Army in Skirts,* 196–97; Olson letter, 11 July 1945; Historical Report, Seine Section, n.d. [1946], NARA, RG 498, TSFET, Provost Marshal, box 4343; US Mission to France, report, 16 August 1945, NARA, RG 498, ETO HQ, box 1488; Harrison, *From the Letters of Robert S. Gerdy,* 320–21, 324, 332.

3. Brown, *Army in Skirts,* 223–24.

4. Comm. Rép., Rouen, to Comm. Maillot, Le Havre, 20 October 1945, ANF, F1a 3305.

5. Comm. Police Central, Rouen, to Sec. Gén. Police, Rouen, 27 September 1945, ANF, F1a 3305; Préf., Rouen, report, September 1945, ANF, F1a 3304; Comm. Rép., Rouen, report, 15 November 1945, ibid.

6. Historical Report, Seine Section, n.d. [1946]; Min. Tixier to Gen. Lee, Chef, Comm-Z, 21 August 1945, ANF, F1a 3305; note from Haas-Picard to Min. Tixier, 5 September 1945, ibid.

7. Sec. Gén. Police, Marseille, to Comm. Rép., Haag, 7 November 1945, ADBdR, 149 W 182.

8. Comm. Rép., Châlons-sur-Marne, report, 15 November 1945; Préf., Chaumont, report, 30 November 1945; Préf., Oise, report, December 1945, all in ANF, F1a 3304.

9. US Mission to France, report, 16 August 1945; AFA, Seine-et-Marne, to AFA, Paris, 28 November 1945, ANF, F1a 3304; Maj. R. H. Hughtt, G-3, 101st ABD, report of investigation of sports arena, Avallon, 20 November 1945, ADY, 1 W 328.

10. Préf., Laon, to Min. Int., 17 December 1945, ANF, F1a 3305; Comm. Rép., Rouen, report, July 1945, ibid.; Comm. Rép., Rouen, report, 28 November, 26 December 1945, ANF, F1a 3304; Préf., Laon, report, 1 October 1945, ibid.; Comm. Rép., Loan–St. Quentin, report, 31 July 1945, ibid.

11. Préf., Orne, report, 21 August 1945, ANF, F1a 3304; Préf., Rhone, report, 31 August 1945, ibid.; US Mission reports, 15 September, 17 October, 15 November 1945, NARA, RG 498, HQ ETO, box 1489; French Liaison, Seine Section, Historical Report, n.d., NARA, RG 498, TSFET, box 4342; telegram from Dir. Port, Marseille, to Chef de Service d'Exploitation, Min. Travaux Pub., Paris, n.d. [1946], ADBdR, 6 S 10/10; Port PC, note, 26 February 1946, attached price list, ibid.

12. AFA, Nancy, reports, 5 March, 3 May, 3 June 1946, ADMM, WM 1521; [Préf.], memo, 25 April 1947, ADA, SC 4290; Comm. Police, Auxerre, note, 27 May 1946, ADY, 1222 W 11; Préf. to mayors in Yonne, circular letter, September 1947, ibid.; circular special, 13 September 1946, ibid. On graves in France, see American Battle Monuments Commission, https://www.abmc.gov/node/1274.

Bibliography

Books and Articles

Aglion, Raoul. *Roosevelt and de Gaulle: Allies in Conflict; a Personal Memoir.* New York: Free Press, 1988.

Alary, Eric, Bénédicte Vergez-Chaignon, and Gilles Gauvin. *Les Français au quotidien, 1939–1949.* Paris: Perrin, 2006.

Amouroux, Henri. *La grande histoire des français après l'occupation.* 10 vols. Paris: Robert Laffont, 1976–1993.

———. *Les Règlements de comptes.* Paris: Robert Laffont, 1991.

Annuaire Statistique de la France. Paris: Ministère du commerce, 1936, 1939, 1946.

Aron, Robert. *Histoire de la Libération de la France, Juin 1944–Mai 1945.* Paris: Libraire Arthème Fayard, 1959.

Azéma, Jean-Pierre, and François Bédarida, eds. *La France des années noires.* Vol. 2, *De l'Occupation à la Libération.* Paris: Editions du Seuil, 2000.

Baldoli, Claudia, and Andrew Knapp. *Forgotten Blitzes: France and Italy under Allied Air Attack, 1940–1945.* London: Continuum, 2012.

Beaufre, André. *La revanche de 1945.* Paris: Plon, 1966.

Bourque, Stephen Alan. *Beyond the Beach: The Allied War against France.* Annapolis, MD: Naval Institute Press, 2018.

Brinton, Crane. "Letters from Liberated France." *French Historical Studies* 2, nos. 1 and 2 (1961).

Brown, Frances DeBra. *An Army in Skirts: The World War II Letters of Frances Debra.* Indianapolis: Indiana Historical Society Press, 2008.

Burrin, Philippe. *France under the Germans: Collaboration and Compromise.* Translated by Janet Lloyd. New York: New Press, 1993.

Busquet, Raoul. *Histoire de Marseille.* Paris: R. Laffont, 1998.

Butcher, Harry C. *My Three Years with Eisenhower.* New York: Simon and Schuster, 1946.

Bykofsky, Joseph, and Harold Larson. *The Transportation Corps: Operations Overseas.* Washington, DC: US Army Center of Military History, 1957.

Capa, Robert. *Slightly out of Focus.* New York: Henry Holt, 1947.

Chandler, Alfred D., ed. *The Papers of Dwight D. Eisenhower. The War Years: III and IV.* Baltimore: Johns Hopkins University Press, 1970.

Churchill, Winston S. *The Second World War.* 6 vols. Boston: Houghton Mifflin, 1949–1950.

Clark, Jeffrey J., and Robert Ross Smith. *Riviera to the Rhine.* Washington, DC: US Army Center of Military History, 1993.

Clark, Mark W. *Calculated Risk.* New York: Harper and Row, 1950.

Codman, Charles. *Drive.* Boston: Little, Brown, [1957].

Cohn, David L. *This Is the Story.* Boston: Houghton Mifflin, 1947.

Coles, Harry L., and Albert K. Weinberg. *Civil Affairs: Soldiers Become Governors.* Washington, DC: US Army Center of Military History, 2004.

Coulet, François. *Vertu des temps difficiles.* Paris: Plon, 1967.

Coutau-Bégarie, Hervé, and Claude Huan. *Darlan.* Paris: Fayard, 1989.

de Gaulle, Charles. *The Complete War Memoirs of Charles de Gaulle.* Translated by Jonathan Griffin and Richard Howard. New York: Da Capo Press, [1984].

de Guerpel, Xavier. *1939–1945, Une Certaine Vie de Château au Bocage Normand.* Conde-sur-Noireau, France: Editions Ch. Corlet, 1973.

Delasselle, Claude, Joel Drogland, Frédéric Gand, Thierry Robin, and Jean Rolley. *Un département dans la guerre 1939–1945: Occupation, collaboration et résistance dans l'Yonne.* Paris: Editions Tirésias, 2006.

Dewavrin, André. *Souvenirs [par] Colonel Passy.* 2 vols. Monte Carlo: Raoul Solar, 1947.

Donnison, Frank S. V. *Civil Affairs and Military Government North-West Europe, 1944–1946.* London: Her Majesty's Stationery Office, 1961.

Dreux, William B. *No Bridges Blown.* South Bend, IN: University of Notre Dame Press, 1971.

Duras, Marguerite. *The War: A Memoir.* Translated by Barbara Bray. New York: Pantheon Books, 1986.

Eisenhower, Dwight D. *Crusade in Europe.* New York: Doubleday, 1948.

Fishman, Sarah. *We Will Wait: Wives of French Prisoners of War, 1940–1945.* New Haven, CT: Yale University Press, 1991.

Flanner, Janet. *Paris Journal, 1944–1965.* New York: Atheneum, 1965.

Foulon, Charles-Louis. *Le pouvoir en province à la libération: les commissaires de la République, 1943–1946.* Paris: Fondation nationale des sciences politiques, Armand Colin, 1975.

Funk, Arthur L. *Charles de Gaulle: The Crucial Years, 1943–1944.* Norman: University of Oklahoma Press, 1959.

Gildea, Robert. *Fighters in the Shadows: A New History of the French Resistance.* Cambridge, MA: Belknap Press, 2015.

Giraud, Henri. *Un Seul But, la Victoire, Alger 1942–1944.* Paris: R. Julliard, [1949].

Giraud, Henri-Christian. *De Gaulle et les communists.* 2 vols. Paris: Albin Michel, 1988–1989.

Grandval, Gilbert, and A. Jean Collin. *Libération de l'Est de la France.* Paris: Hachette, 1974.

Griffiths, Richard. *Pétain: A Biography of Marshal Philippe Pétain of Vichy.* Garden City, NY: Doubleday, 1972.

Harrison, Donald, ed. *From the Letters of Robert S. Gerdy, 1942–1945: A Personal Record of World War II.* Philadelphia: Dorance, 1969.

Hitchcock, William I. *The Bitter Road to Freedom: A New History of the Liberation of Europe.* New York: Free Press, 2008.

Hull, Cordell. *The Memoirs of Cordell Hull.* 2 vols. New York: Macmillan, 1948.

Humbert, Agnès. *Résistance: A Woman's Journal of Struggle and Defiance in Occupied France.* Translated by Barbara Mellor. New York: Bloomsbury, 2008.

Hurstfield, Julian G. *America and the French Nation, 1939–1945.* Chapel Hill: University of North Carolina Press, 1986.

Jankowski, Paul. *Communism and Collaboration: Simon Sabiani and Politics in Marseille, 1919–1944.* New Haven, CT: Yale University Press, 1989.

Juin, Alphonse. *Mémoires.* 2 vols. Paris: A. Fayard, [1959].

Kaiser, Hilary. *French War Brides in America: An Oral History.* Westport, CT: Praeger, 2008.

Kochendoerfer, Violet A. *One Woman's World War II.* Lexington: University Press of Kentucky, 1994.

Lacouture, Jean. *De Gaulle.* 2 vols. Translated by Patrick O'Brian. New York: W. W. Norton, 1990.

Langer, William L. *Our Vichy Gamble.* New York: W. W. Norton, 1966.

Lankford, Nelson Douglas, ed. *OSS against the Reich: The World War II Diaries of Colonel David K. Bruce.* Kent, OH: Kent State University Press, 1991.

Laub, Thomas Johnston. *After the Fall: German Policy in Occupied France, 1940–1944.* New York: Oxford University Press, 2010.

Leahy, William D. *I Was There: The Personal Story of the Chief of Staff to Presidents Roosevelt and Truman.* New York: Whittlesey House, [1950].

Leleu, Jean-Luc, Françoise Passera, and Jean Quellien. *La France pendant la Seconde Guerre Mondiale.* Paris: Fayard and le Ministère de la Défense, 2010.

Lewis, S. J. *Jedburgh Team Operations in Support of the 12th Army Group, August 1944.* Fort Leavenworth, KS: Combat Studies Institute, 1991.

Liebling, Abbott Joseph. *Normandy Revisited.* New York: Simon and Schuster, 1958.

Lilly, J. Robert. *Taken by Force: Rape and American GIs in Europe during World War II.* Basingstoke, UK: Palgrave Macmillan, 2007.

Macmillan, Harold. *The Blast of War, 1939–1945.* London: Macmillan, 1967.

Maginnis, John J., and Robert A. Hart, eds. *Military Government Journal: Normandy to Berlin.* n.p.: University of Massachusetts Press, 1971.

Maguire, G. E. *Anglo-American Policy towards the Free French.* New York: St. Martin's Press, 1995.

Maillaud, Pierre [Pierre Bourdan]. *Over to France.* Translated by Francis Cowper. London: Oxford University Press, 1946.

Marrus, Michael R. *The Unwanted: European Refugees in the Twentieth Century.* New York: Oxford University Press, 1985.

Mast, Général Charles. *Histoire d'une Rébellion, Alger, 8 novembre 1942.* Paris: Plon, 1969.

Maule, Henry. *Out of the Sand: The Epic Story of General Leclerc and the Fighting Free French.* London: Odhams, 1966.

McCarthy, Raymond G., ed. *Drinking and Intoxication.* New Haven, CT: College and University Press, 1959.

McJimsey, George, ed. *Documentary History of the Franklin D. Roosevelt Presidency.* Vol. 47, *Establishing Civil Government in Occupied Europe.* [Bethesda, MD]: University Publications of America, 2001.

Michel, Henri. *Histoire de la France Libre.* Paris: Presses Universitaires de France, 1972.

Mitchell, Allan. *Nazi Paris: The History of an Occupation, 1940–1944.* New York: Berghahn Books, 2008.

Morgan, Sir Frederick. *Overture to Overlord.* Garden City, NY: Doubleday, 1950.

Murphy, Robert. *Diplomat among Warriors.* New York: Doubleday, 1964.

Osmont, Marie-Louise. *The Normandy Diary of Marie-Louise Osmont: 1940–1944.* Translated by George L. Newman. New York: Random House, 1994.

Passera, Françoise, and Jean Quellien. *Les Civils dans la Bataille de Normandie.* Bayeux, France: OREP Editions, 2014.

Pendar, Kenneth Whittemore. *Adventure in Diplomacy: Our French Dilemma.* New York: Da Capo Press, 1976.

Pogue, Forrest C. *George C. Marshall: Organizer of Victory, 1943–1945.* New York: Viking Press, 1973.

———. *The Supreme Command.* Washington, DC: Office of the Chief of Military History, Department of the Army, 1954.

Pujo, Bernard. *Juin, maréchal de France.* Paris: Albin Michel, 1988.

Roberts, Mary Louise. *What Soldiers Do: Sex and the American GI in World War II France.* Chicago: University of Chicago Press, 2013.

Robertson, Charles L. *When Roosevelt Planned to Govern France.* Amherst: University of Massachusetts Press, 2011.

Ross, William F., and Charles F. Romanus. *The Quartermaster Corps: Operations in the War against Germany.* Washington, DC: US Army Center of Military History, 2004.

Ruppenthal, Roland G. *Logistical Support of the Armies.* 2 vols. Washington, DC: US Army Center of Military History, 1953.

Schrijvers, Peter. *Liberators: The Allies and Belgian Society, 1944–1945.* Cambridge: Cambridge University Press, 2009.

Sherwood, Robert E. *Roosevelt and Hopkins: An Intimate History.* New York: Harper Brothers, 1948.

Statistical Abstract of the United States. Washington, DC: Department of Commerce, 1934, 1938, 1940.

Steele, Richard W. *The First Offensive 1942: Roosevelt, Marshall and the Making of American Strategy.* Bloomington: Indiana University Press, 1973.

Taflinger, Nicole H. *Season of Suffering: Coming of Age in Occupied France, 1940–45.* Pullman: Washington State University Press, 2010.

Teissier du Cros, Janet. *Divided Loyalties.* New York: Alfred Knopf, 1964.

US Department of State. *Foreign Relations of the United States.* France, vols. 2, 3, 4. Washington, DC: Department of State, 1943, 1944, 1945.

Vigneras, Marcel. *Rearming the French.* Washington, DC: Office of the Chief of Military History, Department of the Army, 1957.

Vinen, Richard. *The Unfree French: Life under the Occupation.* New Haven, CT: Yale University Press, 2006.

Viorst, Milton. *Hostile Allies: FDR and Charles de Gaulle.* New York: Macmillan, 1965.

Wieviorka, Olivier. *Divided Memory: French Recollections of World War II from the Liberation to the Present.* Translated by George Holoch. Stanford, CA: Stanford University Press, 2012.

Websites

www.abmc.gov/node/1274. American Battle Monuments Commission.

www.theodore-roosevelt.com/trsorbonnespeech.

Manuscript Collections

National Archives and Records Administration, College Park, MD

Record Group 331, SHAEF, G-5

Record Group 338, Third Army, Inspector General Section, Reports and Investigations

Record Group 492, MTO Special Staff Investigations

Record Group 498, HQ ETO

US Army Military History Institute, Carlisle Barracks, PA

Benjamin O. Davis Papers

Chester B. Hansen Papers

John J. Maginnis Papers

Betty M. Olson Papers

William E. Potter Papers

Veterans' Surveys, 2nd Infantry Division

Archives nationales de France, Pierrefitte-sur-Seine, France

Archives départementales de l'Aube, Troyes, France

Archives départementales des Bouches-du-Rhône, Marseille, France

Archives départementales de la Meurthe-et-Moselle, Nancy, France

Archives départementales de l'Yonne, Auxerre, France

Index